"A TRULY IMPORTANT BOOK...

all conscientious parents should read [it] and then leave it on the living room table for their children to sneak off with."

—GRAHAM BLAINE, M.D.
*Chief of Psychiatric Services
at Harvard University*

... No years can be more joyful than the teen years. Yet at the same time, no period of life can be more difficult, as the adolescent—and the parent—must cope with the demands of a self on the threshold of maturity.

It is to help solve the often painful perplexities of the teenager that this book has been written, the product of deep human understanding and brilliant professional authority. At a time when the so-called "new morality" has further clouded the proper course of teenage behavior, this book is of immense value as a guide to present—and future—happiness.

DR. RHODA L. LORAND has been practicing psychotherapy and psychoanalysis for the past sixteen years in New York City, during seven of which she was on the staff of the Vanderbilt Clinic of Child Psychiatry at Presbyterian Hospital. A junior Phi Beta Kappa, *magna cum laude* graduate of Hunter College, she obtained her doctorate at Columbia University, her psychoanalytic training in New York and London. She is a Fellow of the International Council of Psychologists.

Love, Sex
AND THE
Teenager

by Rhoda L. Lorand, Ph.D.

POPULAR LIBRARY • NEW YORK

All POPULAR LIBRARY books are carefully selected by the POPULAR LIBRARY Editorial Board and represent titles by the world's greatest authors.

POPULAR LIBRARY EDITION

Copyright © Rhoda L. Lorand 1965
Library of Congress Catalog Card Number: 65-15578

Published by arrangement with The Macmillan Company
The Macmillan Company edition published in April, 1965
Three printings

TO SANDOR

PRINTED IN THE UNITED STATES OF AMERICA

All rights reserved. No part of this book may be reproduced or utilized in any form or by any means, electronic or mechanical, including photo-copying, recording or by any information storage and retrieval system, without permission in writing from The Macmillan Company.

CONTENTS

Section III

PREFACE

Recently, when asked to give an interview on sex and the adolescent,* I looked through the popular literature written for teenagers and their parents. It was surprising to find how little of the rich material about the unconscious sources of adolescent feelings and behavior with which professional journals abound was spelled out in non-technical language.

In therapy the workings of the unconscious are explained in simple and direct terms to teenagers and parents. Through the years, in my therapeutic practice, I have been impressed by the ease with which young people and their parents are able to understand complicated psychological forces, if these are explained in terms of individual experience. It seemed to me to be possible to do the same in writing. This book represents such an attempt. It was written in the belief that insight into the unconscious causes of behavior is always helpful.

The teenage population is an extraordinary mixture of maturity levels, ranging from those who are emotionally childlike, just barely ready to venture forth from their homes, to those who are married and parents themselves, some already divorced. The bulk of the teenage population falls in between

* Published in *The Why Report,* Edited by L. Freeman and M. Theodores, Arthur Bernhard, Inc., Purchase, New York, 1964.

and is subject to the usual teenage experiences, aspirations and problems.

This book is directed to older adolescents and to parents. It seems to have divided itself into three sections. The first contains an explanation of fundamentals of theory; the second deals with practical applications of theory to the social and sex life of the teenager; the last aims at helping parents to understand what is happening between them and their teenagers and offers some practical suggestions to reduce friction.

In simple language, basic psychological facts about love and sexuality are discussed. Sigmund Freud's discovery and investigation of the unconscious part of the mind, of childhood sexuality and its importance in the life of the adolescent and adult, of the instincts and the different ways in which they may be expressed, provide the foundation stones of this book.

The contributions of Dr. Anna Freud on childhood and adolescence have provided therapists with their most important tools for working with these age groups. I have also drawn on the work of other distinguished analysts, whose publications represent enlargement and clarification of the basic work of Freud.

The writings consulted in preparing this volume are listed in the bibliography. I would however like to record here my special debt to Dr. Helena Deutsch and to Mrs. Selma Fraiberg. In writing Chapter 3 I have drawn heavily on Dr. Deutsch's work in feminine psychology and on Mrs. Faiberg's study of homosexuality, including her case history. When referring to studies which I assumed would be of special interest to the reader, the authors' names appear in parentheses in the text.

I wish to express my great appreciation and indebtedness to Lucy Freeman, whose request for an interview on the sexual problems of adolescents led to the realization that this book was needed. Her enthusiastic interest and careful reading of each chapter were a continual source of inspiration and encouragement.

I am particularly grateful to Dr. Ludwig Eidelberg for his generosity in reading a major portion of the manuscript and his invaluable suggestions which helped to clarify and improve the text.

I want to express my gratitude to Dr. Adele Streeseman, who discussed some of her case material with me and permitted me to make use of it.

Dr. Marjorie Harley very kindly read Chapter 4 and made helpful comments for which I am indebted.

I am deeply grateful to Mrs. Sue Wetzel Gardner for her wise and sensitive editorial guidance.

I wish to thank my husband, Sandor Lorand, who has been a most generous and indefatigable sounding-board for my thoughts. His wisdom and warm encouragement were indispensable to the completion of this work.

Finally, I wish to express my thanks to our teenager, Steven, whose services as special library assistant on adolescent advice books, were, without his awareness, augmented by the daily (and sometimes nightly) reminders of how wonderful and how exasperating a time teenage can be—for everyone!

NEW YORK CITY
August 15, 1964

SECTION I

1

INTRODUCTION

Love and sex, as everyone knows, are the most pressing pre-occupations of adolescents. High-school and college students discuss sex endlessly—not merely for kicks, but also in search of knowledge, reassurance and courage. Most often they are in search of guidance in responding to the compelling, often frightening and bewildering, sexual instinct.

Everyone wants to be sexually attractive and lovable. Everyone wants to love and be loved. At no time of life is it more of a worry than during the teen years.

The first goal of unsuccessful teenagers, and there are many, is to lose their crippling inferiority feelings and get into the social swim. A large portion of this book is devoted to them. The rest of the teenage population, those who are en-joying varying degrees of popularity and success, have their own private insecurity feelings. They generally welcome the opportunity to allay their anxieties and to enhance their so-cial success.

In my psychoanalytic and psychotherapeutic practice, it has been possible to observe in detail the different kinds of problems which beset adolescents.

All adolescents are confronted with the inevitable anxieties arising from the drive to translate sexual feelings and sexual thoughts into acceptable sexual behavior. Plagued by uncer-tainty, perplexed as to how far it is permissible to go in show-ing love and affection, in arousing and gratifying sexual desire, most teenagers (and many parents) feel the need of a much broader and psychologically deeper understanding of the development of the sexual instinct and the capacity to love than they usually possess. Adolescence can be a painfully bewildering time for parents as well as for teenagers.

If we observe at a coeducational high school for any length of time, we immediately become aware of the contradictory and bewildering variety of behavior exhibited by teenagers. The mood swings from elation to despair; the excitement and importance of everything—the generosity, meanness, kindness and cruelty; the need to belong; the need to shut out others; the tremendous self-centeredness; the devotion to an idol; the hours of hair-combing in the girls' room, and the sloppy outfit, the desperate concern about a pimple and the gross neglect of health.

Other puzzles which we observe are the pretty girls whom no one asks for a date; the handsome boy who is always unsuccessful with the girls he approaches; the plain girls who are successful and the other plain girls who are envious, friendless and withdrawn. Overly made-up girls, frantically and vainly hoping to attract a boy; other girls who also have too much make-up on for school but who somehow are given a great deal of attention by the boys; boys who freely ask a number of girls to dance at a school affair, and others who stand on the sidelines in an agony of fear lest they be refused. One sees girls who are obviously promiscuous and others who are plainly scared to death of boys.

If we were to follow some of these teenagers home, we would find a great many of them getting on the phone, with the friends they've just left, almost before they drop their books. A boy or girl, if he deigns to speak to his mother, may make a snippy remark one minute and say something sweet and friendly the next. Younger brothers and sisters will be treated with the same unpredictability.

Should it be a Friday evening with a date or a dance in store, the teenager may spend upward of an hour (sometimes two) washing and dressing and will emerge looking like a dream of cleanliness and grooming, leaving behind a room which looks as though invading armies had ransacked it for hidden treasure. Others who know of the dance but were not invited or couldn't find someone they wanted to invite, may sit home in utter despair and spend the entire evening wishing they were dead. Still others will tell themselves they don't care about going out and will devote all their energy to school work or to torturing the younger children in the family. Many will watch television from Friday afternoon until Monday morning.

We hear boys telling their parents that the reason they aren't successful is that they haven't got a car, or can't drive, and girls asserting that no boy likes you unless you make yourself cheap. "I'm too good for those jerks," a teenager once said to me, "but I can't understand why none of them ever asks me for a date."

If we could watch some of the teenagers long enough, we would soon be asking a number of questions that teenagers themselves ask:

1. How is it that certain boys and girls seem to fall into one disappointing and unhappy experience after another with the opposite sex, whereas others move from one happy encounter to another?

2. What forces impel an adolescent to marry someone of a different race or religion, or from a radically different social class?

3. What makes some teenagers promiscuous? Is this a sign of freedom or illness? Are some parents right in feeling that no price is too high for chastity?

4. Why do some teenagers become homosexual, whereas others, who may have had a homosexual crush or experience, are able to turn away from it to a normal relationship with a member of the opposite sex?

The psychological problems of adolescence are determined by the biological maturation of the individual, over which he, of course, has no control. This body, with which he has long been very familiar, rather suddenly becomes an adult body with a strikingly different appearance. He must learn to know himself and to feel at home with his radically changed outer envelope which forms a most important part of his ideas about himself. And he must learn to feel in control, and not at the mercy, of the strong sexual feelings which flood his body, create erotic fantasies in his mind and impel him to seek ever-increasing contact with the opposite sex. The world expects him to move toward establishing himself as an independent adult, toward finding a mate and having children of his own; and he has strong drives within himself which impel him to seek these goals.

With so much to accomplish, it should not be surprising that even normal adolescence in our society is to some degree, for every individual, an age of anxiety.

Those whose early childhood years have been wisely and lovingly handled by parents whose marriage has been one of harmony and affection will come to this turbulent period of life armed with optimism and the ability to think clearly; ingrained self-esteem will carry them through difficulties and setbacks with a minimum of anguish. Those who enter adolescence in a home which has been reverberating with parental dissension and bitterness, whose childhood experiences have left them a heavy burden of guilt, shame, confusion, anger, distrust and fear of adults, will find the going very rough indeed.

It is probably safe to assume that most teenagers' experiences place them somewhere between these two extremes.

We shall expect, then, to find teenage problems falling into the following categories:

1. Anxiety in relation to the "new" body:
    difficulties in achieving a firm sense of identity as male or female.
2. Anxiety about the greatly increased sexual feelings: the degree and manner of their expression.
3. Conflicts about remaining safely dependent upon the parents as in the past versus striking out for independence in all areas:
    transfer of affection outside the family,
    establishment of an individual moral code and finding one's life work.

The most important task the teenager must accomplish is finding someone outside his family to love. Before he can achieve this, he must first break his childhood love ties to his parents, brothers and sisters. That does not mean that he stops loving them, only that the ties must be so completely transformed as to be unrecognizable. In other words, he no longer is the little child adoring the superior parent and accepting every word as gospel. He must be able to feel that he is a loving friend and equal of his parents and to decide for himself whether he fully agrees with their principles, ethics, morals, ideals, goals and standards. There would be no progress in the world if every child grew up with a simple blueprint of his parents' ideas and proceeded to live by them unchanged.

Probably the most painful experience for parents who do not fully understand the inevitability of this break, or whose own lives are in some way deprived so that they lean too heavily on their children's love, is to watch their youngsters transfer their love to outsiders. And it is to some degree a painful experience for every adolescent. One of the reasons moodiness, depression and feelings of loneliness and despair are so common in the adolescent is that the young person often has moments of feeling desperately alone and longs for new love ties which have not yet been established. This is why adolescents need each other so much—support in their aloneness. Having detached himself from his family, the youngster needs the security of belonging to a group of agemates.

During the years of adolescence the personality is characterized by a high degree of fluidity. At this time of life, and at no other, it is normal for childish attitudes and behavior to exist side by side with those which are completely adult and for a continual interchange of mature and immature responses to take place.

There is also a tremendous increase in energy during this crucial period. The body and mind of the adolescent require the extra energy to accomplish the many important tasks of adolescence: the growth of the body, mind and emotions into adulthood. The fluidity of personality enables important changes to take place with extraordinary rapidity and with relative ease. The changes that take place during the five-year span from thirteen to eighteen, or fourteen to nineteen, or fifteen to twenty are phenomenal—where adolescence proceeds with reasonable normality.

In the mental and emotional sphere, childish attitudes and beliefs give way to reliably adult attitudes, chief among which is the discarding of childhood notions about adult love relationships, and the correcting of mistaken perceptions and beliefs regarding sexual feelings and behavior.

If this period of life passes without the accomplishment of the tasks nature assigns to it, they will be considerably more difficult to achieve at a later date because at about twenty the whole organism quiets down and the personality begins to become fixed or crystallized. It usually requires a relatively long process in therapy later on to break into these fixed but inappropriate childhood patterns of feeling and behavior, in order to enable the individual to accomplish the overdue tasks of puberty. Of course, a person who wants to change can be helped at any age.

2

FIRST LESSONS IN LOVE

The crucial aspect of the early childhood relationship with the parents is that it becomes the pattern for all of the individual's later relationships. As Sigmund Freud listened to his patients' accounts of their current behavior and thoughts and feelings, and compared them with recollections of experiences the patients had had in early childhood, he eventually was able to establish that there is in everyone an unconscious compulsion to repeat in later life the patterns of all the earliest reactions of love, hate, rebellion, submission, loyalty and disloyalty. The emotional attitudes which first arose in relation to the parents are later transferred onto other persons in the environment. Strange as it seems, the individual finds the kind of friends, spouse and career that create almost a repetition of his forgotten childhood experiences.

Since nearly all of the early experiences in a child's life are forgotten after the age of five or six, it is not surprising if people who are not familiar with the evidence proving the connection between these experiences and the behavior of the adolescent and adult find it extraordinarily difficult to accept the connection. It *is* hard to believe that events which one cannot even recall without the aid of depth probing, and then only incompletely, can be influencing one's behavior. But the material unearthed in countless psychoanalyses, not only of neurotic patients but of the scores of individuals who have undergone analysis as part of their training to become

19

psychoanalysts themselves, has proven conclusively that in adolescence, which is the first stage of adulthood, the forgotten relationships of the past are relived in a second edition.

Adolescence is the time when the individual begins to pour out to others outside the home the love he took in as an infant and child. The child who has been the recipient of normal parental love and devotion will have a reservoir at his disposal. The adolescent who as a child was hungry for love may, out of distrust, pretend indifference or seek love in a childlike way, which will not make for a successful social life, or may become promiscuous in a vain attempt to find expressions of affection. The young person who is too closely tied to a parent may be unable to love anyone else or may feel compelled to seek only older people who are obvious substitutes for the parents. The child who has had to turn his love back onto himself because no one responded to his needs, thus allowing a love relationship to develop, will remain self-centered and unable to love.

To understand an individual teenager's attitudes toward love and sex, it is essential to go back to his first weeks of life. The baby's earliest experiences of being cared for by its mother (or mother substitute) are of overwhelming importance to the development of his capacity to love.

Recently, a series of experiments was performed in which baby monkeys were completely deprived of contact with their mothers. (Harlow) Instead of being suckled, held, manipulated and "groomed" by their mother, the only mother they were given was a wire figure into which a nursing bottle was inserted and from which the baby monkeys fed themselves. When these monkeys reached simian adolescence, none of them exhibited mating behavior. In fact, if one of the mother-love-starved girl monkeys was approached by a normal boy monkey who had been reared by his own mother, and whose instincts for mating were entirely normal, she retreated from his wooing in terror or attacked him, apparently unable to understand what was wrong with *him*.

The boy monkeys who had been deprived of maternal care never showed the slightest interest in wooing or mating, no matter how beautiful or how willing the normal young females were.

These studies provide interesting evidence in the animal world paralleling the well-known psychoanalytic discoveries of the importance, in fact, the indispensable need, for body contact and all normal types of expressions of mother love in infancy as a preparation for adolescent and adult capacity to love and to function sexually.

A mother teaches her baby to love from the day it is born. As she holds it, fondles it, feeds and bathes it, pleasant sensations are produced in its little body. It becomes aware of the warmth and softness of its mother's body, the tightness of her arms, the touch of her hands. Babies respond differently to soft, loving tones than they do to harsh tones, and, even more amazing, studies have shown that small babies react by crying or refusing to eat when held by a person who is tense or angry.

These findings are now so widely accepted by pediatricians that the mother who does not breast feed her baby is encouraged to duplicate the affectionate, soothing, nursing situation by holding the baby close to her body, giving him his bottle with the same intimate and comforting contact.

The younger the baby, the more surely is the mother's state of mind communicated to him. If the mother is tense, he becomes tense and the resulting feelings of discomfort make him cry. If the mother is depressed, he doesn't sense the warm, loving relatedness which he needs in order to feel safe and relaxed, and so he feels distress. Under such circumstances, his first lessons in love are very unsatisfactory. The capacity to love and trust does not develop as fully as it does in the baby who repeatedly and continually experiences comfort and satisfaction in the arms of his relaxed and reliable (in responding unerringly to his needs) mother. She sends him an infinite variety of loving messages via the incredibly accurate communication system which exists between babies and those mothers who are sufficiently free of problems to allow their maternal instinct to function without hindrance.

Babies are extremely sensitive to the home atmosphere. In a recent study of crying babies done by a pediatrician, it was found that babies cried the most during the hours when the parents were the most tense and tired. In babies who did a great deal of crying, dramatic improvement was noted after the atmosphere was improved; in one case, the harassed young parents moved out into their own apartment and left the irritating atmosphere created by living with their own parents. Another baby's crying decreased markedly after the mother began to ventilate her feelings once a week to her physician, thus reducing her own tension.

Three Lessons

Thus the first lesson in love takes place at a time when being fed by the mother is the major and most important activity in the child's life. We should not be surprised to find that the child's first great pleasure—the experience of sucking while held in his mother's arms—is carried over into adulthood in the form of kissing (and hugging, holding and fondling).

The second lesson in love, strange as it may seem, takes place in connection with the most unromantic of all activities —training the child to be clean instead of depositing the waste products of his body when and where the little one pleases.

This training process is intimately connected with love and sexuality. It marks the first time in the child's life that he is asked to exercise control over his needs and impulses. His willingness to comply with this demand to please his mother is entirely determined by the amount of love he feels for and from her.

If prior frustrations at her hands have caused him to feel distrustful and rebellious, he will be unwilling to restrain himself in order to make her happy. And every baby in his right mind knows very well just how happy he can make his mother with such cooperation. If his refusal brings about harsh attempts on the part of his mother to force compliance, including the use of shame and humiliation, his attitudes toward the lower parts of his body can become permeated with feelings of shame and dirtiness. These will remain throughout his life and extend to his sexual feelings as well. If the child begins life feeling that he does bad things with these parts of his body, the feeling of badness may remain unconsciously attached to all sensations subsequently experienced in the anal and genital regions.

In adolescence, such feelings of shame and dirtiness can easily be extended to the new products discharged from the body in menstruation and seminal emission, which are then unconsciously regarded as excretions. Since self-esteem in adolescence depends so much on attitudes about the body and acceptance of sexual feeling, it can readily be seen that these childhood experiences exert a long-range influence on the individual.

Even more important, the seeds of homosexuality are sometimes brought into existence at this time as a result of an exaggerated concern on the part of those in charge of the child's bodily care to his bowel training. Frequent stimulation of the anal region fixates sexual interest in that area. When the time comes for a little boy's major interest to center in his genital, he may retain a greater interest in the sensations derived from the anus. This may predispose him to a passive sexual attitude, in which this opening of his body is later unconsciously equated with the female sexual organ.

Similar handling of little girls can confuse them as to which of the two body openings serves the sexual function, and it can also inhibit the transfer of sexual feeling to the genital.

The third lesson the child learns is determined by the reaction of the adults in his home to his sexual curiosity. He wants to know all about his own body, his brothers' and sisters' and also his parents' bodies. He enjoys running around in his birthday suit. He needs to be allowed to run around in the nude and to exhibit himself when he is two and three. It helps him develop pride in his body. He needs to be able to observe other little boys and girls of his own age in order to satisfy his curiosity, and he needs to have his parents respond to his request to see them nude, not by a display, but by an explanation that grown-ups want privacy, that only little children go around without clothes, but that they will explain anything to him that he wants to know. In this way he is not made to develop strong guilt feelings because of his curiosity; at the same time, overstimulation which is produced by seeing nude adults is avoided.

Attitudes expressed by the adults toward his childish masturbation and sexual play with other children have a deep and lasting effect upon his feelings about sexual activity. If his parents understand that such activities are part of normal development, requiring some opportunity for expression, the child will retain his self-esteem and will gradually come to realize that sexual feelings are a normal part of life. If he is taught to feel guilty and ashamed, he is not being helped to acquire mature attitudes toward sexual activity; and moreover, he will be burdened by an unrealistic belief that he is an inferior, defective, wicked person.

Sexual Games

The most difficult point for many people to understand is that while sexual play and exploration have a healthy place in the child's life, they nevertheless need to be brought under parental control. If left to their own devices, children might play sexual games in the garage all day long, especially if an older child (or a child with an incipient sexual problem) is leading them on. Unlimited sex play arouses undue quantities of excitement; this leads to anxiety because the child does not know how to cope with these feelings. Moreover, under these circumstances there is no sublimation of the sexual drive into constructive channels. All other types of play in which skills are acquired and energy is healthily expended are neglected. The child fails to learn anything and remains in a continual state of excitement, which makes mastery of school subjects difficult.

Mothers should be aware of what their children are up to. If they're having a pow-wow in one of the bathrooms or out in the woodshed, she can calmly arrive after a discreet lapse of time and suggest in a kindly and nonthreatening way that they do something else. She can counteract the influence of a seductive older child or a determined little one by being the leader herself in starting some new activities. The children will know that she knows what they were doing before she entered, and her manner, indicating as it will that there is nothing inherently wrong, but that there are many other ways of having fun too, can keep things under control without making the children feel like a band of criminals.

Sexuality, it would appear, is a flame which from the beginning of life must be carefully tended, to keep it from getting out of control as well as to avoid smothering it. Guilt about masturbation and childhood sexual games makes sexuality appear wicked. The outcome may be that the child grows to adolescence and adulthood believing that only inferior people have sexual desires. One sees evidence of this attitude in people who do not feel sexually attracted to those whom they love and respect, but only to those who impress them as being coarse or vulgar or "bad." The cultured man who is aroused only by call girls and the refined woman who secretly finds only rogues exciting are two examples.

It need hardly be said that some of the most important lessons in love are learned through observing the kind of relationship the parents have with each other. If Mother admires Dad or feels contempt for him, if Dad is kind or indulgent toward Mom or suspicious, defensive and hostile, the child sees and feels it all and begins to pattern his expectations of married life and the relationship between the sexes, on what he senses between his parents.

Jealousy

Regardless of the nature of the relationship between the parents, the little girl will want to marry Daddy and the little boy to marry Mommy some day, as children so openly declare. How very intensely the little child feels the love and jealousy which torment him at this time of his life is not generally appreciated. It is natural for children to feel guilt and anxiety over their rivalrous wishes. Nightmares in children around the age of four and five are considered to be a normal outcome of this struggle.

How a father responds to his little girl's overtures to him, and how a mother responds to her little boy's courting of her will have a profound influence on the children's adolescent and adult love life. When the child experiences the love of both his parents, who at the same time avoid the pretense that he can replace either one, he eventually feels able to renounce his rivalry, having confidence that he will some day have a mate of his own.

So many things can go wrong at this crucial period if the parents are unhappy, or lack an understanding of the child's feelings, or if they have a need to keep the child tied to them. Whatever disturbance is created at this time—whether it be a girl's fear of her father and therefore of men, or her extreme jealousy and antagonism toward her mother, or too strong an attachment to the father, or to the mother, as a means of denying the Oedipal rivalry, or as a retreat from a harsh father—such problems will determine the kind of adolescent who will eventually emerge and begin to strive for independence.

Often parents who are unhappily married give too much of an adult type of love to their children. This creates an overattachment which may become permanent or which may cause the adolescent to effect an abrupt break with the family in a desperate attempt to emancipate himself.

Overstimulation

For a long time it has been known that overstimulation of various kinds is harmful to a child. Babies who are continually tossed, tickled, rocked, played with and kept up until all hours of the night do not thrive on this kind of care. The overstimulation has the effect of retarding maturation, or, one might say more simply, of slowing down the normal developmental processes of growth.

Recently it has been found that various situations of stress have an overstimulating effect upon the tiny, immature organism, which has far-reaching harmful effects. An adolescent girl of seventeen had a history of stress and overstimulation as an infant and small child. Not only had she been repeatedly exposed to frightening experiences such as witnessing excited quarreling, but had also been directly overstimulated sexually by medical treatments for a skin disorder in the genital region. She once returned from a trip to report that at the airport she mistakenly thought she heard an announcement that her flight was about to leave at a gate which was quite a distance from where she stood. In great excitement and near-panic she began to run toward the plane station, and suddenly to her utter bewilderment found herself overcome by strong sexual excitement. It seemed quite clear that her body was responding along the pattern of very early experiences. She had many problems. Among others, she froze when in the company of boys and was totally unable to respond sexually under circumstances which would normally elicit a sexual feeling.

Her behavior seemed to indicate that when in a romantic setting she unconsciously put herself on guard against experiencing sexual sensations. She was afraid of them because they would have made her feel helpless. In other words, sexual feelings unconsciously revived memories of a distressed, helpless state. When she was off guard, a strong stimulus for which she was not prepared immediately set off a reaction through the sexual apparatus, as in the days of infancy and early childhood.

Another teenage girl who had spent her childhood years in an almost continual state of sexual excitement caused by a disturbing and sexually overstimulating environment (and had as a result spent a good part of every day masturbating in some form, even in school) finally got herself under control and put a stop to it. When she reached puberty and strong sexual feelings began to arise, she was terrified of falling helplessly back into her former practices and therefore cut herself off from any activity which would bring her into contact with boys or stimulate romantic fantasies. Her fear of being helplessly in the grip of sexual feeling was overwhelming.

From extreme cases such as these, requiring therapeutic help, our understanding of all the factors in a normal situation is enlarged and clarified. The process of enlightenment through studying people who have fallen into difficulties has been compared to studying something under a magnifying glass which reveals features not apparent to the naked eye. It has also been compared to observing the breaking of a crystal. When a crystal falls and breaks, the lines of cleavage are not haphazard, but determined in advance by the pattern within the crystal. The points in development at which breaks occur in the human being and the manner in which they occur have shown us the existence of important links and junctures, some of which cannot be detected when development proceeds smoothly.

A small child may also be likened to a tiny, highly complicated electrical device, containing several circuits, which little by little are put into use, and which can utilize electric currents having just the right voltage required to function. If suddenly too great a quantity of electricity is pumped into it, all the circuits are flooded in an attempt to handle the excess stimulation. Its regular operation stops while it attempts to discharge the overflow, thus valuable developmental time is lost and a measure of permanent damage may result.

Any powerful stimulus to which the very little child is exposed floods the organism with excitement. All the outlets for discharge of tension which the body possesses are automatically put to use. Thus it happens that under situations of extreme stress—such as fear produced by prolonged hunger, discomfort or neglect—the baby's sexual organs may be flooded with sensations it would not normally experience. These apparently intensify the child's feeling of helplessness.

When subject to overexcitement, the helpless baby cries, waves its arms, kicks its legs, trembles all over and experiences sensations in its genitals which this area is capable of producing because of the concentration of nerve endings in the sex organs which exist from birth. However, when such feelings are experienced prematurely, there is evidence that they greatly intensify the baby's feeling of helplessness and therefore create a greater tendency to develop anxiety as the individual goes through life. Individuals who start life under these stressful and overstimulating circumstances have been found to be more sensitive to stimuli of all kinds, and especially to the upsurge of sexual drives at puberty. (Greenacre)

Adolescents with this kind of history are particularly prone to compulsive masturbation because they tend to respond to all the tension of puberty with sexual excitement. In extreme cases the tensions become unbearable in that they reinstate the feeling of utter helplessness. Those few adolescent and young adult narcotic addicts who have come under psychoanalytic scrutiny have all had a history of extreme stress of one kind or another in infancy and early childhood, including a very uncertain and undependable mothering person. This was true whether they came from poor, middle-class or rich homes. These young people all described the same symptom as being responsible for their seeking oblivion in narcotics or alcohol; namely, unbearable tension which led to a feeling of complete helplessness and dread of imminent destruction. Similarly, they all described the feeling of comfort derived from the narcotic as "being wrapped in cotton batting" or feeling comforted and safe and able to sleep without fear of something happening to them. The similarity to the needs of the infant is striking and points to the source of the addiction. (Savitt)

We can see that there is no time in a baby's life when its experiences are unimportant to its future development. The younger the baby, the more far-reaching and unmodifiable are the effects of unusual stress upon it—exactly the reverse of what many people believe to be true.

Early Deprivation

The faster a living thing is growing, the greater the influence upon it of any stimulus. This is a physiological law of growth. Experiments with tadpoles dramatically illustrate this law. The head of a pin placed against a very young tadpole which had just begun to develop produced a marked deformity which was irreversible. The same pressure applied to the body of an older tadpole, in which the growth rate had already slowed down, produced a much slighter effect and one which was reversible when the pressure was removed. The identical pressure on the fully developed organism had no effect. In primitive tribes where heads are elongated, or lips made to protrude, the molding process, as the natives know, must start in early childhood because while the child's body is growing rapidly, it can be permanently deformed in various ways to conform to local standards of beauty.

In early childhood, not only the body, but also the emotional and mental development proceed at a more rapid rate than at any other time. (It is interesting to note that during adolescence when there is again a spurt of rapid development, physical, mental and emotional, the individual is once again highly responsive to pressures of all kinds.) Therefore, all experiences leave a deep impression.

In order to overcome a feeling of helplessness and develop trust and love and interest in the world around him, the baby needs exactly what every normal person instinctively feels like giving to him: tender loving care, satisfaction of all his needs and a continuing relationship. Whenever any of these elements are missing or interfered with, the baby's entire development suffers. The younger he is, the greater the suffering and harm. This explains why babies who spend their first few years of life in institutions, where only impersonal care is available, are so badly damaged.

None of the institutionalized baby's cravings for a warm, loving atmosphere, which is what every healthy mother automatically creates for her child, is satisfied. In fear and depression these babies retreat within themselves from the cold, frightening world. All developmental processes slow down drastically at the crucial time when the organism is developing at its most rapid rate in accordance with the biological time-table. The ensuing severe psychological damage brings about a crippling of the infant's emotional and mental apparatus. To what degree the damage can later be corrected will be determined by several factors: on the one hand, the child's endowment, the severity of the emotional deprivation, the length of time the baby had to endure it, and on the other hand, the amount and intensity of loving compensation the child later receives.

Some adopted children, who were grossly neglected before adoption, baffle their new parents by displaying a prolonged fear of relating to them and of trusting them. If the adoptive parents can be helped to understand why their new baby is reacting to them in this disheartening way, they can do a great deal toward starting the relationship off in a manner likely to make the greatest reparation to the infant and assure the earliest possible development of a loving attachment to them. When a mother approaches her adopted baby with affection and elicits no response (the baby may even turn away from her) it is a shock to her and she may feel that the baby intuitively dislikes her. If she then becomes depressed and discouraged, feeling unable to continue to make warm, loving overtures to the child, the basis for further trouble and unhappiness is established.

If she knows, or can assume, that the baby was neglected or abused in some way which caused the child to turn inward, then she automatically understands that she must prove to the baby that he will not be disappointed if he trusts *her*. Instead of being discouraged, she will redouble her efforts to spare the infant any stress whatsoever, to feed him on a self-demand schedule, to come the moment he cries, to cuddle him in her arms; in short, never to let him experience for one moment more than is humanly possible to avoid, a feeling of abandonment or helplessness.

The neglected baby, having had more than his share of fear and frustration, needs very special care to heal his wounds before he can respond to his mother in a healthy way. The more fortunate baby learns very early, even during the first weeks of life, that the world is a safe place because the moment he feels distress (which causes him to cry) there is a sound of footsteps and warm, loving, soothing comfort is on the way—milk, dry diapers and talcum powder; a visit in the mother's arms; being crooned to, perhaps. It's all delicious and he loves it, and eventually comes to know that the supply is unending. It's a wonderful feeling for a baby to learn that he is not helpless, that one loud wail brings him his heart's desire, just as if he were a king. In order not to be frightened, the little baby needs to have that kind of control over its environment. As his understanding grows and he develops the capacity for self-control, then, and only then, can he wait for satisfaction and comfort without becoming panicky, and, eventually, without getting furious.

With a beginning in which trust, self-esteem, and freedom from fear are allowed to develop, the foundation for the ability to love has been firmly established. Where it has not, the years of adolescence provide an opportunity for alleviating the distressing effects of unsatisfactory early relationships.

Teenage boys and girls can build self-esteem through self-understanding, leading to successful experience. New relationships with people outside the family can help to establish attitudes of trust in others, upon which love depends. An understanding of the behavior of others is fundamental to the development of trust in adolescence. It is especially important for young people to understand the psychology of the opposite sex.

3

MASCULINE AND FEMININE PSYCHOLOGY

Psychological differences between the sexes are grounded in physiological differences. Because of the unmistakable and obvious physical response which the boy experiences as a result of romantic fantasy and sexual thoughts, he is never in doubt about the connection between the two. Boys are aroused quickly, and the pressure of sexual feeling clearly localized in the penis spurs them to seek direct gratification for pleasure and also to discharge the tension. The boy feels great pride in the functioning of his genital. Many of the group sex games engaged in by boys demonstrate the competitive pride boys have in the feats which the penis is capable of performing. Group masturbation is in part an exhibitionistic display of sexual power among adolescent boys. (The presence of others also serves to reduce the anxiety which accompanies the act.)

The boy seeks admiration in displaying his prowess and accomplishments, whether it be a sexual, athletic, school work, job or creative undertaking. He is permitted to publicly display only qualities which are considered masculine, such as courage and daring, perseverance and determination, power, strength and speed. These win the admiration of girls, of his elders, and of other boys his age. In other words, a forthright, direct, competitive aggressive approach is considered masculine, and we should not be surprised to find these attributes coloring the boy's sexual approach to girls.

The psychology of the male can be described as aggressive, uncomplicated directness, a pride in accomplishment, with a clear understanding that sex and romance go together.

Some people believe that these typically masculine ways of behaving are brought about solely by child-rearing methods, but there is an increasing body of evidence obtained from various types of studies which indicates that they have a strong biological basis. Males of all ages have a higher proportion of muscle tissue than girls. Some recent findings suggest that infant girls may be more sensitive to pain than infant boys. Aggressive and destructive play, as any observer of young children knows, is much more frequent among boys than among girls. Girls have been found to be typically more tractable and dependent in their behavior than boys. Even the tiniest cell in human tissue can be identified under the microscope as belonging to a male or a female body.

The psychological differences between the sexes are as great as the anatomical dissimilarities would lead one to expect. Girls tend to suppress sexual feeling. They tend in early puberty to have strong feelings of shame about their genitals. Masturbation often assumes indirect and concealed forms. The young girl's fantasies of romance and ideal love are in the beginning very much separated from sexual feelings. Her sexual feelings when they do arise seem not to have the intensity and compelling quality of the young boy's. However, at puberty the girl's entire body develops an erotic sensitivity to touch and she becomes very much aware and proud of her developing body. The expression of love and admiration for her own body, which is typical of women and very strong during adolescence, is socially acceptable. Emphasizing and displaying feminine charms are taken for granted as normal feminine behavior. The girl's great need is to be loved and admired. Normally, she does not crave sexual love early in adolescence and often reserves her most passionate love feelings for an ideal figure whom she doesn't even know. This doesn't mean that she won't enjoy dating and engaging in the typical adolescent lovemaking. Normally she will not be carried away by it, whereas in her erotic fantasies about her idol (who may be a popular singer or film star), she will imagine everything, and she will be perfectly safe while allowing herself to be completely carried away.

A girl's (and woman's) sexuality is much more emotionalized and spiritual than a boy's. A girl's sexual and sensual feelings are subordinated to being loved. With maturity, sexuality and love gradually become fused. Normally, the adolescent girl is much happier with her fantasies of fulfillment than if they actually take place. Channeling her sensuality and sexuality into other areas of her emotional life, enriches the girl's emotional life and makes it more varied than the boy's. At the same time it does endanger her capacity to experience direct sexual gratification. It is well known how sensitive a woman is to the type of approach utilized by her sexual partner. A woman's ability to respond can be enhanced or blocked by the manner in which the man behaves to her. In other words, the atmosphere which the man creates for her greatly influences her response to his sexual approach.

The indirect expression of sensuality which is characteristic of girls seems to lead to the development of other typically feminine qualities. She is more self-centered, more concerned with what is going on within her mind and body. Her stronger fantasy life, her more personal approach to situations and people, seem to enable her to identify herself more easily with others. Women seem to understand their own feelings better than do men, as a result of which they seem to be better able to understand the feelings of others. In other words, woman's intuition really exists. Effortlessly and unconsciously, she is able to understand feelings, emotions and motivations of others in a way that baffles men. It is interesting to note that no woman is a mystery to another woman. We see through each other like glass. One woman always knows what another woman is up to.

Men and boys are more inclined to take personal situations at face value. They are usually not as emotional as women. Men are often exasperated by a woman's line of reasoning in an emotionally charged situation. Cold logic may not stand a chance. No matter how involved in a situation the average male may be, he usually manages to examine the facts with some objectivity. He isn't as likely to get carried away by an emotional, personalized approach. These differences in qualities are no doubt at least partially responsible for the superiority in mathematics and scientific studies which boys begin to exhibit in the late high school years, whereas the girl's interest in fantasy and beauty draws her to literature and poetry.

A permanent relationship is essential to childbearing and childrearing. Perhaps an unconscious awareness of the dependence which pregnancy forces upon her creates the strong need for love and devotion, conditions which girls require for a full sexual response. These are instinctive needs, linked to the knowledge that there will be times in her life when sexual surrender will result in temporary but complete helplessness —the most threatening situation imaginable, unless she is assured of loving and devoted care. A boy's biological destiny does not include periods of helplessness, so it is not surprising that his sexual instincts lead him to seek gratification with simple directness, whereas the girl's inherent caution leads her to develop many charming techniques for delaying and extending the wooing process. Ordinarily these serve to heighten the man's interest and appetite, while giving her a chance to strengthen an attachment and become reassured of love and devotion, meanwhile enjoying the excitement of being pursued. What a genius nature is!

It is interesting to observe that on the accidental occasions when men are rendered helpless by illness or injury, they respond with a sizable quantity of anxiety. Doctors, nurses, wives and children can all attest to the fact that men make the world's worst patients. This is because the condition of helplessness is one for which men are neither psychologically nor biologically prepared. Woman's greater passivity, which is linked with her biological role of childbearing, enables her to accept pain and temporarily incapacitating illness without anxiety. The man's biological role requires only that he be active, the woman's that she at times be passive, receptive and accepting of pain—menstrual discomforts, defloration and childbirth.

Menstruation and seminal emissions, the two most important events of puberty, both create anxiety. The boy must cope with the anxiety brought on by involuntary, unexpected erections and emissions which at first make him feel helpless, not in control of his body. Old feelings of shame and anxiety about bed wetting are temporarily revived. He feels assailed by the intense sexual feelings which arise. Only gradually does he learn to incorporate them as part of himself; the sexual feelings then become sexual desire, related to his own thoughts and feelings. When this finally takes place his anxiety diminishes. Once the girl has established a regular menstrual cycle, her anxiety normally disappears. She becomes more stable and achieves a better integration and organization of personality despite the fact that her periods may be attended by temporary feelings of depression and greater sensitivity to stimuli of all kinds. She is confirmed as a woman.

Girls who have psychological problems related to accepting the role of woman often express them in connection with this function. Unconscious reluctance to become a woman may be expressed in failure to establish a regular cycle, severe pains, disappearance of menstruation for long stretches of time, even years, or failure to begin to menstruate until quite late in the teens.

Other girls, resenting this confirmation of femininity, will make a point of proving that it makes absolutely no difference in their lives. They become particularly active in dancing and sports for the duration of the menstrual period as proof to themselves that nothing has changed and that there is really no difference between them and the boys. This denial serves to reduce their anxiety about womanhood.

Physiological differences, it can be seen, exert a profound influence upon the personalities of boys and girls. How much of the differences are innate and how much the result of training and experience is impossible to measure. There seems to be little question about the fact that characteristic differences in behavior are present from early infancy.

Normal Masculinity and Femininity

For ease of presentation, men and women have been described as though they each were formed out of a mold, one labeled Feminine and the other Masculine. Obviously there is much overlapping of traits.

What is normal? Is there such a thing as being too masculine a man or too feminine a woman? We all know that there are men who are too effeminate and women who are too masculine to be considered normal.

If we were to sort out the entire population of men and rank them on a scale according to the degree of masculine and feminine traits they possessed we would find the bulk of the population of males crowded in the center and bearing the label: "Predominantly masculine traits, with admixture of some feminine traits." At one end of the scale we would find a relatively small number of men who had only masculine traits, such as strength and competitive aggressiveness, and they could bear the label "brutes"; at the other end we would also find a small number of men who had feminine traits almost exclusively, and among them of course would be the homosexual males who play the role of the woman in their relationships with other men. On the outer edges of the normal group we would find "borderline" groups, one tending toward brutism and the other tending toward effeminacy.

If we ranked the entire population of women on a similar scale, the result would be the same. The vast majority would be found to have predominantly feminine traits with an admixture of masculine qualities. At one end would be the group of women who had feminine traits only: emotional, gentle, timid, romantic, tender, sentimental and dependent (the nineteenth-century ideal of womanhood). At the other end would be the very masculine women, among which would be the homosexual women who assume the male role. At the outer edges of the normal groups we would find the borderline groups, the one tending toward sentimental emotionalism, and the other toward a masculine orientation to people and situations.

We may say that some basic attributes belong to both sexes but that their form of expression differs. For instance, physical activity is considered a characteristic of the male sex, yet baby care and housekeeping require enormous activity.

Active aggression is generally considered to be a masculine attribute, and passive dependence a feminine one. But should anyone threaten her children or her marriage, the most feminine of women can become a tigress. Adolescent girls exhibit active aggression in typically feminine form when they steal each other's boy friends and in the pleasure they find in collecting male "scalps."

Passivity (or inactivity) is regarded as an essentially feminine trait. But a boy must be able to passively listen to his teachers and learn. Boys who cannot engage in this healthy form of passivity have learning problems.

The basically feminine qualities of gentleness, tenderness and sympathy enter into the personality development of the boy, fuse with the basically masculine traits, and add a precious dimension. Loving romantic tenderness toward women and gentle kindness toward children make the ideal husband and father, yet direct aggression and competitiveness enable him to be a forceful breadwinner and protector of his family.

Incorporation of various masculine traits gives the girl invaluable strength and a measure of independence which enable her to be a thoroughly capable scholar, professional, worker and wife. At the same time she expresses her great capacity for tenderness in caring for her children.

The fact that a man or woman has many attributes usually

considered appropriate to the opposite sex does not mean the person is not normal. There are many quite masculine women who are happy wives and excellent mothers, just as there are gentle, passive and artistic men who are thoroughly adequate fathers and husbands.

The overlapping of traits has a physiological basis. Male as well as female hormones are secreted by the woman, just as female and male hormones are secreted in the man's body. The balance between the two types of hormones influences various features of the outward appearance of the individual, as well as his sensitivity to stimuli, his energy and various traits of personality and temperament.

When we think of the great range of variation possible at birth as a result of the constitutional activity type and the inherited mental and physical attributes, and when we consider the equally great number of types of experience to which the child is subject from birth, depending upon the temperament and life situation of his parents and the customs of the community in which he lives, and the hormonal balance which will begin to assert itself at puberty, we can understand why the scale of individual differences is infinite and the range of the normal very broad indeed. The question of sexual normalcy is decided by the individual's ability to function sexually with a member of the opposite sex.

The Myth of Superiority

The great geniuses of the world have been men. All the child prodigies—the lightning calculators and the musical geniuses—have been boys. Does that mean that men are superior to women? Brilliant women have made important contributions in many fields, but it is irrefutably clear that the most highly endowed men are significantly superior in creative intellectual power and artistic creativity to the most highly endowed women.

It has been proposed that the reason great intellectual and artistic creativity and genius, and outstanding capacity for abstract thinking have appeared in men only is that women have never been given a chance to develop their intellectual powers to the fullest. While it is true that in Europe women were restricted in certain activities, they were nevertheless encouraged to study music; but how many sonatas did they compose? Modern American women have not been restricted. Russia gives every intellectually gifted youngster the finest education possible. Israeli girls and women are encouraged to develop their intellectual potential to the fullest extent. Still, all the evidence points to the fact that the most outstandingly gifted men are indeed superior to the most outstandingly gifted women. But intellectual superiority is only part of the story.

The masculine gift of major creative thinking is considered by many to be a limited compensation for the gift of bodily creativity which nature has bestowed on women. A scientist recently remarked, "Nature delivers her message with accuracy." With regard to the sexes nature has with her usual wisdom divided the gifts and tasks equally between them. But from time to time there is a rebellious attempt to deny that such a division exists. Woman's greatest creativity and genius is of the body and the emotions, man's is of the mind. Woman plays the major role in replenishing the earth and nurturing the inhabitants thereof, man in enriching the earth, discovering its secrets and bringing them under his control. Each sex has areas of superiority, and they defy comparison.

Women have a very special kind of genius arising from their adaptability, intuition and greater flexibility. It may not be as striking as the intellectual product of men's genius, but it is nevertheless extraordinary. When circumstances have required it, women have proven that they can do absolutely anything and everything. They can be soldiers, road construction workers and business executives. In all professions once thought to be the province of men women have at some time and in some part of the world proven their ability and excellence. In times of emergency down through the ages the women have given evidence of the limitless range of their abilities, as well as their infinite capacity for enduring hardships.

Woman's intuition is another form of genius. It enables even the simplest of women to be wise in their care of their children and in their relationship with their husbands. The woman, it seems, is ideally fitted to be the heart of a household and the man to be its head. Particularly in America currently, where companionship between husband and wife is the ideal, and where equality between the sexes is assumed, the opportunity for harmonious functioning of husband and wife in their specialized roles is maximal.

The notion of over-all superiority has given rise to the contention that a battle exists between the sexes. People who seriously hold to this concept are usually individuals whose unfortunate experiences have rendered them incapable of enjoying their natural gifts and special sex-assigned creativity. They feel competitive toward and suspicious of the opposite sex. Women who hold in contempt nature's gift of body creativity and regard only masculine creativity as admirable are, naturally, very discontented with their lot. Deriving no self-esteem from their greatest gifts, they proceed to feverishly hunt for gratification in masculine pursuits. Men who lack appreciation of the maternal role may regard women either as an underprivileged group or as parasites. Those men who envy woman's major role in procreation—and they are many— tend toward a hostile and rivalrous attitude toward the (in their eyes) unfair sex.

Mystique or Mistake?

Recently, an angry female voice was raised, deploring the tendency of college educated women of the past generation to devote their skills to homemaking and to raising considerably more children than the career women of their mothers' generation. According to Betty Friedan, in *The Feminine Mystique*, the return of educated women to their homes instead of following in their mothers' footsteps and going on to professions and careers is the result of a campaign to brainwash and dehumanize women, reducing them to the state of animals stupid enough to find motherhood a satisfying career. What has produced this strange retreat of the educated woman back to her concentration camp American home? Mrs. Friedan would have us believe that it's a plot, a conspiracy against women; headed by Freud. American men, American business men especially (who want women to stay in the kitchen so they can buy more housewares), are acting as Freud's willing accomplices. American women have been their facile dupes.

Enraged that educated women should be willing to make a career of motherhood and "overproduce" children, Mrs. Friedan, who obviously finds "occupation housewife" an insult, assumes that it is an abnormal state of affairs indicating regression. It must obviously, therefore, have been produced by some evil, sinister outside forces, undoing all the splendid achievements of the former generation of career mothers.

In her need to prove that her personal feelings of contempt for the occupation of housewife should be shared by everyone, it is not surprising that she has missed the most obvious reason for the complete about-face made by the recent generation of college women. *They are the children of career women.* As a natural reaction to their disappointment in the lack of maternal care which they so vainly craved and sought from their career-minded mothers, they determined to be good mothers to their own children. This they envisioned as always being home and available to their children. To have ideal homes and be ideally devoted mothers, they felt, would spare their children the loneliness and neglect they themselves had experienced.

Girls grew up determined to be just the opposite of their disappointing mothers whose careers were the most important factors in their lives, and whose children had continuous evidence of the fact that they came second. Boys grew up determined to find wives who would be mothers and homemakers instead of competitors in the business and professional world. The new generation were confirmed in their attitude by the growing body of evidence showing the importance to the development of emotional security in the child of a warm, dependable, relationship with the mother, in the early years especially. (It must be confessed that Freudian therapists bear the chief burden of guilt for uncovering this evidence.)

The pendulum swings back and forth as the younger generation reacts to the older, and in America where tradition is not deeply rooted, and where change is regarded as desirable, radical changes can take place very quickly. The coming generation may stop the pendulum somewhere in the middle.

Perhaps we will take an example from the Russians, who, when they observed that nursery-reared children were not developing as well as home-reared children, arranged for "mother's shifts" throughout the nation, thereby allowing all mothers to do the work for which they were qualified on a part-time schedule so that they could spend an important part of their time with their children. Some women, unquestionably, need to work in order to be happy. Vast numbers of others do not. With understanding, matters can be worked out satisfactorily for everyone. People simply need to know in which directions to expend their efforts.

Berating girls for wanting large families, or for being unenthusiastic about intellectual subjects is not going to help the situation at all. There is no reason for women to work after marriage if they don't care to, nor does it make sense for college graduates to feel guilty if they do not go on to graduate school after marriage. A woman should be allowed the freedom of enjoying her fundamentally sex-assigned job of being a housewife and a mother—a "nest-builder," as one Smith College graduate recently described herself, expressing her joy in her children and home.

However, girls who because of feelings of inadequacy grasp at marriage as an excuse to be relieved of the burdens of going to school or going to work may be headed for trouble. This does not indicate "femininity," only immaturity, which bodes no good for the future. Dealing effectively with school obligations and responsibilities is an important preparation and training for the burdens and responsibilities of parenthood. Some girls think: "I found a husband, so why should I bother with this rat race any longer?" But there are very good reasons.

It is perfectly obvious to everyone that dropping out of high school in order to marry is a mistake, yet many people do not realize that it is always a mistake for young people, male or female, to drop out of college if they have any choice in the matter. The entire character development suffers when commitments, the fulfillment of which will enrich the person's whole life, are dropped in midstream. On some level in the unconscious, a feeling of inadequacy is thus confirmed, and self-esteem suffers because the individual has failed to achieve an important goal. This is true no matter how high-sounding the reasons given: "I can learn more by reading and studying everything I want to learn instead of restricting myself to what those narrow-minded, stuffy professors think I ought to know."

It is safe to say that in most cases of college and high school dropouts of either sex, whether for marriage or not, severe emotional problems underlie the decision to quit, regardless of the rational-sounding reasons given. Rebellion against parents, refusal to work because it is parents' desire, inability to live up to social and academic pressures because of anxiety and immaturity are all psychological problems.

The girl who finds the self-discipline and strength to carry through to a successful conclusion a high school or college program before embarking on motherhood is thereby helped to be a much more capable wife and mother. (Of course, the same applies to future husbands and fathers.) From a purely practical point of view, the ability to earn money, now or in the unpredictable future, is made much more certain. From the point of view of intellectual interests, the greater one's knowledge, the greater the number of avenues of enjoyment. However, even these considerations, though unquestionably important, are minor compared to the inestimable advantages of knowing that you can organize work, stick to responsibilities, meet obligations, put up with setbacks of all kinds, and wait a long time for gratifications (diploma).

Running a home and bringing up children is a very big job, fraught with frustrations as well as joys. Lucky are the children whose mother has proven to herself the existence of a reservoir of inner strength which gives her the ability to remain calm and to stay with a frustrating or difficult situation until it is resolved. The less excited and upset a mother gets, the fewer the number of times she gets depressed or blows her top, the happier and safer her children feel.

Recently, the head of a distinguished women's college deplored the fact that its highly trained and gifted graduates married and settled down to child-rearing soon after graduation instead of spending at least a few years utilizing their knowledge professionally and enriching, through their contributions, the various fields in which they had received training. It is clear that the great majority of college girls, even the most brilliant (for which this particular college is noted), have the very normal feminine desire to find a husband to love and with whom to have children. They are responding to the strongest instinctive feminine drives.

To advise all college graduates to work for a few years before raising families seems to me to be going to the other extreme from retreat into marriage and motherhood. This advice may unduly delay the fulfillment of feminine drives and make them appear inferior to more masculine drives.

However, those girls who seriously plan to follow a career or profession when their children are grown will no doubt facilitate their later entry into the professional world if they follow their profession or career for a few years before settling down to have babies. How difficult it will be to enter the business or professional world twenty years later will depend primarily on national economic conditions. If the country is in the grip of a depression it will be very difficult for women to find places for themselves regardless of how much experience they have had. Booming prosperity will mean that even the inexperienced will find many opportunities, if they look for them. The women who really cannot bear to be idle when their children are grown, the ones who truly want to work, as distinguished from the ones who talk about wanting to but can never gather up enough drive to do something about it, end up with something satisfying to do. It is not really necessary to take out "job insurance" when you graduate from college, if the price—delaying the coming of children—is more than you want to pay.

On the other hand, it is always a good idea for a newly married couple to have a year to adjust to marriage and all of its responsibilities before introducing the greatest of all responsibilities, the coming of a child. If the bride's salary is not essential, it is advantageous for her to have the year to give full expression to her feminine joy in her own home and husband. To have time to think and plan for the future as well as to learn housewifely arts is the little girl's dream come true. It would be wonderful if every young girl were able to experience and savor to the full a first year of this kind.

It is a mistake to think that a full-time course of study, such as medical school, or full-time work can be satisfactorily combined with good infant or toddler care. The child is always short-changed. Responsibility for his well-being must be left entirely to others, and this is a serious deprivation. The child who is first in his mother's heart and interests knows it. The child who is second in importance also knows it, and it makes a great deal of difference in the way he feels about her and about himself. There is no substitute for the deep sense of joy and loving pride the healthy mother feels and communicates to the child as she cares for him and observes his progress. This favorable "atmosphere," this warm "climate" which the mother effortlessly creates for the baby day after day by the way she feels about it, cannot be duplicated by someone else, unless of course it is someone who has assumed the permanent role of mother, as in adoption. Whenever the normal feminine desire to nurture the young is interfered with, both mother and child are losers.

Mrs. Friedan, whose aim seems to be to get all mothers out of the house and into the business or professional world, whether they want to or not, described with admiration and approval the case of a medical student-mother who turned night into day for her little one. The child was put to bed for the day while the mother was away at school and was up and around during the night when his mother was home. The assumption apparently is that this mother had no need for sleep and moreover was able to go through medical school without having to study. Even assuming that these extraordinary abilities existed, one might ask whether this child built sand castles under the stars and went puddle wading by the light of the moon. What does it do to the child's developing sense of reality to turn its whole world upside down? He plays in a dark childless world illuminated chiefly by electric light. He goes to sleep when the rest of the world of children and their mothers are enjoying daylight and sunshine and strolls in the park and rides in baby carriages and wars in the sand box. What is he learning about the world while the daylight children are learning to recognize the bell of the ice cream man, the different types of stores and what Mommy gets in each, getting to know the characteristics of other children and other mothers, observing clouds in the sky, the disappearance and reappearance of the sun, rain storms, puddles and rainbows. Normal maternal care given under normal conditions is *not* expendable if the child is to develop normally.

Innumerable women have no career ambitions, and there is no reason why they should. A girl is not wasting her education if she does not go on to graduate work or enter a profession. It is a great pity when girls are made to feel that their brains and talents are wasted if, after completing their basic formal education, they prefer to channel their knowledge and talents into homemaking and motherhood. This desire should be respected, not deplored. It is the expression of an important normal difference between the psychology of men and the psychology of women.

It does not mean a return to the errors of the past when girls were regarded as incapable of serious intellectual interests and therefore as inferior beings. It means acquiring an appreciation of women as females, which precludes the error of encouraging them to behave as if they were men. Such an attitude implies that the development of feminine qualities and the achievement of basically feminine goals are not as valuable as duplicating the achievements of men. This was the inevitable feminist error: an overcorrection of the past.

Penis-Envy and Castration-Anxiety

Angry outcries have been raised in many quarters against Freud's assertion that certain character traits in women, which color their entire lives, are caused by penis-envy. He referred to fierce competitiveness with boys, a resentful attitude toward the male sex and toward feminine pursuits. Did Freud mean that these women, mature or adolescent, actually wished to have a penis as part of their grown-up bodies?

Such a wish would obviously be grossly abnormal, and its fulfillment would result in unrivaled grotesqueness. No such conscious wish was implied. The phrase is psychoanalytic shorthand to describe forgotten early childhood events which have led to a particular type of personality formation in the girl. (Years ago I listened to a report of a study in which hundreds of college girls were asked if they had ever wanted a penis. Naturally, they all said "no." The investigators interpreted the results as incontrovertible proof that Freud was in error.)

Freud discovered that little girls of nursery age were clearly dismayed when observing the genitals of little boys, and would demand to know what had happened to their own. He made a parallel discovery, which was that little boys were frightened when they first saw little girls' genitals and also wanted to know what had happened to cause them to be missing a penis. There is ample evidence to indicate that both boys and girls assume everyone starts life with a penis and that the girl has somehow had hers taken away from her. Little boys become frightened at the thought that the same fate may befall them. Freud called this castration-anxiety.

Little girls go through a phase of feeling deprived, especially if they have brothers and watch them doing fascinating things, such as: a contest to see who can make the highest stream, or how far from the toilet bowl can they stand and still reach their goal. Little girls seem to regard the penis simply as a handy extra gadget which they, too, would like to own. They can't do anything spectacular at all when *they* urinate. It just doesn't seem fair at all when you are a young lady of two, three or four. This is the time when penis-envy arises and *is very real*. This is the *only* time in the woman's life when she actually wishes she had a penis. At this point she feels resentful and jealous of boys and feels deprived.

Of course the idea sounds revolting to adolescents and adults. But if we remember that little children's thinking is characterized by concreteness of ideas as well as by a belief that things can happen by magic, it really is not so hard to understand that such a fascinating and useful feature should be envied by that part of the nursery population which finds itself without it. To put ourselves in the little child's place, we must understand the child's belief that in some magical way it was cut away without her knowledge. (After all, parents do all kinds of things which seem magical to the child, who cannot understand how they know so much.) It is not a far-fetched idea for a child of either sex to perceive the girl's genital as a place that has been cut. Many little boys and girls come to the conclusion that it looks that way *because* a penis has been cut away.

Anyone who takes care of very little children and is present when they first become aware of the differences between boys and girls is bound to hear them give some indication of their shock and concern.

"Where is hers?" a little boy may ask, greatly worried.

"Why don't I have any?" a little girl asks her mother with obvious pique. She watches the little boy urinating, then tries to urinate standing up, and is most dissatisfied with her performance. "I wish I had two penises, one in the front and one in the back," an envious little four-year-old said to her mother.

Sometimes boys become quite frightened at their belief in the power of parents to take away a penis. In order to calm their own fears they simply deny that anyone is lacking one, even though they have been told that little girls don't have them because they have a different kind which is hidden. This castration-anxiety becomes very strong in boys if other experiences reinforce the fear of bodily harm; for instance, stern and punitive attitudes towards the little one for his childish misdemeanors, or actively threatening him for playing with his penis. Children fantasize violent destruction at the hands of angry parents, but the ideas come largely from the child's own wish to be powerful and vengeful.

A toy which is being mishandled is taken away from the child. By making a very simple analogy he can, and does, come to the conclusion that if playing with his penis is forbidden, it may also be taken away from him as a punishment. These castration fears do not grow to great proportions in the child who feels comfortable and safe with his parents and sure of their love and approval. But where difficulties arise between parents and child, and a vicious circle of punishments, anger and guilt feelings, spiteful behavior, more punishments arousing renewed anger, etc. exists, the orginal fear of bodily harm is increasingly intensified and begins to color the child's total personality and character. If he is an inactive type constitutionally, he may become extremely timid and withdrawn. If he is the active type, his fears may make him wild, excessively aggressive and rebellious as a means of proving to himself that he is not afraid and can defend himself against such an attack. If his mother is frighteningly aggressive and threatening in her behavior, the little boy will attribute aggressiveness to her whole body. Her angry mouth will be associated unconsciously in his mind with her genital, and he may thus develop fears of contact with the female sex organ, believing it to be a dangerous place equipped with a sharp set of teeth. An intense fear of being castrated by the vagina itself is often found to be an important factor in the combination of causes leading to homosexuality in a man and to impotence. In adolescence and adulthood, these early fears, although forgotten, have a profound effect upon his ability to function sexually, as well as upon his ability to take his place in the world with confidence.

It is important to remember that although an iron curtain comes down between the conscious and the unconscious parts of the mind around the age of six, a very efficient combination radar-wireless system operates from the unconscious, continually beaming messages to the conscious part of the mind, and influencing the way people and situations are perceived and reacted to, no matter how old the person becomes. And so the little boy who felt great guilt and fear lest he lose his penis because of the naughty things he did with it: manipulate it, wet the bed or his pants with it, have forbidden contests in the back yard or the bathroom, is assailed by the old childhood fears and guilt feelings on the occasions when he attempts to function sexually as an adult. Depending upon the intensity of his childhood fears and the degree to which favorable experiences with his parents and other adults have helped him to overcome fear and build self-esteem, his potency will be more or less restricted and inhibited. This is how castration-anxiety operates. In order to cure it in therapy it is necessary to unearth all of the early guilt-ridden and frightening childhood experiences and reexamine them in the light of adult knowledge, so that the grown man is finally released from the influence of childhood beliefs.

A girl can also suffer from castration-anxiety. If as a child she is convinced that she was mutilated as a form of punishment, it means that similar drastic punishments may follow. She may then grow up having exaggerated fears of pain and injury of all kinds, with no conscious awareness of their origin, while at the same time feeling the need to outdo her brother and other males. It is plain that great tension, irritability and feelings of dissatisfaction with life will result.

Under ordinary circumstances, the little girl overcomes penis-envy by the time she is six. She loses all recollection of it and settles down to identifying herself with her mother and looks forward to the day when she will be a mother herself.

But many events can conspire to greatly reinforce the original feeling of deprivation and dissatisfaction with being a girl. If there is an unhappy relationship between mother and daughter, the little girl is bound to renounce the feminine role, to identify with her father instead and to have strong wishes to be like him in every way, including the physical resemblance. In one extreme case, a girl of seven in whom this problem persisted was discovered one morning, lathering her face and shaving a non-existent beard. A father may unwittingly foster penis-envy in his daughters by encouraging them in masculine pursuits while being indifferent to their feminine interests, or worse, showing contempt for them.

Open preference for the brother shown by mother and nurse may intensify a little girl's envy of her brother. Or he may be an unusually handsome child whose appearance elicits many admiring comments. The girl will almost always equate these expressions of appreciation with his maleness. Or perhaps she is a quiet, serious type and he is a sunny-tempered child who irresistibly becomes everyone's favorite. In her mind his greater success may be connected with his being a boy.

If the little girl was the only child and the center of attraction, dethroned by his arrival, she will interpret much of her parents' joy at her brother's arrival to his being a boy; and if they do express open satisfaction in the fact that the new baby is a boy, it almost always means to a little girl that there is something especially wonderful about being a boy, and she soon finds the evidence to support her belief that her parents have a reason to greatly prefer this new baby boy to her.

There are cases, of course, in which a boy is made to feel that the only thing it's good to be is a girl, by the mother's preference for a girl, which is usually caused by the mother's underlying hostility to men and boys; and it is not infrequently a forecast of a divorce, legal or emotional. The normal reaction of a mother is to feel a very special pride and joy in producing a son. Whether it is the result of a universal remnant of childhood penis-envy which gives to every woman an extra sense of gratification in producing a little male from her body, or the biological fact that there is always an attraction, however subtle, between the sexes which accounts for fathers favoring their daughters and mothers their sons, or a combination of both, or something entirely different and as yet undiscovered, who can say? But the preference and pride do exist and little girls, who spend much more time with their mothers than with their fathers, sense this, and it can inflame the childish penis-envy. ("If I were a boy and had one, Mommy would prefer me.") Moreover, as they grow older, the boy may be given greater freedom. He can climb trees and walls and fences and nobody minds if he gets filthy in the process. His life may seem much more interesting and admirable. All in all, the girl's original concrete and specific envy may be so inflamed and generalized that it becomes an all-pervasive element in the growing girl's personality.

A certain amount of fleeting tomboyishness in prepuberty is considered normal, as the girl retreats momentarily to a denial of femininity just before the onset of menstruation will confirm her as a woman. The girl who grows up with a feverish need to prove that anything boys can do she can do better, greatly resents the biological confirmation of womanhood and may experience all sorts of menstrual difficulties, as has been indicated, or attempt to prove that it makes no difference to her whatsoever.

If we bear in mind that penis-envy arises at a very impressionable time in development, that it becomes unconscious, and that even though it is unconscious, many experiences in the girl's life can continue to augment its original intensity, it should not be difficult to understand how it happens that in a free and democratic society with its unlimited opportunities for women, there are nevertheless a sizable number of females who grow up convinced that women always get a raw deal, that men keep them in inferior positions, and who virtually seethe with a need to prove their superiority in any field considered masculine, feeling contempt for activities or interests traditionally considered feminine, particularly homemaking and child rearing.

Everyone knows of certain types of women business executives who are aggressive, domineering and harsh, to the point where everyone (especially men) shudders to have to be in contact with them. That their manner and attitude are entirely unnecessary and caused by unconscious problems which have shaped their lives, is proven by the women executives who efficiently take care of their responsibilities with courtesy and dignity and feminine charm.

The fact that a woman enjoys a position of responsibility in the professional or business world does not in any way indicate that she is suffering from penis-envy. The *manner* in which she discharges her responsibilities is what determines it. The women who enjoy humiliating their subordinates, and proving the stupidity and inferiority of their male co-workers, it can be assumed do suffer from the life-long effects of unconscious envy of the male sex. Just as the male executive who makes a practice of cutting people down and humiliating them may be suspected of overcompensating for life-long problems caused by castration-anxiety. (Extreme timidity in men is an undisguised expression of castration-anxiety.)

Just as the sexual functioning of the man with severe castration-anxiety is interfered with, so is the sex life of the woman with a penis-envy problem. She often fails to respond to the sexual advances of her husband because she cannot bear the relatively passive and entirely receptive role which is so characteristic a feature of feminine sexuality. We speak of a man making love to a woman, of her being responsive to his caress and of her surrender. Healthy women, no matter how much they enjoy actively participating in love play, derive deep gratification from the ultimate surrender.

Is it so hard to understand that a woman who has always, albeit unconsciously, resented being a female, will have many feelings of resentment against this complete surrender, which is the expression of her femininity? In order to achieve the emotional and spiritual surrender which will permit her to experience the deepest pleasures and joys of sexual union, the woman must be fully accepting of the femaleness of her body —not just consciously, but unconsciously as well. To the extent that the old childhood feelings of envy, resentment and rivalry exist in the unconscious, along with the conviction that her vagina is the result of mutilation, her pleasure in intercourse will be restricted.

Normal remnants of castration-anxiety can be observed in the adolescent boy's typical concern about the size of his penis and worry as to whether it will function properly when the occasion arrives. Remnants of penis-envy and castration-anxiety which are quite typical of normal adolescent girls are to be found in their typical overestimation of the size of the male genital and their anxieties about being damaged by it.

The various jokes about the length of the male genital and the teeth and cavernous depth of the female genital are clear indications of the anxieties, stemming from forgotten childhood beliefs, which adolescents and adults have about the physical properties of their sex organs. Joking about them serves to reduce anxiety.

A fixed and exaggerated concern about clothing often is a displaced anxiety. A degree of exaggerated interest is normal for adolescence when the body is changing and the young person feels uncertain and unfamiliar with himself. In the girl, an inordinate preoccupation with beautiful clothes, hair styles and make-up, not to mention hysteria over every skin eruption, may conceal feelings of dissatisfaction and shame about her genital. A feverish attempt to make the outside impeccably beautiful and perfect from head to foot may be the result of the girl's secretly regarding the hidden part of her body as ugly and imperfect.

Similarly, while it is natural for boys to want to look very masculine, to have broad shoulders and strong muscles, preoccupation with becoming a muscleman, a preference for heavily padded shoulders and sensationally "sharp" clothes usually indicates a deep concern about the adequacy of the sex organs. In other words, it is an attempt to compensate for castration-anxiety. The other extreme—complete neglect of the appearance because of a feeling of hopelessness —can also be indicative of the same problem, as if to say: "What's the use? Nothing can hide my defectiveness."

Homosexuality

Many adolescents secretly worry about being homosexual because from time to time they become aware of homosexual thoughts and impulses. Ideas of what it might be like to be a member of the opposite sex can at times preoccupy the young teenager. It is typical of early adolescents to be troubled by bisexual thoughts and feelings while in the process of searching for their own clear-cut identity as male or female.

It has been found that many adolescent boys have at some point engaged in a homosexual game with a group or with a partner and that such experiences need not interfere with normal development. There is no feminine counterpart for the typical homosexual horseplay that goes on among boys in locker rooms, where boys grab at each other's genitals and exhibit erections to each other. Group masturbation is not found among girls as it is in boys. Perfectly normal adolescent boys have been known to try just about anything they could think of during the experimental period of early adolescence. Girls appear to be more frightened of homosexual activity. Secretly a pair of girls may become involved in breast play, and more rarely in mutual masturbation.

In fact, adolescent girls frequently show an exaggerated dread of body contact and a feeling of disgust for women and women's bodies. Although casual embraces and kisses are typical among teenage girls, they are nonsexual. Should the girl become aware of a sexual feeling as a result of such contact, she normally would feel repelled by it.

The loathing girls feel toward the bodies of women finds a parallel in the boy's morbid dread of homosexual contact with an *adult* male. This dread is found even among delinquent boy groups. These taboos against sexual contact with an older man indicate that for the boy, homosexual activity with an adult male is unconsciously perceived as a dangerous throwback to the boy's original loving attachment to the father (his first homosexual love). Similarly, the girl's disgust with women's bodies in adolescence represents her struggle against an unconscious wish to return to her infantile love for her mother, which would bring her back to the mother-child relationship of the first two years of life.

Since adolescence is the time when the individual is struggling to shed childhood love attachments to the parents, the unconscious wishes for a repetition of childhood love experiences, all of which involve body contact, are vigorously fended off. Fathers and mothers normally hug and kiss their little children, fondle them, squeeze them and hold them close. Teenagers cannot bear to be reminded of that intimate body contact. They dread it because they unconsciously fear the realization of the childhood wish for this bodily affection. Once the body has become sexually mature, as in adolescence, such fondling would have a different meaning, hence the conflict.

What makes a child grow up to be a homosexual? How is it that some homosexual men are glaringly effeminate and others appear to be completely masculine, except for the fact that they love other men? The same questions apply to the feminine lesbian and the masculine-appearing lesbian.

As with all other emotional problems, the roots of homosexuality are to be found in early childhood and the causes are many and varied. Usually a combination of disturbances working together produces it. It has come to be generally recognized that a typical pattern of family relationships found in the early childhood of homosexual men is a fatherless home (or a home where the father is away a great deal and very ineffectual when at home) and a particularly strong attachment to the mother. It should be pointed out that *boys can grow up in fatherless homes and still not become homosexual.* A great deal depends upon the mother's attitude towards men and masculinity and the manner in which she relates to her son and to his innately masculine activities and attitudes.

If the mother treats him as if he were a little girl, lets his hair grow long, gives him dolls to play with, shudders at rough play and teaches him to prefer flowers and butterflies to water pistols and fire trucks, she is propelling him towards a feminine identification. She is teaching him in very obvious ways that only feminine behavior and pursuits are desirable. A mother who is unaware of a little boy's need for masculine interests and activities is probably suffering either from fear of men or hostility towards them (or both). These attitudes will be communicated to the child in a thousand ways through the years as he grows up. He will know that in order to keep his mother's love and approval he must be as feminine as possible.

At the same time, anger towards her will be aroused by her continual thwarting and frustrating of his normal masculine drives. This rage will have to be kept buried in the unconscious part of his mind, for to express it would mean taking the unthinkable risk of being cut off from her love and protection. (He would then be helpless, with no one to care for him. Nothing stands between a young child and destruction save a parent's loving care. Children are quite aware of their helpless dependence upon the mother or her surrogate.) The normal castration-anxiety is intensified in such situations by the mother's generalized disapproval of masculinity and by frequent opportunities to see her nude. This combination is often found in homosexual development. In a situation where these factors are involved, the homosexual development can be described as a feminine identification, coupled with unconscious fear and hatred of women, the hostility usually masked by an exaggerated attachment to the mother.

When a father encourages only masculine activities and behavior in his daughter, a parallel result may be anticipated. But since it is rare for fathers to spend many hours a day with their children, they usually are prevented by circumstances from achieving this effect. An exception was a wealthy father who spent his mornings riding around on his estate with his little daughter by his side and taught her to shoot, hunt, fish and trap animals exactly as her brothers did. An indifferent attitude towards this "education" on the part of an invalid mother, and her genuine preference for the boys, led the girl to reject femininity and to identify wiith her father and brothers. In this case, the homosexuality of the girl can be described as a masculine identification coupled with a deep, unconscious longing for maternal love.

Homosexuality can be caused by too much or too little love from the same-sexed parent, strange as this may seem. For instance, if a little boy is completely deprived of a father, or father substitute's affection, he may become homosexual because of his childhood hunger for love from a man. On the other hand, if he receives love only from his father, or mainly from his father, and it has taken a strong physical form, such as much fondling and kissing as well as intimate bodily care, the little boy may develop such a strong love attachment to the father that only another man can replace him as a suitable person to love. Observation of this connection led Freud to conjecture that the cause of the prevalence of homosexuality among the ancient Greeks was to be found in their custom of having male slaves take care of the babies; that is, of mothering them.

A very harsh father can turn a boy towards homosexuality, especially if the mother is very protective towards the boy and encourages him to regard his father as an ogre. The boy may then identify with her, consciously and unconsciously rejecting the identification with his father. At the same time, he will unconsciously long for his father's love, and it may take the form of his wishing the father would love him in the same way that his father loves his mother. In other words, out of fear of his father and his need for his love, the child adopts a passive, feminine attitude toward the father.

The same homosexual development can take place where neither parent has any special problem and where outside circumstances alone are the cause, as in the following case report. A little boy, born while his father was in the army, lived with his mother and older brother, meeting the father for the first time at the age of four. During these first four years, he had grown accustomed to thinking of his slightly older brother as his only rival for his mother's affections. He did not have to deal with the intense jealousy and the hopeless sense of rivalry which a child often feels towards his mighty father, normally mitigated by the love that exists between the father and his child. The four-year-old didn't have to deal with it until, suddenly, one day, his paradise was invaded by a strange giant who promptly took possession of his mother.

How did he cope with this sudden competition and why should it have led to a homosexual development? In the first place, in the games, in wrestling with his older brother, he was frequently bullied and cast in the role of a girl by his brother; hence, a pattern of submission to a male was established. Secondly, the sudden appearance of the father, allowing no time for a gradual grappling with the problems of overwhelming competition, which the child might have mastered little by little, aided by a growing attachment to the father, had the effect of a severe shock. Rather than risk revenge and retaliation (a little child's Oedipal fantasies, based on what *he* would like to be able to do to *his* rival) in a fight between such unevenly matched contenders, the child gave up all normal competitive feelings towards his father. He adopted a passive attitude towards his father, as if to say, "We're not rivals, just love me the same way that you love mother. That's all I want." However, in so doing the boy relinquished his normal masculine drives. Whenever this happens, a boy feels the lack of masculinity and looks for ways of recapturing it. In this boy's case, as in the case of other homosexuals, he temporarily "recovered" his lost masculinity by identifying himself with the very powerful muscular body of his high school athletic coach who had made homosexual advances to him. Certain attributes of the man, not the man himself, excited the boy, and by identifying himself with those qualities via homosexual love, he attempted to acquire masculinity. He thus "borrowed" masculinity through his relationship with the athletic coach.

This unconscious belief in the power of identification is at the root of the frantic desperation and despair which overtakes effeminate homosexual young men when they are abandoned by their masculine-type homosexual partners. It also accounts for the intense jealousy and possessiveness which appears to torment most homosexual partners. All the evidence points to the fact that they suffer much more devastatingly from the break up of a love affair than do heterosexuals. This is understandable, since they feel they have lost a vital part of themselves. The extremity of their response is also caused by the revival of a very early feeling of abandonment by a parent. These unconscious factors account for the clinging, the harassing possessiveness, the tormenting jealousy and suspicion, the hypersensitivity and proneness to emotional outbursts which so many homosexuals display.

In analyzing homosexual patients, Dr. Anna Freud discovered the existence and the meaning of partial identifications in homosexual love attachments, that is, the identification with a *quality* rather than with a *whole person*. Miss Freud also discovered that what her homosexual patients feared most was that analysis might cause them to lose their homosexual partner from whom they were borrowing their masculinity. Since the patient felt that he acquired masculinity only through his partner, losing the partner meant being deprived of masculinity—in other words, castration.

Castration fears which little boys experience, especially as a result of seeing female genitals, play an important, if unconscious role in their turning towards homosexual development, thereby avoiding the dangers of Oedipal rivalry.

Sometimes a boy copes with an overwhelmingly aggressive mother by identifying with her in order to feel as one with her strength and aggression, and therefore to feel safe. When this happens, the feminine identification will conceal intense fear and hatred of the mother. These attitudes will carry over to all other women. He may then seek young men who will unconsciously represent himself, and he will unconsciously represent his aggressive mother.

A boy who has lost his mother in early childhood may, out of love and longing for her, if he has no mother substitute, identify with her and give love to other boys, the love he would have wanted her to continue to give to him. He then represents his departed mother, and the young boys upon whom he lavishes love represent himself.

Homosexuality may develop as a result of intense jealousy of a brother who was preferred by the mother. The original hatred felt toward the successful rival is overcompensated for by an intense love for the other child, with all future partners representing this sibling.

Freud called attention to the fact that where men like girlish boys, the desired partner "is not someone of the same sex but someone who combines the characters of both sexes: there is, as it were, a compromise between an impulse that seeks for a man and one that seeks for a woman, while it remains a paramount condition that the object's body (i.e. genitals) shall be masculine." Many analysts who have treated homosexual men have found that unconscious castration fears, which make the female genital seem repulsive and frightening, are basic to their avoidance of women; they compromise by loving a girlish boy. This is particularly true of homosexual men who appear to be masculine in every other respect.

Parallel situations create homosexuality in women. A great hunger for mother love, of which they were deprived, has led many girls to become lesbians. Therefore it is not surprising to find that a central theme in lesbian relationships is one of mothering each other.

Too close and seductive a mother-daughter relationship can also lead to lesbianism. This may happen in a fatherless home, or in an unhappy marriage where the mother turns to her little girl for affection and especially where she replaces her father by sharing her mother's bed. Unconsciously, masculine drives are stimulated.

At this point, let me repeat: none of these situations *must* result in homosexuality, but they frequently do in cases where several adverse factors are operating simultaneously.

Fear of men engendered by a very cruel father, or by the terrifying experience of having been molested by an alcoholic father or another adult male in the family, has in many instances caused a girl to turn her affections and sexual desires towards women only.

Disappointment in a promiscuous, unfaithful father is sometimes found to be a prime cause of lesbianism. Many lesbians have grown up in homes where the father's infidelities were continually brought to the girl's attention by the outraged mother. On occasion these girls have spied upon their fathers and seen for themselves that the accusations were true. The idol tumbles from his pedestal. The girl may then unconsciously decide that men are no good and that she will love only women. Her behavior is a form of revenge. It says: "I do not need a man. I can be a man myself." At the same time she may unconsciously identify herself with her beloved father and also love many women. Her homosexuality also denies that she ever wanted her father's, or any man's, love. (Sometimes, daughters of promiscuous fathers simply become promiscuous themselves, as a revenge upon the father; or their great disappointment in him may make it impossible for them to trust any man, yet they do not turn to lesbianism.)

Some active homosexual women, after having identified

themselves with their fathers, choose young girls as love partners. They then behave toward these girls as they wished to
have been treated by their fathers. Other girls become lesbians in order not to compete with their mothers for any man's
love or admiration. They "retire in favor of the mother," an
attitude which conceals unconscious hostility towards her,
as well as despair and lack of self-esteem. This may happen
where the mother has had a series of husbands, or where the
mother has a problem of intense feelings of rivalry with her
daughter, or where a father ignores his daughter and is only
attentive to his wife, or where the mother is beautiful and the
girl very homely; usually a combination of several of these
conditions. Then the girl may choose as love partners very
beautiful girls and "borrow" beauty and self-esteem through
a partial identification in the same way that the effeminate
boys "borrow" masculinity from their more muscular partners.
She may also play the role of good mother to her partner and
receive mothering in return.

This discussion of homosexuality does not pretend to be a
thorough study. Its aim is to indicate some of the major forces
which tend to create it, and to make one important point
clear: regardless of what many homosexuals themselves may
say, it is not a third sex. Homosexuals started life as heterosexuals. It is a neurosis like any other. It is curable and pre-
ventable. Homosexuals are fundamentally no different from
the vast army of people who have serious emotional problems
of one kind or another. Unfortunately for them, their particular type of neurosis arouses a feeling of revulsion and fear in
many people which causes them to treat homosexuals with
uncivilized harshness. Hating is so much more comfortable
than fearing. To what may the fear of homosexuality be attributed? Perhaps to the instinctive awareness that its universal adoption would put an end to the human race. More likely,
it is a reaction to the unconscious knowledge that the seeds
of homosexuality exist in everyone as a residue of the childhood love for the parents. Proof of this is to be found in the
well-known fact that when cut off from the possibility of contact with the opposite sex, many people temporarily engage
in homosexual activity despite having been heterosexual until
then. This occurs in prisons and in other situations where men
or women are isolated for long periods of time.

Nevertheless, homosexuality is a serious problem which
creates great unhappiness. The relationships in most cases
cannot escape being unstable and over-emotional, grounded

as they are in deep disappointment and dissatisfaction with their earliest love relationships. In many of these partnerships, the desperation of the small child who would perish without its parents' love is continually evoked. Distrust, jealousy and possessiveness, excessive clinging and dependence are characteristic. Permanent relationships and lasting contentment seem almost impossible to achieve and the basic problems are intensified by the fact that society forces homosexuals to live in a world of their own.

Since many homosexuals are attracted to adolescents, it is best for teenagers to understand the nature of the problem and to guard against becoming involved. Experiencing sexual pleasure usually creates an attachment between two people. This occurs regardless of whether the sex relationship is healthy or unhealthy. Once such a bond has been established, it may not be possible for the young person to progress to a love relationship with someone of the opposite sex without the aid of extensive therapy. Therefore, it is imperative to seek help if there is any reason to believe that a teenager's own love preferences are distinctly moving in the direction of his own sex, or if he is even flirting with the idea of accepting homosexual advances.

The Male Exhibitionist

Exhibitionism is not a problem common to adolescent boys. A discussion of this sexual deviation is included here because so many adolescent girls experience the shock and fright of being confronted by an adult exhibitionist. Many girls believe that the exposure of his sex organ to her is a prelude to a sexual assault.

Like homosexuality and all other problems of deviant development, exhibitionism has its root causes in early childhood. It starts out as a normal expression of the sexual drive appropriate to a particular phase of life. Anyone who has observed little boys knows what delight each takes in showing his penis to the other, and in showing it to the adults, in displaying its powers. The urination contests of who can shoot a stream the highest and the furthest and the longest are typical childhood games which show the boy's pride in his penis and his wish to have it admired.

Exhibitionists are tied to this childhood form of pleasure. In those who have been analyzed, it has been found that the need to persist in this kind of childhood pleasure stems from childhood experiences which created in the child an overwhelming fear of losing his penis (castration-anxiety), coupled with strong feelings of hostility toward his mother. (She may, for instance, have been very severe about punishing childhood exhibitionism and masturbation or she may have belittled the boy and withheld expressions of admiration for his budding masculine drives.)

In displaying his penis to a girl, the exhibitionist unconsciously expresses all these factors at once: his childish need to display and be admired, his hostility towards females (in frightening the girl); the reassurance by her shock at the sight of his erect penis that he indeed has not been castrated, that it is still very much there. Thus his castration-anxiety is temporarily reduced by the act of exhibitionism. It is as if he were saying to the girl, "You *are* castrated. You don't have a penis, but I do. You have proven this to me by your reaction."

The reason the exhibitionist's penis is always erect when presented to the girl's view is that in anticipating the pleasure he will experience from her reaction of fear and horror, he becomes sexually aroused. But the exhibitionist is not dangerous. He does not seek actual body contact with his "victims," who are usually young girls. His pleasure is derived from shocking and frightening the girl and having her look at his penis. He craves no more than that to gratify his sexual desire.

This is not intended to be a thorough study of the disturbance, but rather, as in the presentation of homosexuality, an indication of the outstanding factors involved.

4

MASTURBATION

There is probably no scientifically (if not socially) acceptable word in the English language which has an uglier sound to most ears than "masturbation"; no word which arouses a greater feeling of distress, distaste, anxiety and remorse. The fact remains, however, that a central problem for adolescents is their struggle with masturbation. The manner in which the struggle to resist is carried on—the degree of success or failure—the adolescent's feelings about his own behavior in this area, all have their roots in childhood upbringing, experiences which exert a strong influence on the way the adolescent copes with this vital phase of development. In turn, the manner in which these strong biological urges are dealt with colors the adolescent's future love and sex life, as well as contributing specific characteristics to his personality and general behavior.

It is not surprising that books on facts of life for teenagers have so little to say about the subject, and that what is said is often contradictory. It is an area of human behavior which creates anxiety in parents and children, and it is only fairly recently that our knowledge of this area of life has become sufficiently broad to clarify its meaning in the total life history of the youngster.

History of Attitudes

According to Kinsey, the historical record of the disapproval of masturbation goes back to the Book of the Dead of the ancient Egyptians, 1550 B.C. In Orthodox Jewish codes it was considered a major sin. Catholic sex codes, as Kinsey points out, originated among the Jewish founders of the early Church and they similarly condemn masturbation as a carnal sin. It was, however, only mildly condemned in Greece and Rome.

In a survey of the literature on the subject done by Dr. Rene Spitz, he states that masturbation is not mentioned in church literature until the sixth century, two centuries after celibacy was required of the clergy. The first Penitentials (treatises listing various sins and their punishments) appeared in the sixth century, and in these, reference is made to "intentional pollution," the punishment for which was "singing of psalms and one day of fasting." For having erotic fantasies the punishment was one or two days of penance.

It was not until one thousand years later that physicians began to be interested in masturbation and alarmed about it. Adopting a moralistic rather than a scientific attitude, they published opinions as to the frightful consequences of what they considered to be a dreadfully sinful act. Masturbation became the cause of every horrible disease known to mankind, including a few which existed only in the imagination of the doctors themselves. Not only did it cause insanity, but one "victim" was described who had, according to the doctor, managed the extraordinary feat of drying out his brains so prodigiously that they could be heard rattling in his skull. Not only was masturbation the brain dryer of 1770 but it also killed people. It is interesting to note, however, that the remedies proposed for this cause-of-all-evil were simply diet and baths. In the eighteenth century there was still no attitude of "retaliation against the sinner," just an attempt to "cure" him. By the middle of the nineteenth century, very cruel and sadistic measures to suppress masturbation were being practiced by physicians—with attention especially directed to girls and women.

These practices included surgical removal of various parts of the female genitalia, principally the clitoris, which is the focal point of sexual sensations in the little girl. They also recommended severely frightening women and children, and the use of mechanical restraints. One physician invented a metal contraption with spikes. This was designed for boys. It prevented the boy from touching his genital, and if erotic thoughts produced an erection, his genital was thereby brought into contact with the spikes. A leading textbook in pediatrics, up until the edition of 1936, advocated circumcision for boys of any age who masturbated, and putting the boy's genital into a double-side splint, such as is used for a fractured leg. For little girls, physicians recommended blistering the inside of the thigh and genitals.

Dr. Spitz points out in his survey that very few people realize how extremely cruel the persecution of the masturbator has been up to our day; "nor is it generally known that these sadistic practices found support among authoritative physicians and that they were recommended up to almost [twenty years] ago in official textbooks."

Freud's *Three Essays on the Theory of Sexuality,* published in 1905, provided the first scientific explanation of auto-erotic activities and their origin. In the essay on infantile sexuality, Freud pointed out that the child has feelings of pleasure in various parts of the body starting at birth (all of which play an important role later in adult love and sex life) and that masturbation begins in earliest infancy as the baby strives to *duplicate pleasurable feelings it has experienced.* Freud discovered that the tiny baby very early becomes aware of its sex organs through the sensations produced by urination and also from the washing and rubbing to which it is subjected in the course of being bathed and cleaned by the mother. He concluded that it was "inevitable that the pleasurable feeling which this part of the body is capable of producing should be noticed by children even during their earliest infancy, and should give rise to a need for its repetition."

This essay of Freud's marks the beginning of a different attitude toward masturbation. But it took thirty-five years before Freudian-oriented psychiatrists were able to influence their medical colleagues to the point of rewriting the medical textbooks. An article by a psychiatrist, describing the problem behavior in children caused by masturbation threats and severely criticizing the attitude taken in the pediatric textbook used in most medical schools, finally brought about a rewriting of that chapter in 1940. The edition of 1940 states that masturbation causes no physical harm but that the harm lies in the worry and guilt which the act calls forth.

One may well ask—if the foremost textbook of pediatrics has for the past twenty-two years authoritatively stated that masturbation is harmless—why the belief that it causes insanity and is harmful in other ways nevertheless persists in the minds of many people? The belief in the mysterious power of masturbation to cause serious harm is still widely held. Some of the anxiety, of course, may be attributed to the aftereffects of the former medical attitude towards it. Just as it took the medical profession thirty-five years to catch up with Freud, it is highly likely that it will take a great many people the same amount of time to catch up with the latest medical opinion. Also, it seems to be much more difficult to eradicate fears than to implant them.

When an idea which has been proven to be false is nevertheless clung to tenaciously, there must be a compelling reason for it. We would say that if the fear has taken such strong root, it must have fallen on fertile ground. Little children are not afraid that auto-erotic pleasures will drive them crazy but adolescents often are. Where do they get this notion? It arises spontaneously in many adolescents as a result of the feelings which overwhelm them in the course of seeking to gratify the drive to obtain sensual pleasure from their own bodies. There is no comparison between the strength of the surges of sexual feeling in the four-year-old boy who enthusiastically plays with his genitals and those of the adolescent. The sexual glands of the adolescents have matured to the point where sexual excitement is capable of adult intensity. The sensation of distance from the world and helpless surrender to the feeling of sensuality, the moment of almost unconsciousness which are characteristic of the peak of sexual pleasure (known as orgasm), are what frighten the teenager, giving rise to the fear that he may remain in that state indefinitely. Moreover, the youngsters often experience a sensation of exhaustion and sometimes a slightly sick feeling afterwards which leads them to believe that they have damaged themselves in some way. How much shame, guilt and anxiety the teenager feels about masturbation will largely be determined by early childhood experiences, and the tenor of the relationship that exists between himself and his parents.

Feelings of shame and disgust about the sex organs frequently arise around toilet training. Also, if the little child's normal delight in running about in the nude is spoiled by disapproval or ridicule, he will develop generalized feelings of shame and inferiority about his body, which will act as a dam upon sexual activity. If his early childhood curiosity about differences in the bodies of the people in his family was harshly repressed, if his childhood masturbatory activities were severely punished, his adolescent sexual drives which impel him towards masturbation will be fraught with intense anxiety. Sometimes the anxiety is so overwhelming that the young person flees entirely from all sexual activities and thoughts into complete asceticism.

Fear of the parents increases the fear of the consequences of being caught by them in auto-erotic activities. Since fear of the parents is usually the result of too strict or repressive handling in the early years, it most usually is accompanied by all of the crippling feelings of shame about interest in the body and the sensations it is capable of giving, as well as fear of retaliation by punishment to the sex organ itself, as is frequently threatened by parents.

The future sex life of the teenager depends to a considerable extent on how successfully he can surmount these fears and come to terms with the biologically determined demands of his body. To the extent that he is unsuccessful they will continue to exercise some disturbing influence on him all of his life. Fears of having damaged one's self through masturbation can be remarkably persistent.

A highly intelligent woman who all through her school life had suffered from a learning difficulty believed that it resulted from brain damage caused by masturbation. At the time of our meeting she was in her forties, and almost the whole of her life had been spent under the shadow of this mistaken belief, which was now beginning to spread to her handling of her children. She was terrified lest anyone tickle the youngsters, believing that the sexual desires thus aroused would lead them to uncontrollable masturbation and they would then share her fate. She had become motherless at the age of five and thereafter repeatedly sought solace in her own body for the disappointments she experienced in her longings for love and affection which were ignored by an indifferent and harassed stepmother. Her harsh reality had caused her to turn too exclusively to her own body for a duplication of remembered pleasurable experiences. Thus, her personality was impoverished and her relationships with others had been somewhat stunted. Her whole personality was stamped by the effects of the unsuccessful struggle with masturbation. Intense feelings of inferiority and worthlessness influenced all her actions.

Healthy Aspects

A most important problem of adolescence is the achievement of a sense of self, or sense of identity. Teenagers often ask themselves: Who am I? What am I? Why do I feel and act as I do? Which behavior is the real me? What is my personality really like? Are the changes in my body occurring as they should? Am I underdeveloped, overdeveloped, never going to start or never going to stop developing? Am I masculine enough, or feminine enough? With regard to the feelings which invade his body, he asks: How strong can they become? Should I be having them or is there something wrong with me? What will they make me do?

Boys anxious about their normal sexual feelings are often heard to say, "I must be a sex maniac." And girls, ashamed and guilty about their youthful longing to be made love to, confess, "I feel like a prostitute"—as though normal sexual desires make maniacs of men and prostitutes of women.

The sense of self or the self-image, as it is often called, which until puberty was reliably rooted in familiarity with the appearance of the body and the more or less predictable feelings in the body, is shaken by the radically changing appearance of the body and by the strange and unpredictable feelings which come unbidden and often cannot be regulated. The young adolescent at first experiences sexual tension as an assault from the outside, an external force which is not part of himself. Gradually, the teenager is able to integrate sexuality, to make it a part of himself. This takes place as sexual tension gradually is transformed into sexual desire. No longer then does he feel helplessly in the grip of a sexual feeling which is taking possession of him. Instead, he becomes aware of his own drive for sexual pleasure.

During adolescence masturbation serves not only in the release of sexual tension, but also the much more subtle function of enabling the young person undergoing rapid physiological changes to become truly acquainted with his body and the sensations which it is capable of producing. The feeling of being on thoroughly familiar terms with his new and dramatically different body gives the adolescent a firmer sense of who and what he is. The sense of identity as a male or female thus becomes clearer and stronger, leading to greater self-awareness and self-confidence. Moderate amounts of masturbation are therefore considered to be of importance to the development of the sense of self in adolescence. Clarification of the sense of identity can be counted as one of its positive aspects. A second is the bringing of the young individual closer to contact with a member of the opposite sex through "experimental quasi-action in fantasy." Total absence of masturbation during adolescence indicates an overwhelming fear of dealing with sexual drives. This can be produced by severe prohibitions against childish auto-eroticism, or exaggerated fear of damaging the genitals.

Differences in Attitudes Between Boys and Girls

Masturbation in girls is often greatly inhibited. It finds expression in indirect forms which may escape notice and perhaps be denied by the girl to herself. The greater inhibition of sexual response in the girl is caused by several factors, her upbringing being one. The fact that her genital is hidden from view and consists of several distinct parts makes it more mysterious than the male sex organ—to her as well as to the boy. Therefore her anxiety about her genital is greater. The little girl is primarily aware of the clitoris because it is the focal point in childhood of sexual sensations.

Although in childish explorations she is bound to have discovered the tiny opening in the hymen leading to the vagina, what evidence there is points to the fact that she suppresses this knowledge because of her conviction that what should be there is the clearly observable sexual organ she sees on little boys. It was at first thought that the little girl did not have sensations in the vagina unless subject to unusual stimulation, but from recent investigations it appears that many little girls are aware of vaginal sensations at an early age. Some girls, for instance, can recall vivid sensations of this type which came upon them as they were flying through the air on a swing.

As the young girl enters puberty, the instinctual, biological drives characteristic of the female begin to assert themselves and stimulate desires for vaginal receptivity. These desires in turn give rise to fears of penetration and of childbirth. Moreover, the girl may unconsciously equate this opening in her body with the adjacent anal one, and the feeling of dirtiness may attach itself to both. At the same time she is taught the great value of her genital. All of these conflicting feelings and ideas contribute to inhibiting the girl's masturbatory activities.

With the boy, the situation is simpler, although the mystery of erections causes much more concern to little boys than is commonly realized. (One little boy of seven confided to his therapist that he hoped she would cure him of this "affliction" which he considered to be the worst of his problems.) The fact that the boy has always been able to see his genital and become thoroughly familiar with it may be connected with the boy's greater confidence and more direct approach to sexuality.

Healthy and Unhealthy Practices

Whether masturbation is to be regarded as a healthy step in the direction of adult behavior or viewed as a sign of maladjustment is determined first of all by whether it can be considered an appropriate and therefore adequate method of gratification for the sexual drive. An evaluation of whether it is serving as a progressive or regressive force in the individual's development can be made in the light of the kind of relationships he should be capable of at that period in his life. Therefore, masturbation is considered normal in infancy and childhood when it would not be normal to have a sex relationship with another person, less so in puberty when it is possible to gratify sexual desire with another person, and no longer normal in adulthood except under circumstances of abnormal deprivation. Our society encourages masturbation beyond the years when it would be considered a satisfactory method of gratifying this biological drive, because we do not officially allow our adolescents to become adults sexually, although we do encourage adult behavior in all other respects.

The second decisive factor in evaluating the progressive or regressive nature of masturbation is the frequency with which the young person resorts to it for solace and comfort as a result of disappointing and depressing events in his daily life. Too frequent retreat to masturbation indicates overly strong ties to infantile behavior.

Compulsive masturbation is another sign of disturbance. Sometimes it is caused by the unconscious fear of having caused injury to the genitals. Repeating the act proves that the genital still functions as it should, then anxiety and guilt arise again, and another vicious cycle is set in motion as the young person continuously and vainly seeks reassurance and relief.

One of the negative aspects of prolonged masturbation is

that it can make the finding of a suitable partner in real life more difficult. Since masturbation requires no effort, it can delay the felt need to find a mate; thus, normal adjustment to reality is retarded. Furthermore, since no real person can measure up to the idealized creatures of fantasy, the giving up of fantasy figures for the acceptance of real people can be seriously delayed, encouraging a generalized retreat from reality and too great a reliance upon make believe.

Sometimes excessive masturbation represents an escape from homosexual leanings. The young person fears being tempted into a homosexual affair and attempts to safeguard himself in this manner. Other adolescents with strong homosexual drives avoid masturbation completely and throw themselves into affairs with members of the opposite sex in a desperate effort to escape homosexuality. However, they have very little actual feeling of tenderness or affection for their sexual partners, using them primarily as a means of proving to themselves that they are not abnormal. Still others, with strong feelings of fear and hostility towards the opposite sex, masturbate excessively as an unconscious defense against being dependent upon the opposite sex for sexual gratification.

A third and most important feature in evaluating masturbation are the contents of the accompanying fantasies. Of whom and of what is the young person thinking? Or is he thinking of nothing at all except the sensations in the genitals? For youngsters just entering puberty, it is not at all uncommon to be entirely preoccupied with the sensations their manipulation of the sex organs is able to yield. However, if boys and girls well into adolescence engage in auto-erotic activity without requiring the presence in their thoughts of a person of the opposite sex, they are not experiencing "quasi-action in fantasy" which would be a step towards heterosexual activity. It can be taken as a clear indication that important psychological aspects of sexual development have been blocked. (Blos)

The next consideration is the type of fantasy involving a person of the opposite sex. If it must always be a scene of violence and extreme aggression in order for it to be stimulating and gratifying, it signifies that the fusion of tender and aggressive elements in the sexual drive, required for mature genital functioning, has not taken place and that sexuality remains on an early childhood level of emotional development.

It is by no means unnatural or unusual for girls to have rape fantasies or for boys to imagine that they are overpowering a girl. Aside from an element of masochistic pleasure, rape fantasies enable the girl to experience sexual feelings while denying responsibility for desiring them. The element of forced submission is exciting because feminine sexual behavior characteristically involves surrender to the male, and masculine sexual behavior characteristically involves aggressive mastery of the female. Freud explains the biological significance of the male desire to subjugate the female as stemming from the need to overcome the resistance of the female by means other than the process of wooing. Perhaps our prehistoric ancestors did a minimum of wooing and a maximum of subjugating. There is no question about the fact that the expression of these components in the sexual drive is pleasurable to both sexes.

It is quite a different story if the girl finds pleasure in the fantasy that a repulsive, criminal brute is painfully assaulting her. When this theme recurs as an accompaniment to masturbation, it indicates a need for help. Patients with this type of fantasy also exhibit marked fears of boys (which is not surprising) and usually have a very unsatisfactory social life. Because of unfortunate childhood experiences, longings for sexual experience immediately become converted into a longing for a sadistic attack. This is sometimes caused by childhood observation of intercourse between the parents from which she assumes that what was seen was a painful attack upon the mother. This type of fantasy also leads to compulsive masturbation because it arouses so much anxiety that the youngster cannot really experience a sense of relief even though she may have achieved a physical orgasm.

Similarly, in boys it is a sign of disturbance in development if masturbatory fantasies are replete with scenes of damaging and torturing women. In boys who enjoy the fantasy that someone is beating or torturing them, there is the obvious problem of the repression of healthy masculine aggression and the turning of it into its opposite.

Masturbation anxieties are not the kind of problems that can be "talked out" with parents or teachers. The young adolescent who has a masturbation problem is an anxious and troubled person, and needs someone to talk to who is trained in psychotherapy.

A young teenager should not be required to tell his parents the exact nature of what is troubling him in order for the parents to cooperate in getting him help. When parents insist upon knowing, they usually get evasive answers, often plain lies, as the adolescent exercises a healthy instinct for privacy in sexual matters.

Effect on Character Traits

It is not generally known that there are very specific kinds of behavior which are the result of the individual's fight against masturbation. It has been found that some teenagers (and adults) become habitual liars as a consequence of feeling a need to deny that they indulge in this practice, of which they feel deeply ashamed and which lowers their self-esteem. On the other hand, lying about it, pretending they never do it, can result in their feeling a need to always confess things about themselves, to be compulsively honest about every unimportant detail in their dealings with people.

Often the adolescent who fails in the struggle to resist develops feelings of inferiority, becomes depressed and devalues and debases himself in his own thoughts. Self-accusations and self-torment may be so severe that they interfere with the development of all other qualities and talents.

The adolescent who wins the fight against masturbation by his own power and not through external prohibitions enhances his self-esteem, sometimes to the extent of developing feelings of grandeur, which then stamp the entire personality. Such an adolescent can become overbearing in his overestimation of himself and lack all self-criticism. Most often, the struggle succeeds only partially. There are periodic breakthroughs of masturbation, and hence there is a shifting back and forth between grandiose and inferiority feelings.

Not infrequently it has been found that the impulse to masturbate finds expression in roundabout ways. The sexual excitement is displaced onto completely unsexual or nonsexual activities. When this happens, the individual has no awareness of the sexual nature of the excitement and so does not realize that the activity has masturbatory meaning. Certain dangerous activities usually serve such a purpose: physical activities which have a certain amount of danger attached to them such as flying an airplane or reckless driving. Children's wild running and violent games may have a similar basis. One youngster who had a problem of compulsive masturbation developed a great interest in building excavations and used to leap into the sand pits time after time, often hurting herself. The gambling of adults often has been found to be another disguised masturbatory outlet. In many of these activities there is the possibility of a catastrophic ending, representing punishment for the forbidden sexual excitement.

There are several theories as to why masturbation, which is accepted as a universal practice in adolescence, should so often have an aftermath of feelings of malaise. One theory is that it is the psychosomatic response to feelings of guilt, anxiety and shame all of which accompany the activity to some degree in nearly all youngsters. Another is that it is at best an incomplete experience for anyone who has become capable of a mature sexual experience with a partner, and therefore leaves a residue of undischarged tension and frustration which continues to have a disturbing effect upon the person, also a pyschosomatic response. (A psychosomatic illness is one brought on by emotional disturbance.)

At one time analysts believed that the problem of healthy adjustment in adolescence was simply a matter of freeing adolescents from their masturbation guilt feelings and hence all efforts were expended in that direction. When children of such progressive homes were later analyzed, however, it was found that the feelings of guilt and anxiety were present all the same, although they were kept out of conscious awareness with the aid of parental reassurance in word and manner. Most analysts now feel that a certain amount of guilt and anxiety are inevitable accompaniments to masturbatory activity because in the unconscious part of the mind there still dwell the forgotten and now forbidden memories of romantic interest in the parent of the opposite sex. In other words, the four-year-old girl who wanted to marry Daddy and the four-year-old boy who was going to be Mommy's husband come disconcertingly close to recall when the teenager first begins to feel strong sexual drives.

There is the added possibility that we may here be confronted once again with the wisdom of nature, goading the individual on to fulfilling his role of propagation by reserving complete gratification for that act alone.

SECTION II

5

POPULARITY

If Cinderella's fairy godmother were to grant to every adolescent one wish, most would choose popularity. It seems to spell paradise to almost all teenagers. Being liked is always important; at no other time of life does it matter so much. The reasons popularity ranks highest on the list of teenage aspirations are not hard to find. Living in a transitional world, halfway between the safety of childhood and the unknown hazards of adulthood, having given up old childhood love ties without having as yet established new ones on the level of the adult world about to be entered, causes even the happiest teenagers to be assailed at times by doubts and fears as to who will love them and whether they are lovable.

The feelings of uncertainty which stem from having bidden goodby to one's childhood self as well as one's childhood loves, lead to a strong need for reassurance. Nothing is more reassuring than popularity. It is the stamp of approval, the confirmation of being lovable, the assurance of adequacy and the guarantee of success in the vaguely threatening adult world of responsibility and achievement. At least it appears to mean all these things to teenagers.

What makes a person popular? A combination of traits— warmth, kindness, cheerfulness and a genuine liking for people are paramount. A popular person has an intuitive and keen awareness of other people's feelings and reactions. It is pleasant to be near these teenagers because they reduce tension in others, reduce feelings of inferiority and make everyone feel accepted and appreciated. No one need be hesitant about approaching them fearing an unfriendly reception; they are usually gracious and tactful, which is why others feel relaxed and appreciated in their company. Their infectious high good humor makes the world seem a happier place. Popular teenagers are not, however, paragons of perfection. They have their faults and their off-moments of course, but in general their friendliness can be relied upon.

The interests of popular youngsters are those of the group, by and large. Thus, they are entirely related to the group. Their spark of originality enables them to offer the group something new. This is what keeps them in the position of leadership, which they seek and enjoy. Leadership is sustained by their great interest in other people, which is entirely sincere, implying of course that they cannot at the same time be, and are not, self-centered.

To a certain extent there is a biological basis for popularity in that these individuals have great vitality and energy. Both are constitutional factors acting as an endless fuel supply for their cheerfulness and activity. Their warmth and enthusiasm for people and activities never wanes. They are able to give continuously of themselves and they are fun to be with because they are not dull or boring.

It might be a good idea to turn about and list the qualities which are conspicuously absent in popular youngsters. They are not bitter, cynical or morose, nor are they unkind, rude, nasty or tactless; they are never selfish, irresponsible or self-centered, nor infantile and demanding; they are not suspicious, hostile and distrustful; they are never two-faced and tricky; they are not tense and easily irritated; they are not overly critical of others; they are not lazy and sloppy; they are not bored and indifferent; they are not fearful and anxious; they are neither vulgar nor ostentatious; they don't parade wealth nor bemoan the lack of it; they are never failing students.

For those who dearly want to be popular, or greatly increase their social success, the single most important quality to understand the dimensions of and to develop is kindness. The person who is kind and considerate is free of the guilt feelings and self-hatred which an unkind person continuously builds up within himself, automatically cutting down on his spontaneous enjoyment of other people, unless he can join them in hate crusades. (Some people are very good haters and fighters but the only people they are popular with are haters looking for someone to fight. That's how we come by popular rabble-rousers.)

A kind person can dare to be completely sincere since there are no guilt-laden motives which must be disguised. The kind person automatically becomes more aware of other people's feelings and therefore his interest in other people is increased. A pretense of interest never fools anyone, young or old, for long.

Not everyone can be gay and bubbling over with vitality. Forced cheerfulness like forced interest does not ring true and is exhausting and irritating for all concerned. It is best for youngsters whose usual behavior is far from cheerful or gay to exert themselves to be pleasant and courteous and leave the bubbling gaiety to those to whom it comes naturally.

Does popularity necessarily spell happiness in the long run? Many teenagers find it hard to believe that popularity is not always the great boon it appears to be and moreover that many boys and girls who never made the hit parade end up being much happier than some very popular idols. The popular youngster returning home after having been the belle or the beau of the ball, and once removed from the excitement and the gratification of being sought after, may suddenly feel exhausted and empty, envying other youngsters who have a steady, or a real romance flowering.

Despite the outstanding combination of qualities required for popularity, it does not mean that the popular youngster is necessarily a well-adjusted person with the world as his oyster. There are many cases in which the gifted youngster is goaded by a need to be loved by everyone because he feels loved by no one, and so he "plays the field" continually, with each new conquest serving as a temporary prop and reassurance. Some youngsters use popularity as a means of proving to their parents that they are indeed lovable, if they have felt slighted in favor of another child, or disappointed in the parents' interest in them. Still others make use of popularity to stave off facing up to fears of close relationships. One can observe this in the adult who continues to behave like a popular adolescent and can never settle down and marry. A less severe form of the same problem can be observed in a married person who must still be continually surrounded by beaux or belles. Popularity may be a sign of well-being and true success, but as the old song goes, "it ain't necessarily so."

6

THE PSYCHOLOGY OF DRESSING
FOR A DATE

The anxiety a teenager feels often reveals itself in his preparation for the evening. It may sound strange, but the amount of time spent on getting ready for a date can have a direct bearing on how good or bad a time a young person (or an old person) will have. It is a serious mistake to spend hours getting washed, dressed, groomed and made-up for a date. It is a mistake because, first of all, tension is slowly being built up during long hours of preparation. Tension cuts down charm, which thrives on an easy-going, friendly, relaxed manner. Secondly, if one spends long hours over every infinitesimal detail of one's appearance, the natural tendency is to rely heavily upon one's appearance for the success of the evening, and to underestimate the importance of what is beneath the exterior. Both of these factors militate against a warm and happy evening, and against popularity.

Is this a pitch for careless grooming? Far from it. Appearance is very important and every youngster should do his sensible best to be clean, neat, attractive, well groomed, with neatly pressed clothing. Doesn't that automatically mean that you must spend the whole day taking care of everything? Certainly not, if you plan sensibly and are realistic in deciding what good grooming and good make-up consist of.

Everything that can be accomplished before the day of the date, should be. The clothing to be worn should be inspected and put into perfect working order a few days in advance.

78

Items in the manicuring and tweezing departments can be done the day before, as can hair-sets. On the evening of the date, one hour or so should be entirely sufficient to shower, dress and make-up.

On the other hand, one often sees youngsters getting the whole household and themselves into an uproar a half hour before they are expected to be ready, demanding all kinds of help—shining shoes, sewing buttons, removing stains, dashing out to buy accessories at the last moment. The result is that they leave for their date with nerves frazzled, the family in a state of near-collapse. Although the youngster may not realize it, it is a poor way to start the evening. The result of this kind of start is that the girl is usually held together by a bunch of safety pins, praying that they won't show or burst open and stab her. Or the boy has gone out with dirty nails, spinach on his teeth and a handkerchief with a hole in it, hoping he won't be called upon to lend it to the girl. In both of these extremes the youngsters start the evening with two strikes against them. If one had to choose between the two, the over-prepared are actually in greater distress than the last-minute men, for the over-prepared are so much less spontaneous. Of course there are exceptions, and some youngsters can manage to be spontaneous and outgoing no matter how they've spent the day or the hours preceding the date.

The youngster who spends all day getting ready, or who goes into an explosive tizzy at the last moment, may be hiding from himself fears and anxieties about the encounter which he dares not think about. Instead, all the thought goes onto externals about which one can think without getting upset, or the excitement is transferred to the much less threatening situation—working up the family into an uproar before the date. Youngsters who feel great turmoil within themselves often find a way of involving the whole environment in it.

Sometimes, quietly given assistance, which is calm and cheerful in tone, helps the teenager to feel more in control of himself and the situation. The world seems less threatening—and every problem therefore less threatening—when one's family rallies round and shows their affection and esteem by helping, but being careful not to be infected by the excitement.

Behind the last minute hysteria or the day-long preoccupation actually is anxiety about the forthcoming encounter. Both boys and girls are probably worrying about how successful they will be on the date. Will they know what to say? Will they know how to act? Will what they say and do be pleasing to their date? The girl may be secretly worrying about how far the boy will try to go, struggling with all of her own conflicting desires and beliefs. Every girl wants the boy to find her attractive enough to want to kiss her and hold her in his arms, no matter how young a teenager she is. Depending on her age, upbringing, attitude and degree of sophistication, she will have varying degrees of fear and anxiety about it. The boy may be concerned about how bold he is expected to be. Sometimes the conflict of very strong unconscious wishes and equally strong fear of those wishes being gratified is so great that no satisfactory solution is possible. In extreme cases it causes adolescents to avoid dates altogether, the withdrawing attitude of the excessively shy or tense and uncomfortable adolescent. The next, less neurotic step is the transferring of all the uncertainty, excitement and anxiety to a situation which can be shared with the family.

It would be unusual for a youngster to discuss the real cause of his anxiety with his parents, even if he were sufficiently conscious of it himself to be able to talk about it. It is a natural and healthy development for teenagers to be reluctant to discuss sexual matters with their parents; in a sense, talking about sex is sharing a sexual experience. At this time of life teenagers become much more self-conscious about even verbal intimacy with the parents.

An adolescent's grooming, or lack of it, is a barometer to his attitudes about himself and his control over the anxieties resulting from the upsurge of sexual feelings and fantasies. The obsessionally clean and neat adolescent, for whom even a speck of dandruff is revolting, seems to be saying, "I've made myself lovable by removing myself from any possibility of being considered dirty." This may be a reaction against an infantile interest in being dirty, which was overcome with great effort. It may on the other hand be a reaction to guilt feelings about on-going masturbatory activities. Then the overemphasis on cleanliness represents a denial of them. "Who me, do a dirty thing like that? You couldn't possibly suspect me of it. See how clean I am."

In extreme cases, dirtiness can indicate hatred of everyone, born of despair of ever finding someone whose love can be trusted. "Go ahead and hate me, because I hate you anyway," is what these unfortunate youngsters are unconsciously saying. It gives them the feeling of having control of the situation, in that they are forcing people to dislike them. Thus, they feel less helpless than if they made an unsuccessful effort to be found attractive or lovable.

The type and quantity of make-up a girl uses may tell many things about her unconscious problems. Sometimes girls who are really timid and basically afraid of boys will loudly deny it by appearing in school with eyelids staggering under the load of mascara and brightly colored eyeshadow. Yet they are girls who are unsuccessful with boys. The conflict is expressed in the difference between their appearance and their manner. Their behavior, whether subtle or obvious, chases the boys away. They may act aloof or unfriendly, or sarcastic, or nervous, tense, anxious and jumpy, all of which are caused by fear of contact with boys. Meanwhile, the overdose of make-up is screaming, "I'm not in the least afraid of being a sexually attractive female and attracting men. In fact that's just what I want." If a boy does approach her, a girl with such problems always finds a way of spoiling it. She either will decide that he isn't good enough for her, or she will do something, however subtle, to repel him. Being unaware of her unconscious fears, this type of girl can never understand why she is unsuccessful.

On the other hand, there are girls who are just as over made-up who *are* successful in attracting boys. These are girls whose dissatisfaction with themselves (arising from anxiety over body development) leads them to use too much make-up in the belief that since it isn't themselves but something external covering or disguising a part of themselves, it thereby enhances them. This "disguise" is all they need to give them sufficient confidence to feel attractive. Their normal desire for romance and male companionship enables them to reach out successfully to boys. The only difficulty here is that the use of too much make-up makes a girl look coarse (in bad taste) to many people, even though she may not really be coarse at all. However, she will fail to attract some very nice boys who have the standards of their homes firmly entrenched in their own beliefs. They will misjudge her because of her make-up and avoid her. She may succeed in looking so sexy that a more timid boy, who would have found her appealing with just lipstick and a simple hairdo, may be overawed by a bleached-blond beehive, and feel somewhat threatened by the boldly sexual look of the eye make-up. On the other hand, she may very strongly attract a young man of refined tastes who, despite them, will fall for the theatrical, glamorous look. The trouble will start when his mother or sister sees the girl and begins to make disparaging remarks about her appearance.

Standards differ among different groups as to what is appropriate in the matter of make-up and dress. If a girl has all the standards of one group (i.e., a group that doesn't approve of heavy make-up for women of any age), and yet feels impelled to look as though she belongs to another group with different standards, she will find herself in difficulties because she won't feel at home in either group. The same applies to boys. The boy from a home that doesn't go in for D.A. haircuts and bohemian clothes, will find himself misjudged, if he feels compelled to look like a beatnik (when in reality he belongs in dress only) because of what the outfit symbolizes to him unconsciously.

In all cases of this type, a battle is being waged between what the teenager consciously wants and at the same time unconsciously fears. Sometimes the fear is so overwhelmingly strong no struggle is apparent, as in the case of the girl who always wears loose, shapeless clothes and no make-up, and pays no attention whatsoever to boys. In these situations the strength of the fear has almost entirely squelched conscious normal desires.

The elements in these situations are clearly observable in the course of therapy. The therapist is in the unique position of being able to see the changes in dress and make-up evolve as fear and guilt are reduced and greater harmony is achieved between the different forces within the personality. When conscious desires for romance no longer come smack up against the unconscious prohibitions of "it is dangerous, bad, forbidden, only for the mysterious world of adults," the teenager is able to be more realistic about taking steps to be attractive to the opposite sex in an appropriate manner. Sometimes fears diminish with increasing age, as the adolescent's sense of reality registers the fact that romance cannot possibly be as dangerous as it has seemed.

7

DATE BEHAVIOR

Dating experiences are an important part of the process of developing into an adult. The teenager is groping and experimenting, learning what teenagers of the opposite sex are like and what he himself is like. Naturally, dating produces anxieties. The young person is uncertain as to how he should behave.

Being out on a date is a host and guest situation. The host has the responsibility of providing a pleasant evening for the guest, and the guest has the obligation of making the occasion as pleasant as possible for the host. These are social obligations which apply to everyone, young and old. When treated with the seriousness they merit, they smooth relationships between people. This is particularly important for adolescents because they are especially sensitive to slights and rudeness.

Often teenagers are very much disturbed by the fact that the date is not repeated, even though they have done their best to be pleasant and considerate. There are many times when two young people will find that they really are unsuited to each other in terms of personality and temperament and no matter how pleasant and well-behaved they both are, the evening just doesn't work out well. There is such a thing as incompatibility. It doesn't exist only in divorce cases. It can be true of family members, fraternity brothers, teacher and pupil relationships, etc. Some personalities grate on each other and the sensible thing is to look for more congenial company when possible. As one teenager expressed it, "I could feel the evening dying around me from the minute we started off." From the distance a boy or girl may seem to be just the perfect date; yet, when the time comes, it is a disappointment. There is nothing to reproach yourself with or feel inferior or anxious about as long as you know that you gave it a chance, and were pleasant and friendly.

When dates are made only to be able to go out and without any real feeling of attraction to the partner, the situation calls for extreme caution. To betray indifference or boredom, to make it obvious that you are looking around for something more appealing in the course of the evening is unpardonable. While it is natural to want to be on the alert, unless it is done with the utmost subtlety it is a great humiliation to your date.

If time after time, with different dates, a young person continues to feel at a loss, then something needs remedying, and usually it is a combination of self-consciousness, inferiority feelings and anxieties. The best remedy is to find some way of forgetting about yourself. How can this be done? Changing the frame of mind in which you go out on the date will help. If you concentrate on measuring up to what you think your date expects of you, you're lost for it will just make you more self-conscious and generate more inferiority feelings as you keep worrying about whether you are living up to what you think is expected of you. Don't forget, these standards have been created by you and then attributed to the other person.

In order to change your frame of mind, you need to be able to view the date situation from an entirely different point of view. Concentrate on getting to know all about your date in as friendly and diplomatic a way as possible. If you charge yourself with that assignment, as though you were a member of the State Department, entertaining an important young foreign guest, with whose country we want to be on the best possible terms, you are bound to forget yourself to the extent that you throw yourself into the assignment. Suppose you were required to send in a report the next day, so that if it turned out that you and your guest were incompatible, the State Department could find a more suitable partner for the following evening. How helpful would your report be? Would it be full of how you felt (which would be of no value) or would you be able to indicate personality traits, areas of interest, certain likes and dislikes? Naturally, you wouldn't find out anything by bombarding your guest with a battery of questions. You would have to be subtle and agreeable, an observant, interested companion and host (or hostess).

It goes without saying that quiet and serious young people will behave differently from gay and high-spirited teenagers. A word of caution is in order about the two extremes of behavior. If being yourself means doing a Jerry Lewis or a Carol Burnett, it would be wisest to give a small trailer of coming attractions to see how the audience responds before presenting the whole show. In other words, if clowning is the only thing that makes you feel comfortable (your problem, even if it amuses your companions), exercise some restraint and don't overdo it. Continuous clowning occurs because the person feels unsure of himself and breaks the tension of uncertainty caused by not knowing how he'll be received, by making everyone laugh at him. When overdone it can be exhausting and irritating to the audience, and it leaves the poor "clown" with less and less self-esteem as he perceives the boredom or annoyance of his companions.

If your natural way of behaving is to be very quiet, then it would be a good idea to familiarize yourself with the latest events of importance in all the worlds you inhabit—from school games and elections to international crises. If your head is well supplied with ideas, you won't feel as much at a loss for something to say. Awareness of your weakness enables you to take steps to correct it.

Saying Yes

An attitude which has a great deal to do with success or lack of it can perhaps best be described as the psychological edge of reserve which distinguishes adult from childlike love. The child's love for the parent is complete and openhearted. He would perish without his parents' affectionate care. In his helplessness he throws himself completely upon the mercy and the love of his parents, even if he's busy disguising it in the guise of a little top sergeant. He can do nothing else. Therefore, these qualities are characteristic of normal childhood love. An abnormal situation prevails when the child has learned through repeated hurts and disappointments to maintain an edge of reserve and distrust, ceasing to openheartedly and completely love his parents, to trust them unconditionally as the guardians of his well-being and happiness.

The characteristic of mature love that should begin to develop in adolescence is that the person has a feeling of independence within himself, born of his newly acquired ability to take care of himself independently, if necessary. (Don't forget that many immigrants came to this country alone at the age of thirteen or fourteen.) The love the young person feels for another person will never again be a love involving absolute and complete dependence upon the loved one. He feels himself to be an adult, capable of coping even with the tragedy of losing his beloved. Women, however, do retain more of the feeling of dependence upon the beloved person than men as a rule.

A boy or girl who has retained a strong element of childlike love and throws him or herself headlong at a prospective date will probably find that instead of waiting with outstretched arms as a good parent should with a small child, the prospective date steps aside and the child-adolescent rams his head against a stone wall, and then needs to heal the bruises.

Somehow, human nature places less value on what is readily available than on what must be striven for. Therefore, a quick, childlike offer of complete availability doesn't work out well for the adolescent or the adult. Part of growing up is coming to recognize this fact, developing the self-esteem and self-restraint required to avoid offering companionship and admiration which does not include some slight margin of reserve. People sense this reserve which indicates self-respect and self-confidence. The young person possessing those qualities immediately rises in the estimation of others. Sometimes it is very difficult for individuals of ardent and impetuous temperaments to keep this principle in mind, as it is for desperately lonely people, but in forgetting it, they leave themselves open to the indifferent regard of others, and even to avoidance.

How to Say *No*

It is often difficult for young teenage girls or older girls just starting to date to know what to do about a boy's attempts to make-out, particularly on a first date. Many girls fear that if they refuse they won't be asked out again, and the fewer their dates the more anxious they naturally become. Some boys, particularly very young adolescents, it is true, have an almost feverish desire to make out. They become impatient and annoyed with the girl who refuses and do not ask her out again. These boys aren't ogres. They simply haven't yet reached the stage of maturity where tenderness and awareness of the girl as an individual can be combined with their sexual drive. Any girl will do; all are exciting. As one young teenage boy expressed it, "All of a sudden one day I looked around and all girls were beautiful."

The more mature a boy is the more self-control he will have at his command in his approach to a girl. He won't feel that unless he makes out the evening is a total waste. He will be able to judge how the girl feels and guide himself accordingly. There is such a thing as wooing. It didn't go out with hoop skirts.

The psychology of females requires that they tame the more direct and aggressive sexual approach which is natural to the male, insisting that he keep it more under control while at the same time encouraging his interest and continued attraction. Many girls understand intuitively how to accomplish this. Others feel unsure and bewildered in the beginning. Girls often ask, "How do you refuse to pet, to drink, to go to unsuitable places in which you wouldn't feel comfortable, and still be asked out?"

The important thing to remember when saying "no" is that your date or the others in the group may feel that you are criticizing and reproving them. Your refusal reminds them of parental prohibitions and criticisms about the very things they now want you to do, such as drinking and going to shady joints. A boy with deep inferiority feelings may be genuinely hurt and humiliated by a girl's refusal, but this does not mean that she has to say "yes."

The manner in which the refusal is made makes all the difference. If you give an impersonation of being a Puritan ancestor exhumed from a New England graveyard, you will make your companions feel guilty, and they will quite naturally want to avoid you in the future. If, however, you remain cheerful and friendly, casual and confident, without a hint of reproach, you shouldn't have much trouble, unless you've picked yourself guilt-laden teenage companions who cannot tolerate any kind of disagreement. In that case does anyone have to tell you you're much better off being compelled to find other company, distressing though it temporarily will be? With reasonably normal adolescents, your maturity will be recognized and you will end up winning admiration and respect without having forfeited your convictions or their friendship.

You should never do anything which you feel is not right for you. It will only make you feel disgusted, guilty and unhappy, so the evening will be ruined anyway. That goes for boys as well as for girls. Many boys feel that they must try to make out immediately or the girl will think them babies and broadcast *that* around town.

A girl cannot feel comfortable or happy about giving in to a boy's demands when she doesn't feel responsive herself. It is bound to lower her self-esteem and also make her especially worried about being talked about. There's no doubt about it, boys not only talk, they brag about their amorous exploits as a way of appearing very grown-up to their friends. "Gentlemen don't tell" applies only to the mature and sophisticated males, not to insecure teenagers, anxious to be considered experienced. And girls, too, like to brag to each other about the trouble they have in keeping various boys under control.

Sometimes a girl makes-out on the first date with a boy because she *is* attracted to him and wants him to know it. This doesn't always work out well for her because if she doesn't hear from him again, as often happens, she feels hurt and humiliated and regrets having engaged in warm expressions of affection with someone who, as events prove, doesn't really care about her. The boy's disappearance from her horizon may be caused by any one of several factors: indifference or another girl, perhaps. Sometimes a boy retreats in alarm because of what he was so quickly permitted to do, and avoids the girl out of fear that he will be expected to go further on subsequent dates. Boys have their anxieties, too. If a boy's self-esteem is not very high, he may attribute the immediate surrender not to his own charms and the girl's open-heartedness, but to a mistaken judgment that the girl must be "easy" and anyone could have been as successful. He then loses interest and looks for a girl who will boost his ego by making him work at winning proof of his attractiveness to her, after which he can feel that he has an accomplishment to his credit. Therefore, a girl never makes a mistake by waiting until the boy shows that he is genuinely interested in her. In this way she spares herself the anguish of feeling "used" as an impersonal object for the boy's momentary pleasure.

A boy who feels uncertain as to how far to go with a girl and who is sensitive about being rebuffed should think in terms of being friendly and considerate. No girl can find such behavior foolish or offensive. He will soon be able to tell from numerous small signs if his caresses are welcome. If the signs are not forthcoming, he has spared himself the hurt of being refused. But a boy has no reason to feel miffed if he is re-buffed by a girl with whom he tries to act semi-engaged with-out benefit of a courtship period. A girl with self-confidence and a good sense of reality knows perfectly well if she is at-tractive to a boy and she does not take it as a compliment—just the reverse—if he is in too much of a hurry to prove that his body chemistry is working properly. Boys who feel that because they take a girl out on a date she's got to "come across" with some form of love-making are thereby giving evidence that their sexual development is strongly tied to the level of greedy demandingness which is characteristic of (and this is not meant as a joke) the kind of love an eighteen-month to two-year-old child has for his mother. If a mother doesn't give the baby what he wants, he sees her as a bad mother. He wants to kick and hit her and if possible get a better mother. Tenderness and the wish to be protective and do things for his mother develop later in the little boy (third and fourth year) with the blossoming of Oedipal love. This is also known as the phallic phase of development because it is the time when the child's interest and pleasure and pride in his body center in the genital. Masculine pride fuses with his love for his mother and the capacity for tenderness begins to develop.

In cases where boys have had frustrating, harsh or indif-ferent mothers the fusion of tenderness with masculinity and sexuality is interfered with. And since in adolescence, all the early love-relationships are revived, the boy will carry on the unfinished fight with his mother in his attitude to his dates. A girl who isn't ready to immediately gratify him arouses his wrath because of a backlog of frustrations. Having been se-verely frustrated as a toddler, his tolerance for the normal frustrations of teenage dating is low. Unless he can learn to separate the present from the past, he is in trouble.

The Tease—Real and Apparent

Some girls show their aggressive feelings towards the male sex by engaging in the provocative and frustrating behavior which is understood by the term "tease." A teasing attitude is their revenge for early disappointments in their fathers' treat-ment of them. Their chief pleasure is in trying to even the score via teenage males. Boys sense the aggressive intent and are angered by it as well as by the frustration to which they are exposed. The girl knows exactly what she is doing and derives pleasure from her power over the boy.

There is another type of girl, however, who is frequently thought to be a tease, but who really has no hostile intent. These girls have a great hunger for being kissed and held close and have blocked out the sexual significance of this type of behavior because their craving for it comes directly from a lack of loving body-contact experiences when they were very little. On a date they always manage to be in a great deal of bodily contact with the boy, with no awareness of what it means to him. The boy naturally takes it as an invitation to greater intimacy. He ends up feeling that he's been made a fool of, and the girl can't understand why he is angry. Boys can suffer from the same hunger for nonsexual affection. It can be seen most clearly in those men who always have their arms around whichever woman is near them. They often give the wrong impression, too!

The Broken Romance

The psychological edge of reserve is that area of the emotions to which the person retreats to heal the wounds of a broken romance. No matter what the age it means anguish. But broken romances are characteristic of adolescence and teenagers must try to be psychologically prepared for them. The heart is experimenting. Love feelings, although intense, are unstable. Suddenly, for no reason, the feeling of attraction wanes; there is an attraction to someone else, not someone who is better, just a different person. It is a healthy process, much more desirable than going steady for years during the teens, but, unfortunately, painful. Be prepared for the inevitable and you won't be as crushed by it.

That edge of reserve gives you a grip on reality when the whole world seems to have come tumbling down around your ears and you feel as though you want nothing so much as to die. It is what prevents you from being completely adrift, because it enables you to remember your own worth and strength at all times. The part of you which you reserved for yourself, that you refrained from pouring into the other person is the storehouse from which you will draw sustenance during times of emotional famine.

Unrequited Love

Sometimes an adolescent falls head over heels for someone who never quite becomes aware of his or her existence. This is quite typical of adolescence because the one who falls so hard is often responding to his own fantasy of what the adored one is like, and pours all his emotions into the fantasy. Getting to actually know the person sometimes is sufficient to cure the infatuation.

On the other hand, a young person may really know and appreciate and be mad about another teenager, while failing to elicit even a spark of interest in return. This can happen to anyone. It is a slow torture from which the healthy young person soon extricates himself when he realizes the hopelessness of the situation. When the teenager cannot give up, or when this sort of thing happens over and over again, it constitutes grounds for becoming suspicious of what is going on in the unconscious of the chronic torch-carrier.

Courting Rejection

Some people always fall for someone who either ignores them or within a very short time breaks off with them. In investigating the backgrounds of people who go from one unhappy experience to another, unerringly scenting members of the opposite sex who will reject them, it always turns out that they have had disappointing experiences in childhood, either with parents or older siblings, as in the following cases.

A little girl whose loving attachment to her father was shattered by a divorce, after which he made few attempts to see her, grew up feeling most unsure of herself with boys. As children do under those circumstances, she believed that it was her lack of charm and lovableness which had led her father to neglect her. As time went on and anger at him arose alongside the love and longing, she felt guilty and even more unworthy. During adolescence she experienced a revival of intense longing, coupled with distrust of the regard and affection of boys. Whether she fell for a boy her own age, or a man who was frankly a father figure, they invariably were selfish, self-centered individuals who had no appreciation of her many lovely qualities, and who treated her inconsiderately.

A girl whose father and brothers were cruel to her, grew

up with the unconscious conviction that men are supposed to behave that way. Although she deplored their behavior, she, nevertheless, found herself attracted to boy after boy who behaved badly to her. Similarly, a boy whose mother was extremely harsh to him always managed to find cold, heartless girls with whom to fall in love.

Many divorced people admit that they have subsequently married the same type of person they originally divorced, which is why some people divorce and remarry many times. What they consciously desire is so different from what they unconsciously seek and find.

Adolescents who have felt neglected or despised as children often have contempt for boys and girls who admire them. If someones admires them, they distrust it, or they assume it indicates that the person is stupid and has bad taste. They find it impossible to believe that anyone with intelligence could think more of them than their own parents or siblings apparently did. So they gravitate to others who can be relied upon to behave in the manner to which they have long been unhappily accustomed. The ultimate pain and rejection also gratifies the need for punishment which has arisen because of guilt feelings stemming from anger and hostility towards the frustrating, disappointing family members. In addition, each painful experience proves that the hostile feelings and distrust are justified.

Teenagers with similar histories need to become aware that the cause of their bad experience is not a lack of fundamental charm, but an unconscious seeking for a repetition of an unhappy childhood love.

8

PSYCHOLOGICAL FIRST AID

Adolescents in their middle and late teens who are not dating and who are not included in co-ed parties need help. The problems, of course, are psychological, but the psychological can affect the physical. It is generally a good idea to begin the overhauling in this area.

Physical Fundamentals

Sometimes the general appearance of a teenager tells volumes about what is wrong, and at the same time is a means of perpetuating the problem. Neglected hair, skin, body cleanliness, and unattractive clothes tell something unpleasant to the world. Often it is a challenge, "If your liking for me is sincere, you'll like me dirty as well as clean. I won't clean up in order to earn your liking." This is an anachronism. It doesn't belong to the present, it belongs way back in the past, at which time it had validity. Parents who love their babies don't or shouldn't stop loving them when they are dirty; however, they still have to teach them to be clean. To carry this attitude along into adolescence means that an unresolved difficulty over cleanliness resulted in the child's feeling that it was not loved unless it was clean. This creates disappointment and anger towards the parents; subsequently, the rest of the world is treated as if it were the childhood parent. Unconsciously, the same battle is fought over and over again. If one is tied to an angry, spiteful infancy, then one is being held back from entering the world of adolescence. Dirty babies *should* be acceptable, dirty adolescents are not.

The unkempt appearance also says something else which is entirely self-destructive. It cries, "See, I am nothing but the dirty baby my parents disapproved of so strongly. I don't deserve to be liked and I don't expect to be." An adolescent who knows that he has been neglecting skin, hair, daily bath, nails, teeth and the use of deodorants, as well as being careless about clean underwear and keeping clothing spotless and well-pressed, must rouse himself and work out a daily routine that will keep him a welcome member of adolescent society. Give your physical self a thorough going over to make sure that no one will find being close to you an unpleasant experience. Greasy, dandruffy hair, noses covered with blackheads, dirty nails and teeth are as offensive to the eyes as body odors are to the nose. They repel other people and the person who is guilty of such neglect in our country where a daily bath, toothbrushing and use of deodorant are standard procedure, is expressing a wish to repel others and will undoubtedly succeed. Those who belong in this group should lose no time in scrubbing themselves right out of it, thereby bringing about an immediate rise in self-esteem.

Overweight teenagers have the most difficult problem to conquer. The underlying problem of many, but not all, obese youngsters is one of depression. Sometimes it is a deep fear of being attractive. They need a great deal of understanding from the people in their environment to compensate for the unbearable feeling of frustration produced by denying themselves food. Many of these youngsters feel happiest when they are eating. They seem to have a great need for the eating pleasures of early childhood and also usually crave the sensation of being filled up. It is not at all unusual for them to feel a deep sense of alarm when they try to cope with hunger pangs.

In the case of young children in therapy, it is possible to observe a youngster go into a panic when the mother attempts to carry out the pediatrician's advice to refuse to give the child more than a certain amount of food. Some children have a food addiction. In order to feel relaxed and safe, they must keep stuffing themselves with food. Fighting fat is undeniably an uphill battle and takes more courage than most people of ordinary weight realize.

The tension, frustration and unhappiness which make some

people over-eat or eat only fattening foods, make others unable to eat. Very thin youngsters are just as painfully unhappy about being skinny as are the overweight about being too heavy. Both situations are caused by psychological problems and usually require psychotherapy. Bad skin conditions, too, may be caused by unresolved problems. If medical care fails to clear up a bad complexion, it is worthwhile to consider psychotherapeutic help.

After one's appearance has been taken care of, the next step is to acquire some fundamental skills required to participate in adolescent social life. No single skill is a more important asset for social success for both boys and girls than dancing. If parents can afford it, private lessons are the best. Being in an agony of self-consciousness because others are watching the beginner stumble and bumble, can render instruction ineffectual. If private lessons are out of the question, then find a friend, or brother or sister, or some young relative to give the instructions. If just a basic fox-trot is practiced literally by the hour, until it becomes so automatic that you can converse while doing it without losing the beat or the step, it will be fairly easy to later pick up other dance routines. Most boys and girls are quite ready to show each other steps of new dances, but you must first have mastered basic skills.

The next point in the program is to become reasonably proficient in a few sports. Swimming, skating, bike riding are especially good because they can all be group activities. Exercise, moreover, has important psychological results. It offers an excellent outlet for tension and aggression and is therefore an ideal tranquilizer. Exercise has often been suggested to boys and men as a means of reducing tensions, both sexual and aggressive, but for some reason it is not usually thought of as "medicine" for girls.

The tingling feeling of health and zest and well-being which vigorous exercise gives immediately puts the young person into a better frame of mind. An outstanding characteristic of popular youngsters is their pep and energy. The youngster who feels physically dragged down and looks pasty-faced and dull-eyed, or who is a jittery bundle of nervous tensions, is not going to find it easy to attract others. Tension somehow has the effect of repelling others. It is catching and everyone unconsciously tries to avoid the source of it. Whether one feels dragged down or overly keyed up, vigorous exercise will make a great difference. Of course, these suggestions are based on the assumption that physical exertion has not been ruled out because of a physical ailment and that you are on a sensible diet. Many teenagers indulge in the self-deception of believing that some inherent superiority to the usual laws of nature prevails in their case; that there is a unique magical quality to their own endurance which enables them to get along on a 4-C diet of cokes, cookies, cigarettes and coffee. During teenage the biological magic which is taking place in the body produces a greater amount of energy than the individual will ever have at any other time in his life. This extraordinary supply of energy masks the harm caused by an inadequate diet because even with its depleting effect on energy, the young person feels the same as he used to. Every teenager should feel full of energy, enabling him to accomplish with gusto all the many important tasks of adolescence: competence in school work, successful social relationships, proficiency in sports, emancipation from childhood emotional ties, broadening horizons with new interests, finding one's life work and finding a mate.

Some adolescents think it is sophisticated (cool) to squander this extra supply of energy through undernourishment and insufficient sleep. How silly! It is a golden time. Every teenager should keep himself in tip-top health so that he can perform miracles of achievement in every area of his development. All of these achievements will remain part of him and add to his sense of worth and to his happiness in providing countless avenues of interest and enjoyment for the rest of his life. The really intelligent thing to do is to ride the great wave of increased energy into as many different ports of interest and accomplishment as possible. Never again will there be an opportunity equal to this one.

Psychological Problems

It goes without saying that teenagers who are unconflictedly eager for contact with others don't need any advice as to where and how to meet them. As unerringly as the roots of trees change direction underground and grow towards a water supply, so do reasonably confident teenagers find places and activities which bring them into the company of the opposite sex. In fact, they will overcome with great ingenuity any obstacles put in their path. But many teenagers have a hard time getting into social life. They may feel deeply inferior, self-conscious, shy, frightened, angry or bitter.

Shyness

Shyness is probably the most widespread general problem of adolescents. For many it is an agonizing problem, one they are quite willing to admit troubles them greatly. A degree of shyness is a normal, inescapable part of adolescence. The dictionary defines it as follows, "A manner which shows discomfort or lack of confidence in association with others. Shy implies a constitutional shrinking from contact or close association with others, together with a wish to escape notice. Diffident—self-distrust, fear of censure, failure."

Why should the adolescent typically suffer from all these feelings? Shyness is the end-result of a struggle with entirely opposite feelings; namely, a strong wish to be extravagantly admired and loved; above all, to be found sexually attractive and to have romantic and sexual experiences. It is entirely natural for adolescents to have all these wishes, yet they create anxiety.

Adult sexual strivings can be alarmingly new to the teenager. These strivings are charged with masturbation and Oedipal guilt. The girl's wish to display the beauty of her body and the boy's wish to display the power and size of his produce some guilt feelings as a rule. Childhood guilt about masturbation and wanting to run around in the nude temporarily casts a shadow of disapproval over the new sexual wishes and the desires for the body to be seen and admired. And as for Oedipus, he's a big boy now—in some ways his father's equal: intelligence and ability to work, in some ways perhaps superior: strength and vigor. The girl may for the first time surpass her mother in beauty, charm and seductiveness. These changes evoke memories of the once-hopeless childhood struggle for exclusive possession of the parent of the opposite sex, and there is a degree of anxiety about the possibility of success because the wish is still there in the unconscious. Shyness denies the existence of these all-important desires.

When the guilt is strong, shyness does not disappear as it does under normal circumstances, with the adolescent's realization that he is entitled to feel exactly as he does and to strive for admiration and romance. Strong guilt makes the adolescent extremely uncomfortable, therefore he must keep on denying by means of his shy behavior that such feelings and wishes exist. Shy behavior says: "I don't want to be noticed and admired." And yet, it gratifies the original wish of getting attention, since everyone notices the excessively shy person's awkwardness, blushing and self-conscious manner.

Teenagers whose self-consciousness was always kept at a painful pitch by being called runts, stringbeans or butterballs as they were growing up will be even more aware of themselves than are others. Being made fun of creates a greater than average need for admiration to undo the damage to self-esteem and the body-image. The best method for overcoming shyness is to try to overcome guilt feelings resulting from pride in the sexual development of the body, realizing it is all a normal part of adolescence and will not end in a fulfillment of Oedipal wishes or rape fantasies, unless the people involved are extremely disturbed. The alternative to shy behavior for a girl is not that of walking unescorted through a dangerous neighborhood late at night, thus inviting a sexual assault. Unconsciously, she may have such a wish, for then her secret longing for a sexual experience would be gratified and at the same time she could disclaim all responsibility.

The acceptance of one's normal sexual wishes, including a wish to display the body and have it admired, a realization that sexually mature bodies are attractive, and that knowing and enjoying this does not cause anyone to lose control over him or herself, should be of help in overcoming shyness.

Withdrawing Behavior

Teenagers who have had difficult experiences of one kind or another as they were growing up often find it difficult to reach out to others with whom their daily activities bring them in contact. When confronted with a live member of the opposite sex, they either behave unpleasantly or retreat into the innermost recesses of their emotional home, as opposed to their behavior in fantasies in which they usually greatly enjoy the company of the opposite sex.

Many of these teenagers have settled for withdrawing behavior, which consists first and foremost of daydreaming by the hour. A certain amount of fantasy serves a useful purpose. It enlarges the young person's horizons, gives birth to ideas which can be put to use, gives the youngster a chance to rehearse in advance and prepare for experiences which he is likely to have in the normal course of events, and generally can serve as a springboard to original activity.

When the adolescent relies entirely on fantasy experiences and fantasy successes he is in trouble. For the duration of the fantasy he is happy and gratified, feels strong, successful, important and proud. Then it all disappears. He is left with nothing but a greater sense of frustration than before and lowered self-esteem when he contemplates the great chasm existing between reality and the fantasy achievements. In an effort to compensate for the ever-increasing sense of frustration and futility, the fantasies usually become more extreme, with the result that the teenager despairs more and more of making the grade in real life.

Some unpopular teenagers whose school behavior is aggressive and unpleasant and, therefore, does not qualify as "withdrawing" nevertheless spend much of their time escaping in fantasy, homemade or commercial. Some teenagers make an overly great use of the ready-made fantasies offered to them in TV shows, comics, novels, movie magazines and movies, spending all of their free time involved in these media which serve the same function as one's own fantasies and promote the same negative purpose, when indulged in to excess, of removing the young person from the world and from reality achievements.

Intellectual youngsters of this type often submerge themselves in scientific and academic studies. These may, of course, serve a very useful purpose later in life, but during adolescence it may be viewed with suspicion as a withdrawing mechanism if the adolescent spends all his time studying and yet is secretly unhappy about his social life. There are some unusually intellectual boys whose scientific interests absorb them so completely that social life goes by the board. They never date and don't care to. They are totally gratified by scientific pursuits and sometimes don't become aware of girls as sexual beings until graduate school. "Suddenly one day he notices a girl on the other side of the test tube." (It is extremely rare to find girls truly satisfied with only intellectual pursuits, although some pretend to be.)

These boys are not unhappy about being outside the social swing and therefore do not require "first aid." Their entire lives may follow the same pattern, all personal matters remaining secondary to their scientific work.

Unsuccessful teenagers observed first hand in therapy can be roughly classified into three groups: those who are convinced that no one could find them attractive, those who cannot understand why they are not liked, and those who insist that the whole trouble is that all the members of the opposite sex in their particular school or neighborhood are a bunch of creeps and crumbs, dogs and drips. When treatment begins there usually isn't one possibility in the entire area; well, maybe one, but he or she is somehow always going steady. Wonderful to relate, after a while many of these revolting young classmates are mysteriously transformed into nice, attractive boys and girls who, it turns out, are exciting to be with and fun to know.

There's hardly a person, young or old, who really wants to change and improve his situation, who can't do *something* about it through his own efforts. The *degree* of success will vary among individuals. The most important factors which will determine the degree of success are the depth and complexity of the problem and the strength of the desire to change.

In the realm of physical accomplishments there are many dramatic examples of people becoming experts in fields in which they originally were handicapped. From time to time in the life history of a dancer or athlete, one discovers that the skill was first acquired in childhood as the determined youngster ceaselessly exerted himself to overcome a defect or injury. And of course there is no more inspiring example of the heights to which will-power and courage can propel an individual than the achievements of Franklin Delano Roosevelt, who in the face of permanent crippling in the prime of his life, moved ahead to the pinnacle of success.

The same principle applies in the realm of psychological handicaps. A therapist cannot help a patient who has no wish to change. That is why adolescents cannot be sent for treatment against their will. They have to want to change something (even if it's the world) in order to have a meaningful starting point. If a young person comes to treatment feeling that all of his unhappiness is caused by his being just a helpless victim of circumstances over which he has *no* control, then the first step in psychotherapy would be to help him gain insight into the fact that he is pushing responsibility completely onto others because it makes him feel so unhappy to realize that his own behavior is not what he really would like it to be.

Unsuccessful adolescents need to learn how to be friendly, how to be relaxed and less preoccupied with themselves and their fancied (in most cases) defects. They usually have had experiences in the course of growing up which have made them feel resentful and reluctant to reach maturity, fearful of the responsibilities and involvements of adulthood, especially relationships with the opposite sex. Of all this they frequently are completely unaware.

When asked to describe unsuccessful teenagers the following emerged as the impression made on others by the youngsters who have trouble getting along socially:

They're terribly tense and self-conscious and always worrying about every word that they say and wondering if they said the right thing. Some are jumpy and jittery. It's hard to be near them. Some have very irritating mannerisms. Some are so mousey that you overlook them, they fade into the wall. Others are just the opposite, aggressive show-offs, or rude and overbearing, or given to making nasty fun of classmates. Some are grouchy complainers and always up in arms against something or other. They are not fun to be with. They can't seem to think about anything but the impression they're making; they are not nice to people. They are not kind. Their appearance is unattractive.

I have resisted the impulse to tone down these estimates. It can only be helpful for unsuccessful adolescents to look squarely at the *impression* they make on the more thoughtful of their classmates. (The estimates came from teenagers who have had psychotherapy or analysis, and currently are enjoying satisfactory social contacts.)

Every type of behavior referred to is actually used as a defense against feelings of anxiety. It is the method hit upon by the troubled young person for coping with anxiety, reducing it or preventing it from becoming stronger. Strange as this may sound, anxiety is at the root of most brands of unattractive behavior.

Troubled Teenagers

High on the list of teenage goals is a good personality. When we say someone has a good personality, it means he has a predictably pleasant way of dealing with people and situations, an attitude towards life which is genial and friendly.

What is personality? It is the pattern of behavior made up of the individual's habitual responses to the demands made upon him from within himself and from the outside world. In other words, personality is a picture of the compromise arrived at by the individual in attempting to satisfy his impulses, desires and needs, while at the same time living up to the demands made by the people in his environment to behave in certain ways which are approved of.

The unsuccessful teenager has been prevented from developing a pleasing personality. Therefore, we can safely assume that the cravings from within himself for love, appreciation, accomplishment and sufficient freedom to develop his unique qualities have not been able to find a satisfactory compromise with the forces which are impinging upon him from his environment. His thoughts, feelings, wishes (both conscious and unconscious) and actions are not in harmony with the environment and, therefore, are a continual source of frustration and anxiety to him. Someone who feels tense and unhappy, at odds with himself and the world, cannot have a "good personality."

Everyone has a certain amount of tension and anxiety to cope with. (It is important to learn to tolerate it and live with it without reaching for a Miltown, a drink or a cigarette.) More than one popular teenager has a great deal of anxiety. These teenagers have learned to reduce anxiety by making everyone like them. They use the very pleasant technique (defense against anxiety) of being agreeable to everyone in order to keep relationships pleasant and cheerful.

What has happened in the cases of those who have either withdrawn from others or become disagreeable in one or several ways?

Whenever one attempts to divide human beings into neat and precise categories one is always in trouble. Thoughts, feelings, emotions, behavior and experiences are all miracles of complexity and endless in their individual variations. Therefore, an individual put in one category is bound to have a few fingers and toes, if not an arm and a leg, firmly in another category. In the descriptions and explanations which follow one needs to keep in mind that most people's experiences and personality traits relate them to all the categories in varying degrees and combinations. For purely practical reasons the groupings are being resorted to with apologies for the oversimplification. The reader will understand that fitting predominantly into one category does not rule out the fact that he partially fits into others as well. The shy teenager, for example, may belong to several other categories.

The Overindulged

Some youngsters have been doted on by their parents and perhaps by very much older brothers and sisters to an exaggerated degree. All their lives they have been taught by the behavior of others to believe that they are unusually charming and lovable. Therefore, they have never acquired an understanding of the need to make an effort to accommodate themselves to another's wishes or needs. The adults have been ecstatic with praise for every normal thing said or done and this has given them an inflated sense of importance. While it is certainly no fault of the youngsters', it makes them self-centered and they anticipate a warm welcome from everyone without their making any efforts themselves, as in their home.

In some cases, where the child has been mistakenly encouraged to believe that any ideas or plans he has must always take precedence over those of the other family members, he grows to adolescence believing in the divine rightness of his being the leader. When he finds that he cannot win a key position in the group, he may retreat from all participation. Kingpin, Queen bee or nothing. It is extremely difficult for teenagers with this kind of history to understand what is the matter when they find themselves ignored by their classmates. Frequently, after the first shock of realizing that others are preferred to them, they withdraw in anger and seek solace at home.

Some parents make the serious mistake when they see that their children are rejected by classmates of trying to soothe the child's hurt feelings by assuring the youngster that it is jealousy or lack of appreciation of the youngster's especially fine qualities which is causing the rejection. This usually happens in cases where the parents are so identified with the child that they find the rejection unbearable, and therefore, encourage the child to deny with them the reality of the situation. Just as popularity is deserved, so is unpopularity. If you can't get along with anyone, if no one seems to like you, your behavior, and your behavior alone, is causing it. If jealousy of a pretty face, a lovely figure, artistic talent or a high intelligence caused unpopularity, a great many successful teenagers would be unpopular.

This kind of upbringing results not only in the youngster's being unrealistic about himself, but also of acquiring distorted notions about the character and personality of others. It also encourages him to remain childish in his attitudes, expecting everyone to be an indulgent parent. Very few teen-agers are willing to baby another teenager, needless to say, and they are unimpressed by petulant pouting and haughty disdain. Sometimes parents of teenagers of this type come to their aid by planning activities for a group of teenagers, occa-sionally winning a certain amount of temporary acceptance for their offspring, but unless they can at the same time en-courage him to be more adult, appreciative of others and will-ing to compromise, their efforts will not be crowned with success.

The task for teenagers who fall into this category is that of learning to understand the difference between the kind of be-havior which is appropriate to a younger child, and the kind of behavior which arises from an awareness of other people, their needs and their pleasures. These adolescents have the job of pulling themselves up a few steps on the maturity lad-der without any help from their parents, whose tendency us-ually is to keep on babying them, helping them to deny reality. They must try to understand that they are a puzzle to their classmates who are baffled and bored by the self-centered immature behavior. The self-centered youngsters don't offer companionship, they look for a continuation of their home experiences. Children who have brothers and sis-ters not too different in age seldom have this problem because they have been forced to share the spotlight, cope with com-petition and to be satisfied with a portion of the parents' love. They have learned how to become friends with other chil-dren as they grew up, all of which is good preparation for group participation in adolescence.

The over-indulged teenagers need to carefully observe the behavior of others and to note how their own differs from it, instead of giving in to feelings of being insulted and mis-treated, attributing hostile intentions to others. Through no fault of their own they haven't learned to share, to give and to take care of others. Becoming successful socially means they first must realize that their expectations are based on mistaken ideas of what the group owes them. They must learn to think in terms of what they can contribute to the group. Instead of continuing to look for indulgent parents, it may help them to try to be indulgent parents to others. Every time they catch themselves feeling indignant and by-passed, they must stop and think about how the situation looked to the other person. They must try to school themselves to be sporting about disappointments. They need to train themselves to stop looking for special treatment. They must work on developing an ever increasing awareness of other people's desires. This will reduce unrealistic feelings of resentment and hostility. It will eliminate the anxiety which is aroused by alienating their classmates and by the failure to which false expectations doom them.

Instead of rushing home to report to oversympathetic parents on the trials and tribulations of the day, the first step in acquiring the much needed maturity is to keep these episodes to themselves, to try with all their might to think about them unemotionally and to have the courage to evaluate realistically their own behavior in the painful episodes, being on the alert to detect their own readiness to take offense. It's hard, but it can be done. The beginning will be painful, unquestionably, but the end result will more than compensate.

The Unsuccessful Rival

Another group of teenagers who often have difficulty relating in a friendly way to others are those who have spent their childhood in some form of bitter rivalry. Girls with exceptionally beautiful mothers often feel hopelessly unattractive compared to them, even when reasonably pretty themselves. Sons of brilliant or prominent fathers sometimes have a hard time acquiring the conviction that they may some day equal their fathers, even if in another field of work. A very successful brother or sister can have the same effect. The sister of a popular or beautiful girl may abandon the struggle to be as successful and turn to nonfeminine pursuits, paying no attention to her appearance or to the usual forms of social life. A boy may have a similar problem with an outstanding brother and pretend indifference to success or to competence in all the areas in which the brother excels.

And of course, there are many other variations on these themes. Sometimes without the parents' having especially outstanding qualities, circumstances can result in unresolved feelings of rivalry between them and their children, as well as among the children themselves. The more favored child may simply be the baby of the family, and, as frequently happens, on that score alone be the greatest recipient of parental attention. It is well known that a middle child frequently feels lost in the shuffle. The eldest is somebody special, so is the baby, and the middle child feels that he is nobody very special. Sometimes one very gifted or exceptionally good looking child in the family draws so much attention and praise from everyone, strangers as well as family members, that the other children feel distinctly inferior and jealous.

These young people arrive at adolescence expecting to take second place with everyone but resenting it at the same time. They carry around a load of anger, jealousy and inferiority feelings, as well as a longing to be top dog, which they continually express to their teachers and classmates. A popular youngster immediately arouses bitter feelings of antagonism and jealousy, and they may sulk in the corner, hating the successful individual without realizing that he reminds them of a brother, a sister or perhaps a parent by whom they have felt hopelessly overshadowed. Many young people from this group have a chip on their shoulder. They are always on the lookout for a quarrel, up in arms about some injustice, or delight in antagonizing others or making cruel jokes. Without realizing what is propelling them, they are trying to even the home score.

The injustice which is really arousing the wrath is the injustice of the home favoritism or overwhelming competition. This is often the basis of the quarrelsome attitude towards teachers and classmates. The antagonism and sadistic humor usually are a displaced expression of the jealousy of brothers or sisters and a wish to belittle and ridicule them, as much as to say, "Look what a ridiculous creature he is, what can my parents find to admire so much in him?" Sometimes this need to belittle is a direct consequence of a parent's belittling of the child, which is then immediately turned by the youngster onto other youngsters. Doing unto others what you hated having done unto you can be a source of great satisfaction. The trouble is that it is an unhappy kind of satisfaction because it brings dislike in its wake, self-dislike as well as the enmity of others. The young person is thus progressively worse off.

Difficult as it may be for many to believe, a surprising number of popular adolescents have unpleasant family relationships. Burning with a need for recognition and having many excellent qualities which went unappreciated at home, or were even disapproved of—as in the case of very gay and outgoing youngsters whose parents approve only of extremely sedate behavior—they are able to seize upon the opportunity afforded by adolescent society to make an important place for themselves. Whatever bitterness, or hostility or jealousy they may feel at home, they manage to shelve it and to devote themselves to friendly, gay, happy encounters which compensate for the unpleasant situation which may be their lot at home. Determined to be recognized and liked, they come ready to put themselves out to be kind and agreeable to others. For them school life and the social life after school hours provide a delicious escape from home. Unpleasant family relationships are not always carried over directly to the outside world.

Teenagers who have grown up under a cloud of disapproval for certain personality traits, or who have lived in the shadow of an unusually endowed or favorite child, or who have unresolved problems of competing with a parent, or those who have the problem of never seeming to be able to win recognition and approval from either parent, obviously have ample reason to feel distressed. It is not surprising to find in them antagonism bursting out towards others, or to find them either retreating from the normal competitiveness of social life, or always provoking punishment.

Unrealistic Self-Estimates

The basic problem of these young people is that their self-estimates are invariably distorted and unrealistically low. They underestimate themselves and usually are unaware of certain fine qualities and abilities either because of the guilt they feel or because these qualities went undetected or unappreciated at home. In addition, self-esteem is further lowered by the weight of the guilt feelings which hostile feelings and behavior towards parents and siblings create.

In order for them to change their behavior, they must first alter their estimates of themselves and their expectations of unpleasant behavior from others. How can this be done? First, by understanding what caused the favoritism at home; second, by realizing that home is not the whole world when one has reached adolescence and that others will respond differently, if the teenager will permit it. The most important thing to understand is that the favoring of one child and the lack of proper appreciation of another's qualities and temperament is not the result of one child's being more lovable or more worthy than another, but a spontaneous response from the parent to particular qualities in a child, based on the parent's personality and life history. It may happen, for instance, that a mother who feels a burden of guilt because of having overshadowed a younger brother in her own childhood may favor and protect her young son from his older sister as a way of atoning for the past. Or a mother who felt slighted in favor of a brother may find herself very much favoring her daughter and even being quite unfair to the boy. Similarly, a father may react in ways determined by his childhood. The children involved do not know what is causing this behavior, but they assume that their own qualities are what make the difference, even while angrily protesting the injustice.

In cases where a parent despises some quality in himself, he may react with exaggerated disapproval when he sees the same characteristic developing in his child, and this can be carried on from generation to generation. A mother who had been brought up in a home where her gaiety was considered vulgar frowned very strongly on her little daughter's strong tendency to engage in rollicking pastimes. As a result, the child grew up feeling hopelessly vulgar and inferior, instead of understanding the advantages of her capacity for merriment and joyous social relationships. Some mothers and fathers are much more at ease with quieter children. Certain coloring appeals more than others. In each case, the element provoking either negative or positive feelings might cause the very opposite response in another set of parents. For instance, in some homes the very quiet and studious child is regarded with worried suspicion and impatience by parents who feel that it is healthier to be gregarious and happy-go-lucky. In other homes, the restrained serious child is considered a gift from heaven. A child may resemble a beloved grandparent who has died, and thus arouse special feelings in the parent. Or the child may bear a physical resemblance to a despised in-law and arouse negative feelings in the parent. The less mature the parent is, the stronger and more uncontrolled the feelings will be.

Without being at all aware of the cause, parents often produce behavior in their child which is extremely disagreeable to them. For instance, a child who is yelled at may yell back. The parent will disapprove of this response. But the child's anxiety, which is aroused by the parent's behavior, may only be reduced by behaving exactly as the parent does. Therefore, no matter how much disapproval the parent shows, the child will feel compelled either to yell back at the parent, or to yell at others, probably smaller fry in the home or neighborhood. As a consequence, the child may soon come to be labeled a loudmouth and a bully. This type of defense against anxiety is very common and it is known psychoanalytically as defense by identification with the (frightening) aggressor. It is as if the child is unconsciously saying to himself, "The only way I can feel safe from my parents' frightening behavior is to be just as frightening as they are, either to them or to somebody else."

On the other hand, yelling at a naturally quiet and constitutionally less active child may lead to strong withdrawing behavior as a defense and the child may become quite silent and sometimes sullen. Such behavior may be extremely disagreeable to the adults who become frustrated in their later attempts to elicit satisfactory responses from the child. This type of withdrawing youngster may go through his childhood years referred to as a sourpuss or a sullen sphinx or whatever strikes the adults as an apt description.

Unquestionably disagreeable behavior is produced in the child. But in none of these cases does the child have control over that which determines his behavior: the manner in which he is treated, and, therefore, the atmosphere in which he grows up. Yet, he will be molded by the treatment he receives and will believe that something inherently wrong with him created the negative feelings in his parents. At the same time, he will develop greater than normal resentment towards them and towards the more favored children, if any, perpetuating a vicious cycle of feelings of guilt and lowered self-esteem.

There is, moreover, a most unfortunate tendency shared by many adults, parent and non-parent alike, to talk about children in their presence as though they were deaf. Unrestrained by the fact that the child hears every word, they describe his behavior as it appears to them. "The big one's a born grouch. She's never been happy since the day she was born. But now you take the boy, he's a real sunny Jim. What a personality. He's a charmer. And that little one is a real conniver. He'll surely be a politician when he grows up. The fat one is going to be the banker of the family, or a miser, we don't know which. He always has all his allowance when the others have spent every cent. He takes after his Uncle Paul who's still got the first dime he ever made. My little girl is a second Aunt Jean. Always taking care of everyone, with a heart as big as all outdoors." (A woman whose children were playing within earshot, actually made these remarks.)

The little girl who is told that she is just like a kindly and generous aunt is given a great spur to develop all the qualities of her aunt. The same promoting of identification goes on when the comparison is meant in a disapproving way. A very disturbing effect of labeling and type-casting is the strong tendency to live up to them which it creates. In the child's mind the parents are always right (even when he also knows that they are wrong); therefore, he feels predestined to live up to the role they cut out for him. Whereas other types of behavior may go unnoticed, the labeled type is continually reinforced by the parents' recognition of it and reaction to it. Moreover, the child who cannot win positive notice will gladly settle for attention of a negative kind. And again the vicious cycle is set in motion.

Frustrated Teenagers

Teenagers with a history of uncomplimentary labels feel a great deal of anger and hostility towards their parents and their brothers and sisters. Frustrating experiences arouse anger; these youngsters have had an overdose of frustration through the years.

Adolescents are also frustrated by parents who are over-involved with them. Their homework, schoolwork, friends, phone calls, letters, clothing, hair style, behavior and activities all are of the greatest concern and interest to the parents, usually the mother in particular. Opinions are expressed continually. The purpose is to direct everything the youngster is doing and thinking. In attempting to live their children's adolescence with them in this suffocating way, the parents find themselves unable to allow the teenager any true freedom. The young individual is usually paralyzed emotionally by this situation and is kept in a frenzy of irritation or becomes completely inactive. Forced to remain in childlike closeness to the parents retards his development and makes it exceedingly difficult to relate to other teenagers on their terms.

A group of teenagers who often feel insecure and distrustful of others are those of divorced parents. This is true particularly in situations where great enmity and hostile criticism has been continually expressed by the parents towards each other, so that the children know that in loving and imitating one parent they are always displeasing the other. Under those circumstances it is difficult to feel lovable, or to be sure of what is truly right or wrong. Still another group of troubled teenagers are those whose parents are unhappily married, and especially where the child has become aware of infidelities on the part of either or both parents. Many emerge from these situations as very prickly young people who find it difficult to relate to others.

Fortunately, adolescence is an ideal time to shed the restricting and depressing influences of an unhappy home, and to form new self-estimates while in the process of enriching one's personality and finding happiness in relating one's self to people whom one admires. Forming a new estimate of one's self where it is depressingly low requires not only understanding of why parents have behaved to you as they have, but also why *you* have reacted as you did. Your behavior, however objectionable, at no time was the result of anything fundamentally wrong with you. It was your intuitive response, dictated by your constitutional type, to pressures from the environment. At birth babies exhibit a characteristic activity pattern. Some are extremely active, yowl if the nipple is withdrawn and search actively for it. At the other end of the scale of activity patterns are babies who are very quiet. If the bottle or breast is withdrawn they may simply cry, or go to sleep, or lose interest in accepting it when it is offered again after being removed a few times. If your constitutional pattern was one of great activity, then the chances are you fought back with vim and vigor when frustrated and pressured. You were harder to handle than the inactive type of baby. Generally, boys are much more active than girls, and, therefore, much more of a challenge to the parent after the first year of life.

Of course, there are very active girl babies and quite inactive boy babies, and this too is entirely within the range of normality. One has only to look around and see the number of gentle, quiet, relaxed men and the number of women who are happy human dynamos to realize where it all starts. These individual differences in activity patterns are necessary for the survival of the world. Imagine, if everyone were a fighter or if everyone were submissive, how exhausting and boring it would be. No intelligent person can maintain that one temperament is more desirable than another, anymore than it can be maintained that the exquisite and perfect design of one snowflake is to be preferred to the perfect but different design of another.

If you have been criticized all your life for having a particular type of temperament or for exhibiting a certain kind of behavior, now is the time for you to strive for some understanding of your parents' blind spots and your own inevitable reactions. Insight about these fundamentals should enable you to stop anticipating the same kind of treatment from the rest of the world, especially if to this insight you add an awareness of the aspects of your behavior which are unpleasant and a determination to correct them. Without insight, the chances are that you will gravitate towards people who will continue the unpleasant relationships you had at home. Look around you and see how many people are always quarreling with every associate and friend, how many others always manage to be taken advantage of by everyone, how many boys and girls always fall for people who are never interested in them. People always find what they unconsciously are looking for. They either provoke it or scent it out as surely as a bloodhound.

Stop looking for unpleasant and unhappy relationships in order to prove that everyone is against you. You have to stop anticipating rejection, give up expecting teachers and other adults to duplicate your parents' behavior and clearly distinguish your classmates from your brothers and sisters. You must try to think about the fact that your home experiences are not typical for the world and you can have very different and much happier experiences out in the world than you had at home.

There is an unconscious tendency to duplicate our childhood relationships even when we think we are doing the opposite. Some people do manage to do the opposite so successfully that others are at a loss to understand it. How can a minister's son become an alcoholic, for instance, or an alcoholic's son become a minister? It happens; it is known as *reactive character formation*. The young person reacts *against* the example of the parent with whom there is an unhappy frustrating relationship. He identifies with the parent's *opposite*. This works out well when the opposite of the parent's qualities are good qualities which are at the same time compatible with the basic temperament of the child. Otherwise, a lifelong struggle ensues within the personality between unconscious identifications with the "disowned" parent and his opposite, frequently leading to escape from unbearable tension in alcohol or other undesirable forms of escape behavior. Sometimes the unfinished story of life with parents is played out for the entire lifetime. The most harmless form is to be found in the individuals whose rebellion takes the form of always having to do odd little things such as eating dessert before the soup as a means of expressing defiance and liberation. Others are always in a fight with the person in authority, whether it be teacher, foreman or president of the company, and still others remain overly timid and dependent upon the authority figures.

In some cases one sees the struggle carried on with the parents themselves for a lifetime. This is at work in situations such as the one in which two sons behave very differently towards their mother, for instance. One son does everything for the mother, sends her south in the winter, pays her bills, and is extremely attentive in every way. The other does very little and is very casual about her welfare. To everyone's surprise, it is the son who does very little for her whom the mother favors and she expresses very little appreciation for the efforts of the son who tries to give her everything. What is going on in a situation like this? The favorite son takes his mother's love and preference for granted, the other spends his life trying to win the favored position. Unconsciously, or perhaps even consciously, he hopes that some day the mother will realize that she has been mistaken and that he is the most deserving of her love. This will never happen, no matter what he does for the mother, and no matter what honors and distinctions he achieves, because her feeling of greater love for and enjoyment of the favored son has come about spontaneously because of unconscious factors over which no one has control.

Should the devoted son stop being devoted? If he gains insight into what is motivating him and understands the futility of it, he will continue to do what is proper and filial, but the energy expended and the continuous frustration experienced in the expectation of finally overcoming his childhood rival and standing first in the mother's esteem will cease to be a driving force in his life. Liberated from the struggle he will be able to devote himself to finding a woman who will love him best of all men in the world. If he doesn't understand the struggle going on within him, he may remain a slave to it, and although he may marry, the chances are that he will always find reason to feel dissatisfied with his wife's affection for him. His demands may be unreasonable and childish, or he may unconsciously select someone who, like his mother, will give him only second place in her heart.

In the overwhelming majority of cases, parents with problems haven't the faintest idea of the effect they have upon their children, nor of the factors which are causing them to perceive the child and behave to him as they do. Difficult though it may be for some teenagers to believe, parents try to do the best for their children *as they see it*. They do not know that they have been blinded by impulses and emotions stemming from their own unresolved problems of childhood which distort their vision and contaminate their feelings.

Parents who are unfair or unkind to their children don't get that way by saying to each other, "Now let's see how miserable we can make Jimmy and Jane." Parents who behave as though they had consciously arrived at these attitudes actually believe they are helping their children to improve by treating them in these mistakenly critical ways. They have a strong drive to continue to behave exactly as they are behaving. A very complicated set of unconscious interacting forces keeps propelling them in the same destructive direction. Yet their conscious intent, in all but severely disturbed individuals where spite and hostility are indeed conscious, is to do what they truly believe is best for the child. The parent who makes his child's life miserable with continuous carping and criticism would nevertheless unhesitatingly lay down his life for that same child, were he faced with the necessity. Parents love all their children, not in exactly the same degree nor in the same way, but the love is there even though very severe problems may prevent the feeling from coming forth and finding the expression in the way that would satisfy the child's needs for affection.

A teenager may well say, "To heck with heroics. I'll settle for pleasantness and friendliness every day and take my chances when the building burns down." The teenager is quite right from his point of view. The little everyday kindnesses do make life happy. But you are not going to change your parents. The only person you can change is you. And it very often happens that when a teenager is able to make an important change in his behavior, automatically there is some change in the way he is treated at home.

Prescription for Angry Teenagers

It would be a very simple-minded therapist who would assume that an explanation to the teenager of why he and his parents have behaved towards each other as they have is sufficient to eliminate the feelings of anger which have been accumulating through the years, or sufficient to prevent new ones from arising. But the teenager who is able to piece together information about his parents' childhood and upbringing, who is able to see connections between the parents' experiences and attitudes toward their children, as well as toward each other, should be able to view his own situation with at least some objectivity so that there is a partial reduction of hostility. This is important because overwhelming feelings of hostility can spill over into all relationships and spoil them.

It is unquestionably a bad break to grow up feeling that other children have been preferred or that one's personality and behavior have never been pleasing to a parent, or that one could never hope to equal a parent, or that love for one parent is displeasing to the other (as in divorce), or that parents will never consider you mature enough to be entitled to privacy and a life of your own. But hundreds of thousands of youngsters are in this predicament. Those who sit around wallowing in a sea of self-pity, discontent and anger get absolutely nowhere, and alienate everyone by their unpleasant behavior. The really intelligent solution is to use the energy generated by discontent and frustration as fuel to propel yourself in the direction of solid accomplishments which will give you continuing gratification. Whenever you start to boil, use the steam to get something done for yourself, even if at times it is no more vital than completely redoing your closets and bureau drawers, or putting every article of clothing into perfect condition, or rearranging the furniture in your room, or perfecting a skill you are in the process of acquiring.

It may be of interest to youngsters whose childhoods have been unhappy to know that a study which was made of men and women whose work and accomplishments have resulted in their being considered outstandingly creative disclosed an overwhelming number of them to have been unhappy in childhood. This study points out of course that parents should not take this as a signal to make their children unhappy. If unhappiness alone were sufficient to produce creative people, the world would be spilling over with them. It does seem to indicate, however, that unhappiness can be a great spur to accomplishment. Whether the creative persons seek solace in work or have a greater than average need to acccomplish, the study did not indicate. But it is likely that both are true. And in social relationships the very same principles apply. Discontent can always be used as a driving force toward outstanding accomplishment.

Instead of nursing grievances (however justified), the intelligent attitude is to face the fact that you've been living under a handicap and to make up your mind that you're going to do something to improve your own situation. You have a measure of independence and can get around to different places and meet a variety of new people. Your home is no longer the whole world as it was when you were a small child. Others will treat you differently if you give them a chance. Look squarely at your own behavior and try to estimate the extent to which you live up to your home reputation. Many unhappy teenagers have acquired a fool-proof set of irritating, exasperating modes of behavior, some the direct result of childhood labels. There is a natural tendency to grow into them no matter how unfair you have believed them to be. All your courage is needed to assess the unpleasant aspects of your behavior in order to decide what you would like to get rid of. Changing one's behavior at home is the hardest job of all because of the intensity of emotional relationships between family members. It's best to begin by concentrating on changing your behavior in contacts outside your home; school, of course, being the most important place.

A Time to Change

Adolescence is the ideal time for making radical changes in one's behavior and personality. The structure of the personality, which has been fairly fixed and rigid during the years from six to about eleven, suddenly becomes fluid as the behavioral patterns which were appropriate to childhood are suddenly shattered by the upsurges of adolescent drives towards maturity, necessitating an entirely new approach to the world which has begun to make totally different demands upon the individual.

Suddenly there is emotional chaos, but chaos which serves a most important and healthy purpose. The adjustments you made to your environment during the preceding years were appropriate for the childhood world you are leaving. The uncanny wisdom of nature which has fashioned the marvelous patterns of which all life consists, and yet within which are to be found an infinite variety of individual differences, has arranged for a breaking up of this fairly rigid behavior which has served during the years from six to eleven. That was the age of the concrete and the predictable, the time for acquiring mental skills, sport skills and learning to have social relationships, with dependence upon parents and other adults for approval and guidance. Home was the most important place in the world and school the second most important.

Now there are completely adult stirrings: the imminence of sexually tinged relationships, the drive for independence with its concomitant need to find one's life work. Life outside the home becomes of the greatest importance. The old behavior patterns are no longer useful and a state of fluidity and flux ensues which allows for the greatest opportunity for reorganizing, changing, enlarging and enriching your personality.

Adolescence is truly the crossroad of life. It is the first time you are in a position to make decisions about yourself which will have an important influence on the rest of your life. It is the first time you have the power to change your own behavior without adult support. In the past it was parents' or teachers' continuing demands upon you which kept you going in a particular direction. At this point a great force influencing your behavior is your own concept of the kind of person you would like to be.

The Importance of Identifications

For all teenagers, not only the ones who are dissatisfied with their social success, adolescence is the time for absorbing new qualities and characteristics through identifying themselves with other greatly admired people, either older, or the same age. The parents, who provided the models for early childhood identifications, recede into the background and other individuals in the outside world begin to replace them. This is the normal situation, and with youngsters who are relatively untroubled, one usually sees a series of these identifications taking place, by means of which the youngster draws into himself, as it were, qualities of the other person which then become a permanent part of his own personality.

The process of identification may begin with a crush on the other person, and feelings of great admiration and reverence. Frequently the manner of dress, and in the case of girls, the hairdo of the idol is copied. Mannerisms are also imitated, types of speech and gestures. The next step in the process is the most important: identification with the attitudes, behavior, achievements, standards and philosophy of the idolized individual. All of these identifications are incorporated by the teenager; they fuse with existing personality features or are added to them.

Adolescence is the time for worshipping not only the living, but for being inspired as well by the life stories of great people who have either changed the course of history or brilliantly illuminated one tiny corner of the earth, or whose spirituality has fired the hearts of mankind, or whose compassion and self-sacrifice have ennobled all of humanity in disclosing the sublime heights which the human spirit may attain. Heroes and heroines in great works of fiction can also serve as subjects for identification. Great writers, as is well known, are intuitive psychologists and are able to portray real people. Sometimes one particular aspect of a fictional character can provide inspiration.

A young adolescent from a home in which aggressive quarreling with everyone was the order of the day, so that people were entertained at their own risk, where the host or hostess might pounce on any guest for expressing an opinion contrary to theirs, was particularly struck by a description in a Tolstoy novel of an outstandingly successful hostess. She made careful note of the qualities described, determined to acquire all of them—and did. Needless to say, they were diametrically opposite to anything she had learned at home. But the lesson she took from a great novelist was so well learned that it stayed with her, greatly increasing her success and happiness.

The adolescents most in need of this series of identifications are often the most fearful of making them. In troubled teenagers this natural and important development often tends to be restricted because the young person feels disloyal to his own parents if he allows himself to adore and emulate other parent figures. This happens when the tie to the parent is fraught with conflicting feelings in which anger and hostility born of humiliation, disappointment and frustration mingle with feelings of affection and craving for love. Without being aware of the causes, the troubled young person often feels as guilty as if his emotional and spiritual "adoption" of another parent figure meant the physical destruction of his own parents. Such strong guilt feelings interfere with the identifications needed in order to broaden the teenager's concepts of himself and to deepen his understanding of the adults in the world outside his home.

The guilt feelings experienced by troubled youngsters at this phase of their development are often reinforced by the parents' actual resentment of the adolescent's enthusiasm and admiration for certain outstanding people in the teenager's environment. Such resentment creates obstacles to making the best use of channels for normal development. The adolescent in that position must remind himself as often as need be that it is in no way disloyal to idolize others. It is a normal, healthy and much-to-be-desired occurrence, provided, of course, that it does not go to the extreme of becoming an obsessive adulation of only one person, in which case it indicates an underlying strong fixation to a parent. The intensity and the duration of the violent crush will indicate whether or not the young person is in need of professional help in order to be able to relinquish the one attachment and move on to others. In some instances where a teenager is very much in need of a good parent substitute, a long-lasting attachment can provide him with important experiences missed during his childhood. But eventually he must be able to take other people as models, too.

Respecting Your Personality Type

None of these suggestions are aimed at changing your basic temperament and type of personality. If you are a volatile person of fiery temperament, it is a mistake to try to be a mouse no matter how much you may wish you were. And if you are a quiet mouse or sedate and thoughtful, it is senseless to attempt to be a rollicking extrovert. Whatever type of temperament you have, be familiar with it, respect it, appreciate it and enjoy it. The world needs your type just as much as it needs any other type, regardless of what your choice would be if you could pick yourself a brand new temperament. Kindness, courtesy, dignity, cheerfulness and seriousness will be expressed within the framework of your special personality and character.

Differences in temperament, of course, mean different types of faults to correct. The very outgoing and excitable types may tend to err in the direction of bombast and overly dramatic behavior and the very quiet and reserved types may tend to be insufficiently friendly or gracious. Knowing your type means knowing what areas of behavior will need the most thought in the process of training yourself to behave in the most agreeable and attractive manner harmonious with your basic personality type.

If you feel like a devil and try to act like an angel, you may be sure your horns are going to be clearly visible under your halo. Learning to feel differently about yourself and others is the most important part of learning to behave differently. Happiness and a sense of fulfillment lie in the direction of the broadest and highest development of your own type of personality. When inspired by another person to develop qualities like his, those qualities will have to be grafted onto elements within your personality in order for them to become permanent. If you can identify yourself with those qualities strongly enough, some version of them will become your own. Ironing out defects, strengthening positive attributes, extending one's range of responses through identifying with other types of behavior, which may also bring about modifications in one's own behavior, are all constructive processes and, needless to say, bear no relationship whatsoever to pretense, insincerity or artificiality.

Changing Everyday Behavior

Your behavior outside your home can fairly easily be changed if you are truly determined to change it. This can be accomplished by making use of the psychological process called identification, in a conscious way.

Step No. 1. When you're lying in bed at night think about the kind of situations and encounters you are likely to have the following day at school or wherever you are going to be if it is a weekend. Think about what your characteristic way of behaving in each situation would be.

Step No. 2. Then think of someone whom you greatly admire and imagine that person in your place in each of those situations and think about how your idol would behave, what he would say and do, and the manner in which it would be done. Think of what your idol's attitude towards the people involved would be, and the points at which it differs from yours.

Step No. 3. In your mind go through all those situations again, this time adopting your idol's attitude and making it your own. Note the differences in the way you handle each encounter this time. You will become aware of tendencies and impulses that need to be counteracted.

In the morning, try to find at least five minutes in which you can be alone and quiet, and spend the time thinking about the person you greatly admire: his manner, his voice, smile, carriage and bearing, his characteristic behavior. Let your mind and heart be flooded with the essence of this individual's personality as you see it. Don't, for heaven's sake, write yourself a script, and plan in advance exactly what you are going to say to anyone. It would be disastrous because it would not be spontaneous. Starting off the day wrapped in the aura of a revered individual's personality, after having unconsciously worked on identification with it during the night as a result of your bedtime psychological exercise, is all that you need to do to bring about a fairly rapid change in your attitude and behavior. The right words will come of themselves as you become more accustomed to your changing self. They will be the right words for you, if your feelings toward people are the right ones. If you don't feel at all friendly, it is hard to find friendly words of conversation. If you're new at feeling friendly, you may not immediately find the words you want, but they will come after a while, and there's nothing wrong with just standing around feeling pleasant towards everyone and listening to what they have to say. A gentle, friendly, sweet, gay or dignified smile is most eloquent. People respond to the feelings which they sense from you. Unless they are very troubled themselves and unable to perceive others accurately, they will tune you in very clearly. It was the static of tension, fear and hostility which made it unpleasant for them when they tuned you in in the past. You don't have to be ready with a bright remark every minute of the day. That can be exhausting for everyone. All you need is a little store of kindness and graciousness in your heart. It will significantly raise your lovability rating.

Getting into the Swim

All teenagers have some anxieties about everything pertaining to sex, a sweeping statement, to be sure, but true. Is my body developing as it should? Are the feelings and sensations which overtake me normal or is there something wrong with me which makes them arise? Will I be attractive to the opposite sex? Will I be found lovable? How much making-out is permissible? Will sexual excitement carry me away so that I won't be able to stop myself from going all the way? Are boys dangerous? Are girls dangerous? Will I know what to do? How bold does the girl expect me to be? How willing does the boy expect me to be? Will my reputation be ruined if it gets around that I made-out with a boy? Will I be considered chicken if I don't try to do a real make-out job with a girl?

In some young people these anxieties are so strong, so overwhelmingly difficult to cope with, the youngsters completely withdraw from the possibility of having to face up to them. Since all teenagers have these fears to a certain extent, one may ask, what has happened in the cases of those who cannot manage to master them sufficiently to be able to be part of the social life of their peers—to get into the social swim. The very shy and withdrawn teenager does not feel able to cope with boy-girl relationships, and retreats from them. Here, it is important to point out that many of the "angry" teenagers have great anxieties about sexuality which are masked by a fighting and aggressive attitude towards the opposite sex. The unpleasantness keeps them from being involved in a sexual relationship, fear of which may be the basis of their unpleasantness. Converting fear into hostility is an unconscious defense against experiencing the feeling of fear. Thus, some girls who are inwardly terrified of boys behave in an extremely antagonistic way to them, and vice versa. In this way they disguise their fear and at the same time eliminate the possibility of becoming involved in a romantic (sexual) encounter.

The overindulged girl with excessive sexual fears may use the excuse, to herself as well as to others, that the boys are rude or don't behave properly. The overindulged boy may complain that the girls are too demanding and stuck on themselves. The hostile teenagers often use the rationalization that all the teenagers they know are drips and creeps.

What can be done to help teenagers who have exaggerated fears of sexuality to overcome them sufficiently to become part of the social life of their school? What follows will apply to all troubled teenagers in varying degrees, just as the examples explaining some of the situations causing unpleasant behavior in the group designated as "angry teenagers" apply to many of the "withdrawn" group as well. Withdrawn teenagers can be just as angry as the openly hostile. The former keep it bottled up, the latter give vent to it all the time.

In discussing stages of early childhood development, it was previously pointed out that each stage of development presents its own specific areas for difficulty later on, if mishandled; overstimulation leads to feelings of helplessness in the grip of sexual feelings; guilt over difficulties in toilet training, including bed wetting; guilt and anxiety over sexual curiosity; sexual explorations and sexual play with brothers and sisters, as well as other children; and guilt and anxiety about masturbation. The manner in which these situations are handled by the adults in the child's environment has a great deal to do with how comfortable the child feels about his body; in particular, about the sensations which the sexual parts of the body produce. If the child has been subject to overstimulation repeatedly as an infant, he may dread the normal adolescent upsurges of sexual feeling as they will reinstate the feeling of helplessness he experienced as an infant.

All of these early experiences, as was explained, enter into the manner in which the child will deal with his Oedipal rivalry. If he is very frightened and guilty about his past "crimes," he may very likely feel overwhelmed with guilt about his feelings of rivalry with the same-sexed parent or overwhelmed with fear and feel the need to repress his feelings instead of being able to come to terms with them, knowing that some day he will have a spouse of his own. When this happens, childhood attitudes of fear and anxiety and feelings of inadequacy remain fixed. And the individual goes through life feeling like a little child, even at fifty, with regard to the opposite sex and all sexual matters. Everyone knows unmarried people well on in years who blush and go into an anxiety state when in the presence of an attractive member of the opposite sex. They may be very attractive themselves, but they never seem to be able to find anyone with whom they are comfortable and happy and whom they feel able to love. They are tied to the parents and fear unconscious sexual wishes. The roots of these problems are always to be found in the experiences the individual had during the first five years of his life.

A severe father, or a father with a terrible temper, may very easily instill in his little daughters the conviction that all men are frightening and dangerous, particularly if a great deal of angry quarreling takes place often between the parents. A boy whose mother has been given to aggressive acts and violent threats may very likely enter adolescence with deeply ingrained fears and hostility towards women which can make him withdraw from social life because he feels unable to relate to girls. A girl who felt unable to love her father as she grew up may have similar difficulties with boys.

Children who are overly attached to a parent find it difficult to make the necessary break at adolescence. Some appear to, in that they eventually make dates, but they never break the childhood emotional tie, and reveal it in being attracted only to married men or women, who unconsciously represent the beloved and forbidden parent, or they lose interest the moment someone becomes seriously interested in them.

Sometimes a fear of growing up arises in children who have been either too much or too little babied. The one who has been babied too much lacks the incentive to accept adult responsibilities, the one who has had too little may keep on searching for babying from the frustrating parent or other adults. Therefore, one frequently sees teenagers (and younger children) who are perfectly at ease with adults and completely charming in their company, but never able to get along with age-mates.

In some cases the girl whose father has been treating her in many ways like a girl friend or a junior wife cannot break away from this relationship, and, similarly, with boys who have been encouraged to be the man of the house in their father's frequent absences. These situations encourage the play-acting of being grown-up without becoming grown-up. The fantasy and the pretense are so strong and give so much gratification that true progress towards maturity is impeded.

The eight or nine year old boy who goes out to dinner with his mother and pays the check, who is encouraged to be the man of the house during father's absence, comment on her appearance and share her adult interests, very quickly makes a practice of pretending he is entirely grown-up. It is very hard for him to relinquish these fantasies and get to work on the very slowly acquired everyday accomplishments such as competence in school work, learning sport skills, and learning the give and take of social relationships with friends his age, all of which are true preparations for adulthood, and indispensable steps on the road to maturity.

Similarly, the little girl who is given too much freedom and responsibility in handling the baby and pretending it is hers and who is also allowed to monopolize her father's attention and be treated by him in many ways as a tiny wife finds school work and other childhood attainments very unappealing by comparison to the drama she enacts at home and continues in her daydreams. Although these fantasies provide them with a great deal of pleasure, these children end up feeling very frustrated because they know they are only children and also because they usually are retarded in age-appropriate accomplishments which would build real self-esteem. In addition they suffer deeply from guilt feelings which are created by the intense feelings of rivalry towards the same-sexed parent which these situations inflame. The boy wants to play man of the house, and the girl wants to play Mother and also play Daddy's best girl *all* the time, not just when it is convenient for the parents to participate in the little drama.

Far from preparing them for adolescence and adulthood, the anxiety created by the pseudo-maturity, to which they know they cannot live up in reality, has the effect of making the children feel more and more inadequate. One observes these reactions time and time again in the course of therapy. When youngsters with this type of history reach adolescence, they feel quite unequal to coping with the problems, frustrations and anxieties typical of adolescent social life (and they usually have a school learning problem of long standing). One finds that they have skipped over most of the usual childhood problems and challenges, resulting in what may be described as a short-circuiting of development. Their accomplishments consist mostly of being able to play-act an adult, but they are far behind their age-mates in real maturity.

Sometimes in an unhappy marriage or divorce a parent turns exclusively to a child for love and companionship and the child reaches adolescence feeling it his duty to continue to satisfy the parent's needs. Or an embittered divorced parent may actually teach the child that all men, or all women, are untrustworthy or worthless.

Some teenagers whose parents seem to have done nothing but fight, argue and quarrel come to adolescence dreading adulthood, convinced that marriage can be nothing but the one which they have been observing and shuddering under all their lives. Some youngsters reach teenage full of fears and anxieties about sexual and romantic encounters purely as the result of exaggerated feelings of anxiety which they have sensed in their parents towards their budding adulthood. If parents are full of fears of what may happen to their teenagers when they are invited to co-ed parties, or go to the movies, or for a drive in a car, they send undercover messages, as it were, to the child as it nears that time of its life, to the effect that all sorts of hidden dangers are lurking in social encounters. Instead of the teenager being able to overcome his own natural timidities and the residue of his childhood fears, the fears are continually renewed and refreshed by his parents.

Some young people have been type-cast as "old maids" or "women haters" and enter adolescence feeling a compulsion to live up to the labels. The opposite can happen, too. These young people may fling themselves into promiscuous sexual activity either to prove how wrong the type-casters were or fearing that they may have been correct.

It is hoped that in thinking over how you became anxious and fearful about dating you will realize that the fears and feelings really belong to an earlier part of your life, when you could not judge situations accurately. No matter how painful, difficult or overwhelming it may seem to the timid, shy or withdrawn youngster to engage in activities which bring him into contact with young people of the opposite sex, he simply must make every effort to do so. The first attempts will undoubtedly create anxiety; there may well be awkward, unpleasant and disappointing encounters. But it is far better to weather these initial storms with determination and learn how much you can do to improve your social situation, how much more fun you can have and how much more successful you can feel than to continue withdrawing, missing all the fun and building up more and more anxiety about social contacts.

The person who undertakes to give advice has the responsibility of knowing the possible outcomes of following it, and ideally, should be familiar with the way in which it is likely to be interpreted. Advice can be completely misapplied.

If one has a patient in psychotherapy, one has the twin advantage of knowing in advance something of the manner in which the suggestions may be carried out, and of also later receiving a report from the patient as to what actually transpired. Thus, one can deal with misunderstandings, misconceptions and *the new anxieties which attempting to follow the suggestions may have aroused.* How different the situation is when one attempts to give advice by means of a book! Yet, the responsibility is equally great. To talk to invisible teenagers as though they were present, asking questions and bringing up problems which flesh and blood teenagers have done, has the serious drawback of lacking the intermediate questions which each teenager, out of his unique personality and experience would ask, enabling the therapist to relieve the anxiety which frequently is aroused when a young person first begins to look squarely at problems towards which he has hitherto maintained a staunch ostrich-like policy.

It is imperative to stress the fact that if the suggestions made here are not helpful, it simply indicates that you need to discuss your feelings and problems with a trained person. If your community has a child guidance clinic it will most likely include help for adolescents. The psychiatric department of any hospital will probably have people specializing in adolescent problems. The psychology department of a university often has a guidance laboratory or counseling center connected with it, in which counseling and psychotherapy for adolescents and their parents are available. Don't let fear or false pride or a mistaken notion of what courage consists of prevent you from seeking help if you have tried and failed to pull yourself up by your own bootstraps. You condemn yourself to keeping up an endless struggle which will consume and waste your energy. Some people's anxiety is just too great to be coped with alone. Any teenager who has tried for a few months to help himself and finds the results unsatisfactory should not hesitate to seek professional help. He may even find that he is more anxious as a result of trying to get out into the world, but this is not cause for alarm. It is the result of taking the first step, and he may be more quickly able to utilize therapeutic help as a result of having taken that first step by himself.

But you may be surprised to discover how much you *can* improve your situation through your own determined efforts once you understand your situation a little more fully. In many cases, just understanding what is causing the difficulty can be sufficient to enable a teenager to make a giant step towards correcting it.

Withdrawing adolescents must consciously force themselves to make contact with others on a sustained basis. These are the youngsters who never know where and how to meet people, because they have a strong fear of becoming involved with other teenagers. They may be completely unaware of the fears and insist that they want nothing more than to meet nice boys and girls. On a conscious level they are stating the truth. Of course they want to meet boys and girls and have a good time. But the unconscious reluctance to make contact with the opposite sex is so strong that it wins out. It must be very consciously fought against.

Any club that can possibly be joined in or out of school, should be joined, as well as any service committee at school or in the community, or any group activity in athletics or dancing, or any hobby-type club or group. School or community outings should be participated in even if at first you feel as if you won't survive the ordeal. If tension and unhappiness become so great that you *really* cannot bear it and must have some relief, you can always come home where you can think over the situation and try to understand why you felt under such a strain. Think about how you might have handled the situation better, and then try again when you have rested up a bit from your labors. But don't delay too long before trying again. It's like falling off a horse. In order not to let the fear crystallize riders are always made to re-mount immediately. The same psychological principle applies to propelling yourself into social situations.

The beginning is the hardest part. *The beginning is the hardest part of the process!* Don't forget that, otherwise you may become discouraged, feeling that your courage and en-ergy won't hold out because you can't keep on doing some-thing so difficult all the time. If in the beginning, when the going is the roughest, you fight it out with yourself and don't give in to fears and all the physical symptoms which may assail you in order to keep you from leaving the house, you will find them arising less and less. Remember, the uncon-scious is determined to have *its* way. Headaches, nausea, dizzy spells, sudden feelings of weakness, stomach-aches, back-aches, kinks in the neck or various muscles, sore throats are all psychosomatic reactions to your struggle. The feelings of dread and anxiety will become reduced as you prove to yourself by actions that you are not going to be intimidated by the childhood beliefs which have determined your actions until now. There are psychological reasons why fear and anxiety are reduced through conscious efforts to cope with the anxiety-arousing situations instead of avoiding them.

What Goes on in the Unconscious

The unconscious part of the mind is the reservoir, among other things, of all the frightening childhood ideas and con-cepts which have been pushed out of conscious memory. It is the reservoir also of all the memories of early childhood experiences, pleasant as well as unpleasant, which everyone forgets after about the fifth year. Freud discovered that at the time in each child's life when he realizes that he must give up the rivalry with the same-sexed parent and try in-stead to be just like him, he represses all memory of the strug-gle, and along with it, he represses the memory of the entire first five years of his life. That is why most people have only the most fragmentary recollections of their early childhood,

nd it is also the reason why it is so very difficult for people
who do not have the opportunity to observe little children to
believe that such a thing as Oedipal rivalry exists. People
who take care of nursery-age children in a permissive setting
where the children may freely express their ideas and feelings
see evidence of it all the time, a fact which led Freud to say
that it was his fate to discover only those things which every
nursemaid knows.

One may picture the mental apparatus as containing a mini-
ture of the little child the individual once was, the little
child's attitudes and beliefs influencing in varying degrees the
person's current behavior. The great importance of childhood
experiences lies in the fact that they determine attitudes and
may strongly influence behavior all through one's lifetime,
even though the person has forgotten them.

Once an idea, belief or awareness of a feeling is repressed
into the unconscious part of the mind, it is much more difficult to modify by later knowledge and understanding than if
remains conscious. For instance, a child undergoes an op-
ration and is terrified by having an ether mask put over his
nose and mouth. Having believed at the moment that he was
bout to be suffocated, the recollection of the experience is
so painful to bear. Therefore, the memory will automatically
become repressed into the unconscious where it will continue
to influence his behavior in various ways. He may develop a
sudden aversion to being bundled up around the neck, or he
may become hysterical if the sheet and blanket are pulled up
close to his chin when he is tucked in. He may refuse to put
on a pullover sweater or become desperate if his mother
uses a wash cloth on the center of his face.

If nobody knows what is causing this strange behavior, the
chances are he will provoke irritation and coercion on the
part of the adults and the buried fear will continue to plague
him. The situation is quite different when the adults understand that on his return from the hospital a child needs to be
encouraged to talk of his fears related to his experience. If
he can reveal the fear of being suffocated, and go over the
experience verbally in the reassuring presence of his parents,
ventilating his feelings, being comforted and reassured by
them while acquiring a better understanding of what actually
took place and why it was necessary, the experience will lose
the shock effect and the death fears will be dissolved. He
will then have no need to find substitute channels for expressing the repressed fear connected with the belief that he had

narrowly escaped being suffocated. Having his nose a
mouth momentarily covered will not activate a memory of
fear of death.

Another constructive way of handling the situation, if
were not possible for the parents to find out what was cau
ing these sudden peculiarities in behavior, would be to e
courage the child to tolerate what seemed intolerable. The
could explain and demonstrate that there was actually not
ing to fear and encourage him to try to overcome his anxie
by experimenting with the very things of which he w
afraid, proving to himself that no harm came to him as a r
sult. This is not as effective as uncovering the actual fear e
perience, but it is of considerable help because the chi
would be using his knowledge of reality to master unrealist
fear. In this way he would be taking a step forward in em
tional development (technically known as strengthenir
his ego) instead of a step backward (regression).

Strengthening the ego means making more proficient th
part of our mental apparatus with which we view and judg
the world around us, including our own thoughts, feelin
and sensations. The psychoanalytic use of the term is qui
different from the popular use of the word which denot
vanity or conceit. The ego is that portion of the mind throug
which we learn and have acquired all the knowledge whic
we possess. A person with a healthy, strong ego is therefo
able to learn without difficulty. He is able to accurately pe
ceive, assess and judge reality; that is, people, actions, even
and himself.

He does not have exaggerated fears which hamper hi
in moving about freely in the world. He is afraid of what
truly dangerous but not filled with unrealistic anxieties, suc
as fear of being in an elevator, fear of strangers, fear of crowe
—disasters of all kinds. These stem from unconscious idea
The more accurately reality is perceived, the less one's rea
tion to it has been influenced by childhood notions, hen
the more mature and integrated is the ego.

The person with a healthy ego is able to accurately judg
his behavior and to be aware of its effect upon others. A
praisals of his own appearance and personality are realisti
He is able to accurately judge other people and proper
evaluate their behavior as well. During adolescence ever
thing is seen in a rather exaggerated way. This applies t
self-perceptions as well as perceptions of others. These di

tortions mark a disturbance of the ego which is normal to adolescence, when the ego, as was explained earlier, becomes fluid. The safe, familiar world of preadolescence has vanished and the adolescent who is suddenly in limbo, his equilibrium shaken by the upsurge of sexual feeling, the rapid changes taking place in his body, the new role he must suddenly play, tends to temporarily lose his bearings. Strong emotions and insecurity influence the way things appear to him. But as one moves into the late teens the ego should have made strides toward consolidation and a sober, realistic appraisal of the young person's life situation. By late teens, the young person with a healthy ego has a sound and accurate grasp of the world in which he lives, the approximate place he occupies, the relationships between men and women and a knowledge of his own unique value as a human being.

He knows he can do a job, whether at school or out in the business or professional world, and he feels ready to tackle his responsibilities. He knows that life doesn't usually run smoothly for long periods, but he is prepared to handle whatever difficulties arise. He knows that sometimes he'll handle them well and at other times, when he is under strain, he will not. But he won't go around in a stew of self-hatred or brood incessantly over poor handling because he will have a normal tolerance for his own weaknesses. Thus, he will be able to accept others with their faults and be able to evaluate their responses to him in the light of their own personalities. He will know that a person who is habitually rude and unpleasant has no special grudge against him when exhibiting that brand of behavior toward him. He won't imagine that the world is against him because he meets unpleasant people on his job or at school. In other words, he sees the world as it really is, through his adult eyes and not through the eyes of a confused, angry, suspicious or frightened child, which is what some people do all their lives.

When a person's unconscious contains a great many disturbing beliefs and ideas which have been carried over from childhood, other people usually become aware of peculiar behavior and attitudes on the part of that person and wonder what makes him so odd or eccentric. It is obvious to them that the person doesn't behave in the usual, predictable way that most others do. He doesn't because he is not guided in his behavior by the usual evaluations of situations. He is guided by beliefs and judgments based on ideas, thoughts and memories of experiences he doesn't even know he has. Therefore, he views the world differently, and hence, responds differently.

Teenagers who continuously display an extreme form of behavior, such as withdrawing behavior, are responding to childhood ideas and beliefs about themselves and others which make them misjudge the nature of social and sexual relationships. They may have no true idea of why they feel inferior, inadequate, distrustful, anxious or hostile as the case may be, although they can offer many so-called reasons. My bosom isn't big enough. I'm ugly. I'm stupid. I'm too tall. My legs are too skinny or too fat, I don't have enough money, I haven't got a car, and so forth.

The girl will seldom, if ever, be consciously aware of believing, for instance, that going out with a boy means she runs the risk of being sexually assaulted or that she may completely lose control of herself. Nor does the boy realize that his fears of girls may, for example, be related to a childhood notion that women can turn into witches who will cut you to ribbons and whose bodies contain dangerous openings. Children do acquire troublesome ideas of this type under certain circumstances, and there are many other varieties as well. By the time the child becomes a teenager he is aware only of anxiety and discomfort in the presence of the opposite sex and has no idea of what is causing it. Even if he has no idea of what has caused him to feel as he does, he will be making a big step forward if he can force himself to make contact with his own age-mates. In that way the conscious teenage part will be asserting itself over the unconscious childish forces which have been controlling, or at least greatly influencing, his behavior. In this way he will learn to be less afraid through actual experience, in much the same way as the little operation patient could have been helped to cope directly with his anxieties, even if the root-cause was not uncovered. Of course, the more insight he can acquire, the easier it will be, but even without any insight at all, just fighting the fears with determination should produce some results. He will learn to be less afraid, through observing that nothing dreadful happens.

Your own daydreams and fantasies will give you many clues as to what the underlying difficulties may be. After all, daydreams are thoughts we consciously dwell on because they give us pleasure. What kind of thoughts give you pleasure? Only grandiose deeds and heroic acts? Or being madly sought after by innumerable suitors? Then you may suspect that perhaps your main problem is one of having carried over a strong feeling of inadequacy as a result of childhood rivalry with a parent, and that rivalry is being compensated for in fantasy, while nothing is being accomplished in reality.

If your fantasies are of kidnapping and rape or any other form of violence related to sex, is it any wonder that you are afraid to be with the opposite sex? Every sexual feeling reminds you of your fantasies and you then become frightened that they are in danger of coming true. You need to use your reasoning powers to reassure yourself that this is not so.

Instead of giving in to the impulse to indulge in your favorite fantasies which keep your fears or inferiority feelings at high pitch, try instead to think about a successful youngster whom you have been able to observe at school in social situations. Imagine yourself in that person's skin. There is always a certain amount of sexual excitement and pleasure in the company of the opposite sex at adolescence. How does the successful young teenager deal with it? Imagine yourself dealing with it. Go through encounters of this type in your thoughts, *keeping the situations absolutely on a reality level.* Resist the temptation to go off into the clouds. Just keep trying to experience via your thoughts and your powers of identification the normal social encounters with the opposite sex. These rehearsals and quasi-experiences can be of great help in preparing you to relate to others. In this way, you cope in advance with anxieties which might paralyze you if you were not already familiar with them and if you had not had the experience of fighting them, at least mentally.

During these rehearsals for life situations, whenever you feel in doubt as to what would be appropriate behavior in any situation ask yourself what would be courteous, friendly and kind. These are infallible guides. Even if you're trembling and perspiring with anxiety in the real-life encounter, they should provide you with some reliable cues as to what to say and do, or what not to say and do. In order to apply them you have to think about the other person or the group. Automatically, your attention is wrested away from yourself, making you less tense and self-conscious, two prime killers of social success.

Words of Warning

Teenagers with strong feelings of inadequacy and inferiority feelings may find as they begin to move out into the social world of adolescence that they feel comfortable and acceptable only to those distinctly inferior to them in intelligence, academic success, range of interests and general background. This may be all right for a start, but the disadvantage is that people of sharply lower intelligence and vastly different aspirations as well as strictly limited interests are not nearly as much fun to be with and not nearly as stimulating as are those with whom you can have a more equal exchange of ideas and ideals. And in your heart you will still feel that you haven't made the grade.

The real danger in seeking companionship exclusively outside the group which truly shares your interests and goals is that you may find yourself admiring teenagers who exhibit cheerful contempt for teachers, school regulations and traditional forms of behavior generally. If you find yourself being attracted to these very troubled young people, don't walk, run in the opposite direction. Nothing constructive will be gained by involving yourself with them. Adolescence is the time when you can ruin your character through bad company because the same identification process which enables you to greatly enrich and expand your fluid and developing personality also *operates when you are in the company of undesirable people.* You cannot be in the company of others at teenage without identifying with them to some degree. In adolescence the standards of the group replace the standards of the parents. Group standards become the authority and give support for certain kinds of group-sanctioned behavior. Therefore, they often are performed without the guilt and anxiety which a teenager would feel if on his own, comparing his behavior with his parents' ideals. When human birds flock together long enough their plumage comes to have a strong resemblance, even if they were birds of a very different feather to start with. This is particularly important for "angry" young teenagers to bear in mind.

Teenagers who fall into the category of "bad company" are disturbed youngsters greatly in need of help, but the help of adults. Occasionally one finds a teenager with such a strong "rescue complex" that he may compensate for his own anger and frustration by trying to influence a delinquency-prone class-mate towards more constructive behavior. Even if you feel a very strong call to save your fellow-teenagers from delinquency, it is much safer to leave it to the adults, whose attention you can direct to the need. There is a danger of the uncommitted teenager, filled with anger, discontent, discouragement or rebellion being ignited by flames which he had intended to extinguish.

Teenagers beginning to have social relationships should try to become friends with youngsters whose overall friendliness and pleasant behavior can be counted on by one and all. If you approach such youngsters *and aren't too demanding nor too humble and apologetic,* you can be reasonably certain of a friendly reception. People who like people will like *you* as long as your approach is casually friendly and free of tension.

Teenagers from quarrelsome homes will need to be especially on guard against gravitating towards quarrelsome youngsters. They will provoke in you the same old objectionable kinds of behavior which you cannot refrain from exhibiting at home and which fill you with guilt feelings. The reason it is so very difficult to change your behavior at home until after you have achieved a certain measure of success on the outside, is that the same old stimuli produce the same old responses. This tendency is especially strong where responses have been strongly reinforced by highly emotional relationships such as exist between family members. Therefore, it is best to first try to change patterns of behavior in a neutral atmosphere. But be on guard against looking for failure to unconsciously prove that you were right in the first place in believing that people are unfriendly, or that no one could possibly like you. As your self-esteem rises with successful effort and you feel encouraged and happier, you will not be quite as vulnerable to the same old irritations and provocations. Instead of hanging around to fight out the bitter but juicy aspect of every quarrel, you will feel much more able to depart from the battlefield, amuse yourself in your own room, go out and take a walk, or get busy doing something that needs to be done. You will find that as your self-confidence increases through outside-of-home successes, you won't feel such a desperate need to defend your honor at home, and prove that you are right, even if you are.

Don't throw yourself at people. They'll duck and you'll hit the wall. Some youngsters find it so difficult to bear the tension of waiting to see what the outcome of their efforts will be that they nervously rush into things to get it over with. The results are not good. Everyone must learn to bear the tension of waiting, of being patient in his efforts, knowing that sooner or later the results will appear. It is part of maturity. Little children need immediate reassurance. The younger they are, the less able they are to wait for things, to postpone satisfaction. As their egos become stronger they learn that they can depend upon having something in the near future, and they learn to wait for it. You will need self-control to hide your tension and to work at gradually being accepted. It takes time to make a place for yourself in the group. People need time to grow accustomed to seeing you in a different light, and unconsciously getting to know that you are more like one of them than they had realized. Remember, it's hard in the beginning, so be prepared to make great efforts for small results at the start. In that way you will safeguard yourself against hurt feelings, disappointment and discouragement.

If in doubt as to what friendliness without throwing yourself at someone consists of, think of being friendly while maintaining a discreet edge of reserve. That will subtly tell others that you have self-control and self-respect and, therefore, will not be a burden to them. People are reluctant to become friends with those in whom they sense a desperate need to cling. You will notice that as soon as you get your tension under control and send out self-control signals instead of frantic s.o.s.'s, you will receive quite different responses.

As one sixteen-year-old put it, "It's so unfair. When I was miserable and dying to be asked for a date, nobody paid any attention to me. Now that I'm relaxed because I have a steady and don't give a hoot, boys are calling me and inviting me out." It's cruel, but that's how it works.

9

OFF-BEAT RELATIONSHIPS

When adolescents are able to relate socially only to people from groups strikingly different from their own, it invariably indicates unresolved problems with their own family. If temporary, it can be merely a reflection of typical adolescent interest in discovering what other groups are like, plus a dash of normal defiance of traditional codes of behavior. When it is persistent and represents the exclusive interest of the teenager, it may safely be assessed as a distress signal. The causes may be spite and rebellion; flight from overattachment; guilt and inferiority feelings, or a combination of all of these factors.

Often the drama of rebellion against the parents is enacted with striking clarity, as in the following episode. A young American white girl who might have been eighteen years old but looked fifteen was sitting in a little café in Paris with a young Asiatic boy. Her long blond hair was in need of a combing and hung down her back. She looked like a sloppy Lady Godiva in baggy slacks. An otherwise attractive face had the telltale expression of brattishness as she conversed with her companion in a manner that was a mixture of petulance and self-importance. The instant she caught sight of an American couple who had entered the otherwise empty café, she fell to passionately kissing her companion, pausing (fairly often, it must be confessed) to shoot a look of insolent triumph at her fellow Americans, who probably were about the same age as her parents. Here was a picture that told more than a thousand words.

Her grooming, her dress, her facial expression, her behavior when unaware of being observed as compared with her reaction to her American "audience" suggested, if not volumes, at least whole chapters of her life.

Defiance and rebellion were the outstanding motivators of her appearance and behavior. In going about in public like a slob she was flouting the usual requirements of dress. She was not on the Left Bank of the Seine, where she would have disappeared in a crowd who looked very much like her. She chose a café on the Right Bank where the likelihood of being with people in conventional dress was extremely high. Moreover, the café was situated quite near important tourist attractions so that there was a strong possibility of running into Americans. What better setup could be found by a youngster seething with unresolved antagonisms towards her parents (her manner and childish facial expression indicated pronounced emotional immaturity) than to find substitutes for her parents to shock and anger, as she so clearly was hoping to do. The only circumstance which could conceivably have made the situation more satisfactory to her would have been for her observers to have known her parents and given them a blow by blow description of the "love scene."

This may have been one of those situations in which overinvolvement with the father and subsequent disappointmet in him, coupled with extreme jealousy and antagonism between mother and daughter, resulted in a strong desire for revenge. Crossing religious and racial lines can serve not only for rebellion, it may also be a way of running away from an unconscious incestuous attachment. If a partner can be found who is diametrically opposite to the parent in every possible way, then the young person unconsciously can assure himself that the partner is indeed not the longed-for parent of early childhood. This selection usually happens entirely unconsciously. The two young people simply feel drawn to each other for reasons of which they are unaware. Sometimes they fall very much in love. In the case of the teenage girl under discussion, it was quite plain that what she was up to had nothing to do with love for her partner. She was using the young man as a vehicle for her spite and defiance. He seemed both dignified and intelligent, and whereas his own history as a member of a racial group which suffers from social prejudice in the Western world probably contributed to his enjoyment of the little drama, one could judge from his facial expression that he was somewhat embarrassed. Perhaps it was caused by the obviousness of his date's exhibitionistic behavior, or because he knew that her apparently enthusiastic kisses carried little personal conviction and that he was being used as a stage prop.

Two young people can, of course, come from widely diverse backgrounds and be initially drawn to each other because of an unconscious need to escape a childhood problem of overattachment to a parent or brother or sister and nevertheless have an enduring marriage of love and dignity. But the chances of compatibility and lasting happiness are considerably less than under more normal circumstances. Some off-beat marriages are held together by the couple's satisfaction in continually fighting the world. All antagonism and hostility which might have been turned against each other is turned outward in fighting the common enemy: conventional attitudes towards the crossing of religious, racial and socioeconomic boundaries. The only victims in such marriages are the children born of it, since they cannot possibly have the warm, easy security of an unconflicted home in which the parents feel at ease with a sizeable segment of the community. The child's problem of establishing a clear-cut sense of identity may be impossible to resolve, since the difference in attitudes with which various races are regarded is overwhelmingly strong. Children never have an easy time under conditions of war, and in racially mixed marriages there is always some kind of war going on with society. As long as there are societies of human beings, there will always be a plethora of customs, rules and regulations serving as vehicles for rebellion against the family—the first "society" and the first "government" the child comes to know.

The following history also illustrates several of the psychological factors described above:

Sara, a girl from an orthodox Jewish home and John, whose parents were high-church and anti-Semitic, fell in love. They both had been "problem teenagers." The girl was never asked to parties and always returned home from school dances in tears because no one had asked her to dance. The boy was a source of concern to his parents because he always spent his time with teenagers who were not of his religion, never seeming to be able to be on friendly terms with any of the young people in his parents' church group.

The history of these young people, who were highly intelligent, is most instructive in that it clearly shows a flight from an incestuous attachment. The boy's parents were unhappily married and the young mother lavished all her affection on her little boy. Unaware of her unconscious needs and of Freudian discoveries, she cuddled in bed with her young son even when he was eleven and twelve years old. Thus, through the years she unconsciously strengthened the bond between them far beyond normal proportions.

The years away at college loosened the tie sufficiently for John to determine to try to be on his own and live away from home after graduation. His unconscious fears of the unresolved Oedipal relationship with his mother (which had already been signaled by his rejection of the girls of his own religious group) were beginning to emerge in other disguised, intellectualized forms. This product of a devoutly religious Christian home decided that he didn't believe in marriage, he didn't believe in religion, he didn't believe in bringing children into this dangerous and evil world.

The one thing he firmly believed was that those attitudes had been rationally arrived at through a realistic appraisal of life's values and the state of the world. Actually, they were the outgrowth of his childhood belief, buried in the unconscious part of his mind, that his wishes to marry his mother might come true, since she openly preferred her son to her husband and treated him as a "little husband." The father had been so completely pushed aside by the mother that he did not loom as a rival and was not a safeguard against the little boy's wishes. In a normal home, John would have been frustrated by the father's claims to the mother, but at the same time he would also have been made to feel safely out of the running, because he would know his father would not permit him to attempt to take on his responsibilities. (The fear common to children whose mothers are seductive is that they will succeed and then be faced with the need to assume an adult role with the mother.) All of John's beliefs and his behavior were attempts to ward off the danger of realizing his childhood ambitions against which there had been no protection.

If he didn't believe in marriage, then he certainly couldn't be in danger of attempting to marry his mother, and no one (his father) could accuse him of such designs. Another outcome of John's childhood experiences was to regard his mother as faithless, and, therefore, all women were faithless because his mother obviously did not love his father. Unconsciously, he believed that all women were like that. No husband could trust in his wife's love. The best thing was always to be her little boy. Another reason for his not believing in marriage was that he wanted to be obedient to his mother, and she did not want him to marry. She claimed that she wanted him to, but in her heart she couldn't bear to give him up to another woman.

This young man exhibited an extraordinarily hostile rejection of religion. Any passage in which the word God appeared was offensive to him, indicating a frantic flight from his religious father's authority. John could not escape having deep fears of both his father's and God's punishment. Over-attached children always feel guilty towards the parent of the opposite sex and live in fear of punishment from Daddy and God. In the little child's mind, God is just a more powerful edition of Daddy. In his rejection of marriage he was saying in effect, "I don't want to marry anybody so how can Daddy possibly accuse me of wanting to take Mother away from him. Besides, it isn't safe to be a husband. Your wife doesn't like you; she only loves her son, so it's best to always stay a son and never be a husband." In his rejection of religion he was saying, "I don't have to be afraid of my father. He can't punish me. He has no authority over me, and neither can God punish me because He doesn't exist. Therefore I am safe from all harm and there is nothing to fear." This is whistling in the dark with a vengeance. This is not meant to imply that all people who are atheists are atheists out of fear, but when there is such an extreme reaction against religion in someone who has been reared in a religious home, one may suspect a serious problem with the father.

John's stated reasons for not wanting children (the world was too dangerous and evil a place) actually had nothing to do with nuclear warfare, although it seemed to him that this was his true reason. The world seemed particularly dangerous to him, because although he had banished all such ideas from consciousness, he lived in the fear of imminent destruction by the bomb which would be aimed directly at him by "Our Father which art in heaven."

Another case illustrates this particular point. An extremely bright seven-year-old boy, who also was overly involved with his mother, had so great a terror of thunderstorms that he shook uncontrollably at a rumble of thunder, and wept with fear if the sky was dark with "threatening" clouds. He was at a loss to understand why he reacted this way. He could see that other children seemed quite unconcerned about the weather. Months had been largely devoted to discussing his expectation that something would come out of the clouds and mash him to a pulp with a sledge hammer. Why this should happen to him of all the boys in the world, and who would want to do this to him were questions to which he could find no answer. One day in his therapist's office his eye fell on a make-believe diploma from a toy medical kit. As he read the diploma, he came to the passage "in the Year of our Lord." He stopped, repeated the words "our Lord" and then went on to murmur "Lord in heaven . . . Our Father which art in heaven . . . Father in heaven . . . Hey!" Turning to his therapist, his eyes brilliant with the light of discovery, he shouted, "We've cracked the case!" And indeed he had. The realization that he harbored unconscious fears of his father arising out of his strong jealousy created by an overattachment to his mother, whose bed he shared whenever the father was away, had been extremely difficult for him to acquire. Because his father was a kind and friendly person, it didn't seem possible to fear him. How could he believe that he expected such terrible punishment at his hands? But after the flash of insight described, he began to recollect some of his own very angry feelings towards his father when he was sent back to his lonely bed. He could now realize that he attributed to his father the rage he had felt within himself. The next step was uncovering his belief that because this great big guy *could*, he therefore *would*, mash him to a pulp. The child's guilt feelings caused him to believe that he deserved this fate. He kept pushing these frightening thoughts out of his mind, but every rumble of thunder was a threat that the danger and punishment he unconsciously feared were about to be visited upon him.

The wish to be without children has many meanings. One finds this attitude in people who have felt unloved as children, and in others who have felt too much love from the parent of the opposite sex. To someone who has felt unloved as a child it is difficult to understand the joy and happiness that reasonably normal parents experience in loving their child and doing their utmost to help him grow up to be happy and healthy. Many children grow up believing that children are nothing but a burden to their harassed parents because their own parents were unable to show joy or express love and tenderness. One sees this often in homes where tense, frustrated, harassed and unhappy parents are continually shouting, carping, criticizing, punishing, threatening or ignoring the children, and complaining about the cost of everything required to clothe and feed them. Life is one long dreary round of arguments, nagging, quarreling and complaints. Of course, in that type of home the children usually fight continuously amongst themselves, carrying on the parental tradition as well as expressing the need for continuous outlets for their own anger and misery. Often these children grow up afraid to love, and dread becoming parents themselves.

In situations where there is an overattachment to the parent of the opposite sex, one may also find a rejection of the role of parent, for several reasons. The first is the unconscious wish to remain the little child and not be displaced by another child (one's own). A second reason is the inability to think of one's self as an adult and as a parent. If a little girl is encouraged by her daddy to think of herself as his girl friend whom he prefers to Mother, this prevents the girl from renouncing her struggle to win Daddy and from settling down with the ideal of becoming just like Mother and waiting until she grows up to get a husband just like Daddy all for herself. She remains in a continual state of rivalry with her mother, making her more and more resentful and bitter towards her mother as the years go on. This, in turn, prevents her from identifying herself with her mother, and Mother's role in life. Also, since her whole childhood is spent in a bitter feeling of frustrated rivalry with the mother, her guilt is very great. She feels guilty about becoming a mother herself and about surpassing her own mother. The same is true of boys in relation to their fathers.

It so happened that John, with his high-church background, found a Jewish girl whose experiences and problems were in many ways identical to his. Overattachment to a tyrannical father, and a very bad relationship with an unfriendly mother who openly preferred her brothers produced many problems. Sara also did not believe in religion, marriage or children. Why did they marry?

The most important factor was the opposition to their marriage by both sets of parents. The desperate attempts made to separate the young couple made them anxious. Unbeknown to themselves, they still were very much under the domination of their parents and secretly feared that somehow the parents might succeed in separating them. So they hunted up a Justice of the Peace in an off-beat section of town, and took as witnesses, not friends, but two workmen who were making repairs on the Justice's garage. Somewhere deep down under layer upon layer of rational reasons for this kind of wedding ceremony must have been the belief that it wasn't really a valid marriage. In this way they satisfied their unconscious and conscious needs.

John and Sara might just as easily, it would seem, have become communists. Rebellious turning against everything the family stands for often produces young communists, devoted only to an organization of rebellion. The saving grace was that each was very much loved by one parent and was running away from that attachment. The communist youths from noncommunist homes vent bitterness and hostility towards both parents by rejecting everything their parents stand for. They reject the parent country and its rules and regulations (the government) as well.

A few years ago a series of articles on Russian adolescents depicted youth in revolt against parents in a communist country. What do communist youths do to express their rebellion and resentment towards parents? Imitate the capitalist American youth as nearly as they can. Their disloyalty to their parents and the Kremlin (and it is noteworthy that many of these youths in revolt were the offspring of high government officials) consists of wearing blue-jeans, listening to rock 'n roll, twist, jive and all manner of swing recordings, and loafing instead of being actively engaged in some government sponsored cultural or work program. (Salisbury)

But just as the capitalist American father is usually ready to blow his child's brains out for becoming an extreme leftist, or making an obviously rebellious marriage, correctly understanding the hidden message to him contained in the move (i.e. "I herewith reject you and all that you stand for. You've never given me the love I've needed and this is where I'll find it.") So, too, the harassed Russian parent understands the message of rejection beamed to him by his children's behavior. It is a thousand times worse, of course, in a dictatorship where it exposes the parent to the real danger of possible punishment by the government, if the youth's behavior arouses sufficient suspicion of improper upbringing, encouraging disloyalty to the State. The irony of the situation is that the Russian party big-wig has no doubt been too devoted to the State in responding to the demands his position has made upon him, similar to his American "capitalist" counterpart. His children, too, must feel deprived of love, companionship, interest and devotion as is so often the complaint in the families of big business men. When the calendar rolls around to the period when a certain amount of revolt and rebellion is a natural yet temporary state, disappointed and frustrated youngsters may go to an extreme on the scale of rebellion, sometime taking up a permanent position.

Do all unusual marriages indicate rebellion or over-attachment to the parent? There are special circumstances which can bring about a crossing of many barriers, chiefly situations in which the young people are thrown into each other's company daily. One characteristic of youth is the readiness to fall in love. During the last decade the world has had occasion to witness the falling in love of several couples from widely divergent backgrounds. In each case, the young people involved lived in the same household. Circumstances which bring extremely attractive young people together day after day during a period in their lives when they are somewhat in a state of rebellion against convention, when their hearts are more open to love than at any other time in their lives, are bound to result in their falling in love in a percentage of the cases. It is still possible, although one would have to study many cases to be sure, that overattachment or rebellion is nevertheless an underlying factor. If newspaper pictures can be relied upon in order to judge resemblances, the beautiful young working girl who captured the heart of a prominent and wealthy young man bears a striking resemblance to his mother, and in the case of a high-born young lady, her working-class husband's photos could pass for photographs of her father when he was a young man. These love stories which electrify the world by their unusual character apparently contain an ingredient relating to the first powerful love in the child's life. This may be the spark that ignites the flame. Freud observed that we always return to our first loves.

The situation is quite different from that perceived by the cynics who see these marriages only as the triumph of ambitious self-seeking people, cold-bloodedly capturing the hearts of the wealthy and the prominent. In the case of one wealthy young girl who had been orphaned, it is very likely that the employee in her guardian's household whom she married was the only person who had ever showed her kindness. A love-starved girl may easily find this irresistible. In her case, the heartless cruelty with which her guardian pursued her and her fiancé and the measures employed to separate them, gave a clear indication of the unsympathetic, un-

understanding and frozen atmosphere in which the girl must have been raised. It enabled one to conjecture how great must have been her need for love, especially from a parent figure. The fact that the man with whom the young girl had fallen in love was married and considerably older can be taken as evidence that, unconsciously, he must have fulfilled some of her yearnings for a father.

Some girls who have a serious problem of unresolved childhood longing for the father's exclusive love fall in love only with married men. Sometimes as soon as they have succeeded in taking the man away from his wife and becoming his wife he ceases to be attractive and they find themselves again falling in love with another woman's husband. It is not a question of an evil creature out to wreck as many homes as possible. In the course of treatment of women with this kind of history, whose unhappiness finally leads them to try to find out what is wrong with them, it invariably turns out that the married man represents the longed for father of early childhood. Either the girl had lost him at a very early age through death, divorce or desertion and felt compelled to keep searching for him, or an overly close and seductive relationship made it impossible to renounce the childish rivalry with the mother and the girl unconsciously sought her father in every married man. When the man became her husband, he was no longer the married man who belonged to someone else; hence, he ceased to represent the unattainable father of her childhood, and *another* married man became the unattainable father whom she then felt she had to have. The same is true of men who are attracted only to married women.

All marriages contain an element of mother and father love. And many a happy marriage exists where there is a strong component of this kind of love. The factors determining whether such a marriage turns out to be happy or unhappy are many and varied, just as in other marriages in which there is no difference in age.

The degree of rebellion and resentment on which the choice of marriage partner is based provides the strongest clue as to whether stormy weather lies ahead. Marriages made primarily out of spite are short-lived, as a rule. Sometimes the very thing which cements other marriages, namely, the coming of children, is the detonator which blows a spite-marriage to bits. The birth of one's own children, reviving as it does all of one's own early childhood experiences with parents, is a critical time for those whose early experiences were painful and frustrating.

Under usual circumstances, in addition to the joy and pride and excitement of the first child, a young couple experiences a certain amount of anxiety about taking proper care of the child, and also about having moved into a new relationship with each other. No longer do they live only for themselves and each other. They now become oriented to making all their own wishes secondary to the child's needs. That's quite a shift and requires their being truly grown-up emotionally. The young couples who have been fortunate enough to have spent their childhoods in atmospheres of warmth and love and devotion shift quite effortlessly into the role of parents. All their lives they have been learning how to be good parents without even knowing it. The love which was given to them they now lavish on their child, and there is plenty to spare for each other.

How different the situation is where either or both parents have brought with them into their marriage all the unfinished fights and frustrations of their childhood homes: rivalries with parents, with brothers and sisters; disappointments in the amount of love which was received, and anxieties caused by quarreling or divorced parents. These young-people-in-distress often find themselves resenting the baby who takes so much of the other parent's attention. The baby is felt to be an intruder, a rival—in other words, a replica of a brother or sister, or even a parent who was the recipient of the coveted love and attention. Immediately, the immature young parents become very critical of each other and the marriage is in trouble, and so is the child.

Sometimes a young person is seething with the desire to prove to his parents that he can not only be a good parent, but a much better parent than his own. The child then becomes a project handled with the utmost tension and a complete lack of intuitive understanding of the child's individuality and emotional needs. The results are never good. Ambition born of spite interferes with spontaneous expressions of affection for the child and enjoyment of the developing little person. Frequently this type of situation produces discord between the parents if they do not happen to share the same problem. Or they may blame their obvious lack of success on each other's handling of the child.

In extreme cases, where a girl has had a very bad relation-

ship with her own mother which has left her full of feelings
of anger and guilt, the coming of her first baby can produce
a depression so severe that she is unable to care for her infant, but must herself be taken care of as a helpless child.
In less severe cases, the young mother may temporarily develop mysterious temperatures and undiagnosable ailments,
which last only for a few weeks, but necessitate someone else's taking complete charge of the baby for those first
weeks, during which time she is able to assimilate the shock
of her new role, and the threat which its responsibilities mean
to her. When she reaches that point, the ailments disappear
and she begins to take charge of her baby. In these situations,
the young mother usually has not the faintest idea that anything is wrong psychologically. These psychosomatic symptoms are nearly always accepted at face value, except in the
severely depressed, where it is quite obvious to everyone that
something is seriously the matter.

The sexual life of the couple whose choice of marriage
partner is based primarily on unresolved childhood problems
runs a hazardous course. Sometimes, as soon as they become
man and wife, they unconsciously become Mother and Father, for a married man is always Father and a married woman
is always Mother in the primitive thinking characteristic of
the unconscious part of the mind in which childhood ideas
are stored. Since a sexual relationship with a parent is forbidden, suddenly the young couple may cease to find each
other sexually attractive.

In some cases this occurs only after the birth of a child. The
act of becoming parents is the powerful stimulus which
brings forth the underlying problem. Sometimes the problem
afflicts only the wife, who may lose sexual desire after she
becomes a mother because of a deeply rooted, unconscious
childhood belief that mothers do not engage in sexual activity. In other cases, it may be the young husband who reacts
to his wife's motherhood by loss of sexual desire for her
because of these same factors.

The moment the young couple cease to be sexually attracted, the marriage of course begins to be shaky. Tension
and dissatisfaction with each other mount, leading to quar-
rels, intolerance of each other's quirks, fault-finding at the
slightest provocation and feelings of emotional desertion. In
some cases, at this point a search begins outside the marriage
for reassurance, appreciation and sexual gratification. To the

young couple's bewilderment, what began as a flaming romance within a very short time turns into an unhappy marriage, often ending in divorce.

In most cases notice of trouble ahead is signaled by the nature of the adolescent's relationships, and ideally should be corrected at that time.

10

DRINKING

There is an old folklore tale about Noah and Satan. When the flood was over, Satan disguised himself and went looking for Noah. He found him planting grape vines in his garden. Satan asked Noah if he could go into partnership with him, promising that he would show him how to make a juice from the grape that would bring joy and gladness to his heart. Noah agreed. Satan killed a lamb, a lion, an ape and a pig and poured the blood of each in turn on the ground. Noah asked Satan why he had done this, and Satan replied, "The first cup of wine will make its drinker mild like the lamb; after the second he will be boastful and courageous like the lion; the third will cause him to dance and leap and act foolish like the ape; and the fourth will make him bestial, filthy and degraded like the mud-wallowing pig."

Many ill-advised and unfortunate sexual experiences take place as a result of the influence of alcohol. For this reason, it seems well worth while to explore the problem of excessive drinking. Why do people need potions to make them feel like lambs or lions, and what eventually leads them on to the ape and the pig stage?

It is well-known among professional workers that alcoholics are people who feel excruciatingly tense and inadequate when sober. Feelings of inferiority, depression and anxiety continually assail them. They begin to drink, knowing that relaxation will follow and that they will soon feel big and important enough to lick the world. If it were possible to reach this stage and still maintain good judgment and self-control, most alcoholics would restrict their drinking to the amount necessary to maintain this level of unreal courage. But since their judgment has been affected, they usually just keep right on drinking.

All people who regularly need the relief which alcohol provides need therapeutic help. But sad to say, many who could secure it, reach instead for the whiskey bottle for instant therapy. Like their adult counterparts, the teenagers who drink heavily are always escaping some problem by a means which paralyzes their development.

Since adolescence is an age of anxiety, and since drinking is a part of the social life of our culture, it is not surprising that the more anxious a teenager is the more tempted he might be to rely on alcohol to calm his fears and uncertainties, particularly if his parents use these same crutches. Every time he resorts to it, he not only brings his emotional development to a standstill but he moves backward. In relying upon alcohol, he tells himself that he cannot make it with his own inner resources, that they are insufficient to meet the problems of life. Each succeeding time he confirms to himself his own helplessness, he actually becomes weaker. The more often he uses the crutch, the weaker his psychological muscles become and the more he feels the need of outside aid. Thus, he moves back in the direction of childhood helplessness. Who is more pitiful and helpless than an alcoholic or a drug addict? Alcoholism is an addiction, the same as drug addiction, although somewhat more responsive to curative measures. These poor unfortunates gradually destroy their minds and bodies. How is it that young people will nevertheless flirt with such a catastrophic situation?

Student drinking often represents the carrying on of a home tradition. The children of parents who rely heavily upon alcohol tend to do the same unless they have been so revolted by their parents' behavior that they have made a complete about-face.

Teenagers in trouble frequently discover its opiate qualities on their own. And there are some angry, rebellious adolescents who drink as an attack upon their parents. Drinking is a two-edged sword with which they hurt their parents and punish themselves at the same time, although they usually aren't clearly aware of either of these drives. To this group drinking spells complete emancipation from their parents (or so they delude themselves into believing) simply because it is something their parents deplore. Drinking serves, thus, as an avenue for expressing spite, defiance and rebellion, the casting out of parental standards with a vengeance.

To some fearful immature teenagers, the dangers involved in losing control of one's self appear as a brave and daring and grown-up thing to do. "I'm really quite a courageous person, after all," such an adolescent may think to himself; and therefore will take pleasure in exclaiming to all who will listen, "Boy, was I potted—absolutely stinko. Did I ever tie one on." For a while the youngster really believes he's done something admirable.

Moderate drinking among older adolescents, which comes under the heading of social drinking, confined to weekend dates, is not the drinking referred to here. The crucial determinant of whether alcohol is dangerous for someone is whether the person relies upon it in order to feel confident and cheerful, and whether he feels he is proving something to someone by drinking or getting drunk. Under those circumstances, alcohol, much less benignly, serves the same purpose as the endless fantasies of troubled young children, who instead of acquiring skills through which they would develop true self-esteem through pride of accomplishment, enjoy themselves only in fantasy to which they must retreat with ever increasing frequency because they despair of ever having anything to be proud of.

Alcohol provides a fantasy escape. Successful social encounters under the influence of alcohol are only make-believe, because the person's brain is not functioning normally. He literally is not himself. People who can't bear to be themselves are in trouble. They fail to develop their inner resources. They don't come to grips with difficult and frustrating experiences and thereby develop strength and pride in mastery of difficult situations, so that eventually they may learn to face similar difficulties with relative equanimity.

There is another important unconscious lure that drinking embodies, the one which relates most pertinently to the subject matter of this book. In his own mind, the young person is absolved of the responsibility for acts of aggression and for forbidden sexual behavior. "I didn't know what I was doing. I had too much to drink." A survey recently made of vandalism and delinquent behavior at the parties of privileged young people revealed that two adverse factors were always operating: one, there had been considerable drinking; and, two, there was no adult present to exercise a restraining influence, either on the drinking or the destructiveness.

Without being consciously aware of it, many young people with conflicts about sexual behavior find in excessive drinking the neurotic solution to their sexual conflict—a very poor solution but it appeases their conscience. "I wouldn't have done it if I were sober and knew what I was doing because I know it is wrong. But I had no control over myself, so you can't blame me." But if one has such an adolescent (or adult) in treatment, it becomes apparent even to the patient, that somehow and in some part of his mind he *always knew* what the outcome was likely to be. Not being able to make a conscious choice, either to undertake the responsibility of a sexual relationship or to bear the frustration of renouncing it, he plied himself with alcohol and let what would, happen.

Being under the influence of alcohol doesn't absolve anyone from guilt or responsibility for his actions. It is the weak person's way to self-destruction. Any young person who finds himself tempted by the thought, however fleetingly it may have crossed his mind, to get stewed as a means of solving the dilemma of how far he should go, should know that he is treading on very dangerous ground and should lose no time in finding some responsible and trained adult with whom to discuss his sexual problems.

It is especially important for adolescents, looking forward to parenthood as they all do, to understand the devastating effects upon little children of habitual drunkenness of parents. To a child the parent appears to be insane when drunk. Not only has the child lost a loving protector to safeguard him from the dangers of the outside world but he fears destruction at the hands of this lurching, uncomprehending, glassy-eyed, mumbling, stumbling creature who has almost lost the power of speech and may have lost control over bladder and bowel functions.

During the time that the parent is sober, the child feels in contact with him, and forms certain ideas about the type of person the parent fundamentally is, and lives in dread of the moment when the "insane" version of the parent will appear. Since all children unconsciously identify themselves with their parents and build an important part of their personality traits as a result of the process of identification, the child of an alcoholic parent develops two entirely different concepts of what a parent's role is and what he himself wants to be like.

The child keeps fluctuating between these two sets of ideas and so his personality cannot achieve the integration and solidity needed to enable him to function effectively. The parent's weakness, the helplessness and the lack of control and responsibility all communicate themselves to the child eventually, and he must struggle against an unconscious identification with these qualities. Under such adverse circumstances, a child's struggle to build his own reliable inner controls by means of which he achieves self-respect and a clear-cut sense of identity (who and what he is) may be overwhelmingly difficult.

All people, young and old, who feel the need to drink to the point of intoxication, or who regularly rely upon alcohol in order to feel at ease are very much in need of help. They need to find and eradicate the causes of their feelings of inadequacy so that they can experience life as it is, instead of through an alcoholic haze which makes life experiences unreal, progressively weakening the person's chances of coping with the challenges of daily existence.

Teenagers with an alcoholic parent tend to avoid the company of their classmates after school. They suffer from the twin dread of exposing their parents to criticism and themselves to the humiliation of a drunken scene. For the sake of their own personality development, however, they should fight the tendency to isolate themselves from the young people of their community and should try to be in contact with people outside the home.

It is natural that they do not want to bring classmates home. Simply stating a preference for other meeting places and indicating that home is rather hectic is sufficient explanation with casual acquaintances. With real friends, a knowledge of the true state of affairs will increase their admiration for the young person who, although beset with so much cause for unhappiness, manages to carry on with dignity and friendliness in the outside world.

It has been found that the children of alcoholics harbor a feeling of guilt in relation to their parents, clinging to the totally unreal belief that in some way they have contributed to the parent's alcoholism. Often this results from a parent's accusation. Ashamed of his weakness, many a drinking parent will feel the need to blame his symptom on the behavior of his spouse or his children. In other words, he (or she) finds relief from the intolerable guilt feelings by unconsciously projecting them onto others.

These accusations fall on fertile ground because the frustrations and disappointments of daily life in such a household inevitably give rise to hostile feelings towards the parent who causes so much distress. And, as has been explained, children always feel anxious and guilty when circumstances arouse intense feelings of anger toward a parent. The child thinks that his hostile thoughts have harmed the parent. It is the old belief in the magic of thoughts.

Adolescents are not psychologically equipped to deal with an emotionally ill parent, which is what alcoholics are, and therefore should enlist the aid of a responsible adult. Since alcoholism is such a widespread problem, many communities either have a set-up for helping those afflicted, or have people who are familiar with the problems it brings to the entire family. Some alcoholics respond to psychotherapy; others do extremely well with the aid of Alcoholics Anonymous. And teenagers often need help in arriving at the realization that nothing they have done or failed to do has contributed to their alcoholic parent's plight.

11

GETTING ALONG WITH PARENTS

Nature has decreed that during the adolescent years you will break the childhood ties to your family and find a place for yourself in the world outside your home. For some youngsters this period will be predominantly a happy time, for many it will be an agonizingly painful period, and for the majority it will be some mixture of the two extremes. A principal difficulty will of course be the changing relationships with parents. It is plain from all that has been said so far that childhood experiences will have a great deal to do with how young people react to their parents at this time. Another very important feature in the picture is how happy a teenager's parents are with each other. Each youngster knows best whether or not his parents are happily married, whether they love and enjoy each other, simply tolerate each other, or if they are bound by ties of hatred.

If your parents are happily married they will be able to sustain each other during this period which is at times painful for them as well as for you. They can watch you spread your wings and leave the nest with much less regret and much more enjoyment of your happiness in your new found freedom than can parents whose only satisfaction has been in caring for you.

You must become increasingly independent as you move through your teens. Your parents may find it very difficult to allow you to do so, but do so you must. However, if you know that your parents cannot count on each other for loving support during this period of losing you (temporarily, because you can come back as a young adult and as a loving friend), there are ways of making it easier for them to let you grow up.

Girls whose mothers have let themselves become household drudges, who never go anywhere or do anything, can try to help their mother spruce up. Fix her hair and nails and don't take no for an answer if she tries to refuse. Go shopping with her and help her pick out some becoming clothes. Try to find some organization that she might join and take her there. If necessary, sit through the first encounter with her. Get her on her feet, get her moving out into the world, too. You may have to work against a great deal of resistance, but the results will make both of you happier. If your best efforts get you nowhere, drop the subject for about a month. During that time your mother will have had time to think over your offer, to begin to see advantages in it, and probably to regret that she didn't accept it. She may not be able to bring herself to say anything, but the chances are that when you approach her the second time, she will have done a few psychological exercises, imagining herself out at various meetings and picturing herself in the new role of a woman who participates in community activities, and she won't be quite as negative.

The situation of moving towards middle age and having a rambunctious adolescent in the house is not as difficult for fathers. Their business and professional lives continue undisturbed. In fact, it may be the period in which they feel the greatest security in their work, as a result of years of experience. But they can feel outclassed by their son's vigor and discouraged at seeming to serve only one purpose for their daughters: bigger and better bill payer.

Boys can begin to show some interest in the father's work and the problems he encounters on the job. A father may be very much interested to hear from both sons and daughters what's going on around town, and also at school.

It's a good idea to good-naturedly encourage father to pry himself loose from the television set and take mother out on a Friday or Saturday night. You can suggest movies, plays, meetings, concerts and offer to pick up the tickets for them in advance so that they'll be sure to go. If you have only one parent, you can suggest a friend or relative who might be glad to be invited. Try to pull your parents out of dreary ruts. In most cases they will be very pleased and grateful.

All of this presupposes that you are able to spend some time in their company without feeling as though you're going to jump out of your skin, as some teenagers do who are having a particularly difficult time with unconscious conflicts and have all they can do to keep themselves in one coherent piece. If you are going through a period of feeling as though you'll burst if you have to be anywhere near your parents, don't force it—you'll only end up being churlish. It should, however, be a temporary state, which eases up as you make a place for yourself in the outside world.

Some days you may feel so irritable, every time you open your mouth it will only be to bark at someone. It's best on those days to quietly say that you feel jumpy and keep to yourself. There are days when young teenagers need to be alone and quiet when they get home from school, to deal with difficult moods and regain their equilibrium. Instead of snapping and snarling at everyone, try to get off by yourself.

This is also of importance to your social life, because the less you snap the less guilty you will feel, the higher will be your self-esteem and, therefore, the more at ease you will be in your social relationships outside the home. Any teenager who allows himself to distribute nasty responses impartially around the family from parents to little brothers and sisters is going to hate himself for it and be discouraged about his lack of self-control. Safeguard yourself from the possibility of this happening whenever possible by being on the alert for signs that it is one of those days when you can't stand anybody or anything.

What can teenagers do whose parents are overly interested in everything the teenager is doing? Mothers are usually the worst offenders, sometimes using their own experience as a blueprint the daughter is expected to follow. If your mother insists that you dress, wear your hair and behave exactly as she thinks best, reads your mail, listens in on your phone calls and expects a blow by blow description of everything you do on your dates, you really have a job on your hands.

Usually in these situations, the teenager feels so rebellious that there is a strong tendency to do the opposite of everything the parent advises. Your first step will be to evaluate whether or not you are a slave to this negative kind of obedience. You are actually obeying your mother in reverse, which makes you just as helpless as if you blindly followed her every suggestion. As long as you feel compelled to do the opposite, you have no free choice. So try to calmly judge the merit of her suggestions and to accept whatever is a reasonably good suggestion even as regards your appearance. That will be a sign of your own maturity and it should impress your parents.

Then you can just as calmly insist upon having the other items of hair, dress and make-up as you find them most attractive, and try to satisfy your parents with a brief account of your date. You may be able to stop the telephone and letter snooping by suggesting that it become standard procedure for the whole family. This may make your parents aware of the invasion of privacy.

If none of these suggestions work, and sometimes they do not, you might try writing them a friendly letter explaining how you feel about the situation and asking for the privilege of being treated as a young adult, with privacy and trust in your intelligence and judgment. If you put the letter on their pillow at night when they are out, they can read it when they return, presumably in a good mood. Having the whole night to think about it consciously and unconsciously (in sleep) may result in some shift in attitude by the time they talk with you about it.

Or, you might try to get an adult whom your parents respect to talk with them tactfully and help them to see that they are keeping you a child. Speaking with another adult may help to reduce their anxieties about allowing you adult privileges. If that doesn't work, you can consult a guidance counsellor at school who may call your parents in for a consultation and perhaps be successful in helping them to be less controlling of you.

If none of these measures work, and if your parents can afford it, perhaps you could persuade them to let you go to a boarding school. It can be the best solution. Your parents know you will be supervised and protected, yet you will not be suffocated by parental anxiety and the need to keep you in the position of a small child.

If they are averse to boarding school and nothing else has been effective, then you might suggest that you and your parents together consult a psychiatrist or psychologist specializing in the treatment of teenagers to work out a more harmonious relationship. By this time you and they are probably tense, irritable, worried and harassed and might welcome and profit considerably from professional help.

It is a great temptation for many people—often irresistible

—to use on their family and friends any bit of insight or psychological knowledge which they have picked up. Don't try to psychoanalyze your parents. Don't tell them what you think is going on in their unconscious or what childhood experiences you think may be influencing their behavior to you. First of all, they will think you are out of your mind because most likely they haven't the slightest awareness of it. Secondly, if perchance you should be correct in your diagnosis, far from effecting a change for the better, you will succeed only in disturbing them very much and making them extremely angry at you, *justifiably so*. For one thing, you have no business practicing without a license, and, for another, they didn't come to you for help with their problems. Both are essential for successful therapy: professional competence on the part of the psychotherapist, and, on the part of the patient, a strong desire to be helped to change. Correctly interpreting the unconscious causes of behavior has no value whatsoever unless the patient has reached a point in self-understanding enabling him to fully grasp what is involved. A therapist may know in the first consultation hour what the underlying unconscious factors may be in a particular case, but were he to immediately communicate this to the patient he would succeed only in baffling and confusing the patient and making him more anxious and on guard.

If you feel that you understand the psychological factors causing your parents to act to you in a way which is disturbing to you, the only way you can use that insight is in enabling *you* to be more tolerant of their actions towards you and less affected by those actions. Throwing diagnoses at people is just a sophisticated way of attacking them. The people who are most inclined to do it are those who cannot bear to turn the flashlight on themselves to illuminate a troubled and dark corner of their own unconscious. It's always so much pleasanter to see what's wrong with somebody else and to keep busy working on them instead of on one's self. The fact that your parents may be suffering from neurotic problems is no reason to lose respect for them. Neurotic difficulties are not contemptible, either in your parents or in you. They come unbidden and cause suffering, endured as well as inflicted.

12

THIS THING CALLED LOVE

"How do I know if I'm in love?" If there's the slightest doubt in your mind, don't worry, you're not.

As in all other matters, the temperament of the person will have a great deal to do with his reaction and behavior. But even for the most placid and mild people, the surge of emotions which accompanies being in love is overwhelming. The fact that this state defies description is responsible for our most beautiful poetry and songs as well as for some of the funniest, as people of all levels and temperaments record their attempts to grasp the essence of the greatest of all human experiences.

Being in love is above all things stimulating and exhilarating. The natural tendency to greatly overestimate the beloved is what makes people say that love is blind. The person you are in love with is the greatest and most divine person in the world. And the fact that this extraordinary, heaven-sent creature loves you makes you feel like a very special person yourself. Boys feel that no feat is too difficult, girls feel that no sacrifice is great enough to prove their love. One's heart is open, the world is paradise and everything is possible. Lovers are lunatics is just another way of saying you're usually slightly out of your mind when you're in love—the most delicious form of insanity known to man.

In a sense, one's ego stops functioning. It temporarily ceases to judge reality with any degree of accuracy. Your be-

loved is an angel, you feel like a King (or Queen), and you're
sure that the greatest obstacles will crumble before your determination. The mere presence of the one you love keeps
you ecstatically happy. All of your mentality and your emotions are wrapped around the other person. Your whole being
is poured into his. You are thoroughly identified with him
and everything that he is or likes, or is interested in, or appears to be. When you are apart he is always still with you
in your thoughts, and in your mind you relive every word and
every caress, savoring them over and over again as you put
the steam-iron in the refrigerator and the bread in the broom
closet.

Love may come gradually, as when friendships ripen into
love. It may erupt suddenly, after a short acquaintance. And
there is such a thing as love at first sight. The love that gradually evolves out of a long friendship is usually the most enduring because the "love blindness" comes after the two
young people really know a great deal about each other's
qualities.

Unconscious Deception

In the more impetuous who are inclined to throw themselves into all situations quickly, the tendency to fall quickly
in love may not have as good an outcome because the overestimation of the loved one which is so characterisic of the
lover may blind the two people to faults which make them
truly incompatible. Everyone has faults. It would be foolish
and unrealistic to search for a human being without them.
The important factor in a happy marriage is that the faults
which do exist are not the kind which are unbearable to the
other person. It is also safer if young people have a chance
to test out the compatibility of their interests. When they're
in love it's too late. The presence of the one you love makes
everything enchanting and you may think you enjoy an activity, which later you find you simply cannot bear. One
young woman expressed it as "unconsciously deceiving my
husband before marriage." She explained that she had fallen
in love with her husband very quickly, in a school setting.
After they became engaged they spent long happy Sundays
at his favorite sport: fishing in an uncomfortable rowboat,
having started out for the excursion in the dim, damp, chilly
morning hours. But everything glowed with the warmth of
her love and she would have taken an oath that she was mad

for fishing. Shortly after they were married she recalled, "I was spoiled by having the pleasure of my husband's company every day in the week under very comfortable circumstances. I began to realize that I absolutely hated sitting in that awful rowboat and waiting for hours for those stupid fish to bite. It now seems crazy to me to get out of a nice warm bed at three in the morning to go out into the raw morning air, in order to ruin a perfectly good Sunday."

In this particular case the "unconscious deception" did no harm, because the husband was quite content to fish with male cronies and his wife didn't object to spending some of her springtime Sundays puttering around the house by herself.

But one can see from this example how many later difficulties in marriage, for which the young people reproach each other and themselves, and lead to feelings of having been deliberately deceived, can happen without anyone being guilty of insincerity or guile. Not that some people (by which I mean girls!) don't sometimes very consciously pretend they adore something, like a baseball game, for instance, in order to see as much as possible of some wonderful boy on whom they've set their heart! But that's a harmless part of the game of love, and when a deception of this type comes to light the man is entitled to feel only one emotion: flattered.

Love at First Sight

Love at first sight, while very real, is the potentially most dangerous kind. How is it possible to fall in love at first sight? It is possible because the person to whom it happens, is, without knowing it, already familiar with and psychologically ready to love a particular type of person. The moment he meets her (or she meets him) certain facets of the appearance and personality and general demeanor touch off a series of "boing!" responses, going back to the earliest love relationships of the person's past. Old love feelings which may have been slumbering undisturbed for years are suddenly electrically revived, and infused with all the intensity of adolescent or adult passions. Whether or not love at first sight will turn out to be long-lived or slated for disillusionment will depend upon many factors, most important of which will be the kind of love relationship the person had in early childhood and what the final resolution was. If there is a strong physical resemblance to the parent, or a brother or sister, it often is the

sign of an unresolved tie, then there is a strong possibilit
that marriage and a sex relationship may bring forth guilt an
anxiety related to old guilt-laden childhood rivalries or for
bidden sex games with brothers and sisters. To the uncon
scious the beloved person may be a clear representation o
the family member and all the old taboos will apply and spo
the expression of sexual love.

On the other hand, love at first sight may be rudely de
stroyed within a short time, long before marriage becomes
possibility. This can happen when only the outward appear
ance is a strong reminder of a former love. With greater fa
miliarity, the true personality characteristics have an oppor
tunity to emerge. If there is no attraction in this area, the dis
illusionment is usually swift.

Sometimes love at first sight takes place because the be
loved is exactly the opposite in appearance and personality t
an early love which had an unhappy outcome. For instance
a girl whose childhood was spent in fear of a very harsh and
frightening father (whom she also loved and craved lov
from) may fall instantly in love with an appealing young man
who is outstandingly kind and gentle, if he happens to ad
dress himself to her in an interesting and engaging fashion. I
is as if the voice of her frustrated childhood love suddenly
said to her, "At last there is exactly what you've always
wanted, what you wished so much your first love could have
been like."

Here again the situation is fraught with uncertainty be
cause that one quality which is so overwhelmingly important
to the unconscious, filled as it is with a hunger for gentle
kindly love from a man, may not be sufficient to assure a
happy long-term relationship unless many other features of
compatibility are present.

While love at first sight is entirely possible and in fact fre
quently happens, it calls for very careful testing of the rela
tionship before marriage is seriously considered. Often it is
love based on false recognition because of surface similarities
(or the reverse) to an earlier and all important love.

Infatuation is somewhat related to love at first sight; it re
mains superficial, however, whereas love at first sight can be
very intense and involve deep emotions and all the facets of
the lover's personality and feeling.

Infatuation is an intense yet superficial excitement about a
person, usually based on a single feature, such as extreme
beauty in a girl, hero status in a boy. Because of some unsat-

isfied need it strongly captures the imagination of the young onlooker who immediately begins to weave fantasies about the object of his infatuation and relate himself to it more on a fantasy level than anything else. There is much more excitement and admiration than tenderness and affection.

The Love-Hungry

The poet who said of love that for a man it was a thing apart, 'twas woman's whole existence, understood the psychological differences between the sexes with regard to love. Generally, women are more emotional about being in love and find it harder to pull themselves away from the reliving of the expressions of tenderness in fantasy.

The young people who have felt warmly loved all their lives by their parents seem to take the overwhelmingness of being in love much more in stride than do love-hungry youngsters. The girl-in-love who has always known love in some form is much more likely to do an even better job of her studies and work and be able to exercise some control over her daydreaming.

With the love-hungry one of two extremes may happen. The youngsters may be so ecstatic at finally finding what they have all their lives been yearning for, that nothing else exists. They stop studying, and if working, become ridiculously inefficient on the job. Everyone can see that they are off in a dream world and it occasions much teasing and mirth. On the other hand, a youngster who has never been able to find the spirit and the motivation to work hard at anything, out of discouragement at ever pleasing his parents or being recognized as lovable, may react to being in love by becoming a human buzz saw in regard to studies and work of all kinds. Now that the young person feels loved, admired and appreciated his desire to excel becomes powerful. Anything which brings recognition, pleasure or approval from the beloved person is tackled with the greatest enthusiasm. This kind of reaction of course implies an admixture of parental love. All love relationships have a bit of it, these unquestionably have more, but it need not pose a threat to married happiness. There are many happily married couples who manage to mother and father each other all their lives without feeling that their children are competitors. There's enough love to go round to satisfy everyone.

Is adolescent love real love? Of course it can be real love.

But it is usually not stable or enduring love, as mature love is. Therefore, it is not wise as a rule to commit one's self to a permanent relationship on the basis of it.

The love that we feel for another is real at every stage of our lives. The quality and the dimensions change with maturity. Just as there is a type of sexual activity appropriate to every stage of development, there is a type of love. Love is always a strong emotion and brings jealousy in its train. Love that is not adequately returned is always a source of sharp anguish. Adolescents of passionate temperament can fall deeply and passionately in love and experience the tortures of the damned, if it is unrequited, or when the romance breaks up. The less self-confidence and the greater the hunger for love, the more acute is the agony of the break-up.

Maturity in love means the ability to offer love without first having a guarantee that it will be returned. Many young people are afraid to love and will only allow themselves to have feelings about individuals who first prove a strong interest in them. This of course very greatly narrows down their choice of mate.

Mature love means loving without fear and anxiety, without an admixture of suspicion and hostility which creates continuous doubts of being loved. In other words, mature love is, first of all, dependent upon healthy self-love which creates self-confidence. Mature love is able to give and receive openheartedly; and it involves a total relationship, a sharing and appreciation of spiritual qualities, goals, intellectual interests and personality characteristics, and a strong sexual attraction which makes the other person appear overwhelmingly attractive. The sexual expression of love in a life setting of tenderness and devotion is an indispensable part of mature love. To the extent that people are inhibited and restrained in expressing this facet of love, their maturity is restricted and the marriage is threatened.

Happiness in marriage is very much dependent upon the emotional maturity which permits the couple to freely offer and receive complete expressions of love from each other all their lives.

13

MORALS

Teenage Marriage and Divorce

The number of divorces resulting from teenage marriages seems to point to the fact that many young people marry primarily to be permitted to have a sexual relationship. They very soon find that living happily together requires more than a mutual sexual attraction, which in the teens is inclined to be undiscriminating. It is the time of life when almost any member of the opposite sex who doesn't strike one as unattractive may temporarily appear overwhelmingly desirable. That is why the current college credo "if it's love, it's all right to go all the way" doesn't make sense. Adolescence is the time for falling in and out of love. The overall excitement and attraction gradually give way to a discriminating choice.

Among mature people, a strong sexual attraction is a most important and vitalizing aspect of marriage, enriched by appreciation of personal qualities as well as compatibility of temperament and ideals. The ability to discriminate and select a compatible mate evolves from experience in social relationships with many different people. This is one of the important functions of the adolescent period of life. Those who fail to make use of the opportunities offered by adolescent social life usually have reason to regret it, although, of course, there are high school romances which end in happy, enduring marriages. But they are the exception.

According to a recent article in *Ingenue*, the divorce rate is three times higher for couples who marry in their teens than for those who marry later.

The teenagers who marry to escape an unhappy home, usually do no more than establish another one. Many teenage marriages are forced marriages—the result of pregnancy. A considerable number of marriages are drifted into because no one else asks the girl out after she has started to go steady. For many emotionally immature teens, marriage means effortlessly and magically becoming a respected member of the adult world, a shortcut which is lined with pitfalls. Trouble looms ahead for most of these young couples. But as usual, if the marriage breaks up the girl faces the greatest difficulty. She can never go back to the teenage crowd because she is no longer acceptable to the girls. Her marriage has removed her from their circle. Insurmountable psychological barriers prevent her return. To the teenagers she is no longer a teenager, but a married woman. They are jealous and fearful of her new status and authority. Since she was successful in getting one boy to marry her, they fear she may succeed with their boy friends. They are also aware of the fact that she, like all divorcees, is likely to be regarded as an available sex partner by many of the boys in the group. This is unwelcome competition, and to many of the teenagers it seems unfair competition.

The unbearable loneliness the teenage divorcee usually must endure is frequently a strong factor in propelling her into a second bad marriage. Of course, the unconscious reasons for the first one usually play a role in the second, too.

Cultural Differences

All societies, from the most primitive to the most cultured, have rules and regulations governing sexual activity. In some societies which isolate their budding adolescents from any contact with the opposite sex, unless chaperoned, our adolescent dating customs would seem immoral. At the other extreme are the primitive groups which provide dormitories in which all the adolescents are free to engage in all phases of sexual activity. Thus, a different morality exists in each society. Mental health will depend on how happily and constructively an individual can live within the framework of his particular society's demands.

Adolescence is a preparatory stage of life in our culture where the adult has so many responsibilities and must meet so much competition. Therefore, it is primarily a time of learning social, intellectual, physical and mechanical skills, of acquiring psychological and emotional awareness.

In primitive societies, pubertal boys and girls are tortured in some ceremonial way to symbolically prove their readiness to assume adult responsibilities. They thereupon become a part of the adult community. Duties and responsibilities are fixed and traditional, therefore preparation for adult life is clear and simple, although it frequently involves submitting to severe physical pain and discomfort in initiation rites. But the life of a young adult in our society is brimful of complex responsibilities and goals which are not readily attainable. For that reason a long period of preparation, namely, the teens, is required for competence.

Out of our learning to control the expression of primitive drives of all kinds, including the very important one of seeking sexual gratification, have come the highest achievements of civilization: scientific knowledge, inventions, art, literature and music. These become possible when the tremendous creative energy which is at the disposal of the sexual instinct is directed into other channels; in other words, is sublimated. This is the condition *sine qua non* for intellectual achievement.

In those primitive societies where children are permitted to do whatever they like all day long without supervision, guidance or instruction by adults, the children show a very low level of imagination and originality in their play, an impoverishment of personality and a lack of creativity. Our goals of high achievement are made possible by our system of child rearing and formal education which channels all the derivatives of the life instincts into learning. Sexual curiosity is pressed into the service of a quest for intellectual knowledge, which starts with the ABC's. Sexual impulses for mastery (masculine) and receptivity (feminine) are used in assimilating knowledge. Aggression finds a healthy and constructive outlet when work is attacked and conquered. In learning to postpone gratification and tolerate frustration and delay, the individual acquires self-control which gives him power over his impulses, and, therefore, power to achieve. The pleasure-seeking instincts which are so readily satisfied in primitive societies, in ours find gratification in gradually acquired accomplishments which are a source of pride and self-esteem, and of lasting pleasure.

The individuals who come through these formative periods

of youth, having utilized them to the best advantage, are individuals to reckon with. They make their mark in the adult world because they come equipped for its challenges.

When teenagers engage in a complete sexual relationship, their own individual self-civilizing processes come to a halt. Academic and scholastic achievements become unimportant. The energy and interest needed to master them are expended in a premature sexual relationship which, except for very rare instances, adds nothing to the teenager's development. In fact the guilt and anxiety aroused by the illicit romance have an additional disorganizing effect upon whatever efforts might be made to study.

When a major adult goal is thus attained without true preparation for it, everything suffers. The goal is not fully understood, appreciated or enjoyed and the short circuiting of the process of maturing permanently impoverishes the general development of the individual. You can understand if you gave rare French champagne to your ten-year-old brother or sister it would be completely inappropriate, largely wasted and somewhat harmful. The ten-year-olds might get a great kick out of the idea of the champagne, perhaps even enjoy something of the taste, and even be thrilled at the experience of getting a bit tipsy and feel terribly grown-up and sophisticated because of it, but if it makes them lose interest in ice cream sodas and football, school clubs or dancing school, and if from then on their idea of a great time is only to get high on champagne, you would know that you had seriously interfered with the course of normal development from which they would derive much more genuine pleasure and profit.

Intercourse is an adult activity in our society where we do not arrange for pubertal marriages and where individuals, not a tribe, are responsible for the children born to them, where abortions are illegal and dangerous, where crushing stigma attaches to the illegitimate child and the unwed mother, where feelings of depression and longing may continually haunt the young girl who has no alternative but to give her baby away; and the father's life may be blighted as well. Many girls can never find peace once they have given up their babies. They spend their lives trying to find and reclaim them. Whatever the outcome of the search, there is heartbreak and tragedy for someone.

Premarital Sex

Premarital intercourse is fraught with problems and responsibilities. Many young people who are preparing for a profession have to spend more than half of their twenties in school, during which time the majority are dependent upon their parents for support. Many of them find the frustration of waiting until they can afford to marry too great to bear and engage in sexual relationships, some of which end in marriage, some of which do not.

This is a problem which adults must settle for themselves. Anyone over the age of twenty-one is legally an adult, therefore legally responsible for his actions, and therefore entitled to make a decision. A wise decision in this very difficult matter requires a fully devoloped adult sense of responsibility.

In order to be savored to the full the important experiences of life must be treasured. There are appropriate times and circumstances which provide the perfect setting in which significant and meaningful events may be experienced in all their richness.

For a girl or woman to give up her virginity is an important emotional experience, regardless of how sophisticated and worldly she considers herself to be. Under normal circumstances, it causes her to feel a very special attachment to the man to whom she has given it, and, therefore, is an excellent beginning for a marriage. Sharing a precious experience with a beloved person to whom one belongs forges strong emotional and psychological bonds. These will be strengthened as their sexual embraces gradually involve more and more of a feeling of total relationship and truly become a rainbow of emotion in which love and devotion, ardor and ecstasy mingle in an indescribable way, adding new dimensions to the personalities of both as they learn to know the depths and the range of exquisite loving sensuality of which the body and the emotions are capable, and which deepen and broaden their love for each other.

Some teenagers try to convince themselves that sexual intimacy is not a serious matter and should in fact be a normal part of college life.

Sex on the Campus

In a recent survey of the sexual activities of college girls, the evidence is unmistakable that most of the girls who are having affairs feel anxious and distressed, despite their valiant attempts to deny such feelings to themselves and to anyone who will listen. Further, a report on the psychiatric problems of college girls indicates that many become depressed and unable to work after being shed by their campus lover.

It is clear that while a great many college girls think they can cope with an affair, very few of them actually can. When the boy moves on to another flame, their distress, as one would expect, is overwhelming. Whether the few who can take it in stride are unusually secure or from homes where the satisfaction of sexual appetites is regarded as no more significant than eating, or, more likely, whether they are girls who are strongly masculine in their orientation—which means that feminine needs for tenderness and devotion are repressed, has not yet become clear.

* What is clear is that the girls who are sleeping with boys have not thereby found happiness, contentment or self-realization. Even in the cases where it is real love leading to marriage, the uncertainty of her position is bound to create anxiety in the girl and give rise to periodic doubts about her partner's devotion to her.

Many girls are, unfortunately, being pushed into affairs by the combined pressure of the boy's impassioned demands and protestations of love, along with their dorm-mates' example and urging. Because of the insecurity which is so typical of adolescence, sensitive, intelligent boys and girls who wouldn't think of having an affair if left to work out their own relationships as they saw fit may, because of ridicule and threats of being left out of social life, abandon their principles. Far from the stabilizing influence of their homes, they succumb to the new "authority." Girls are particularly vulnerable. Exposed to the double threat of being on their own, worried about social success, they all too frequently are victimized by the propaganda of the co-eds who are already having sex relations.

Girls going to out-of-town colleges need to bear in mind that the co-eds who have been having affairs, no matter what they say to the contrary, almost without exception feel insecure, anxious and guilty about it. Their feelings *uncon-*

sciously impel them to pull as many girls into the same boat with them as possible. The more companions in guilt they have, the lighter their burden of individual guilt feels. Girls who can look around the dorm or the classroom and say to themselves, "Most everyone is doing it; I'm no different," momentarily feel less guilty and anxious.

(People who are really sure of themselves and their actions, whether they be indulgence or abstinence, do not feel the need to talk everyone else into a course of action similar to theirs.)

Awareness of the chastity of other girls is experienced as a reproach and they are unconsciously driven to eliminate the source of such discomforting feelings. As a result of this vicious cycle, colleges from coast to coast have become breeding grounds for depressions and breakdowns of girls who have been pressured into sexual activity for which they were not psychologically ready and which went against their moral principles.

Another reason why sex on the campus so easily gets out of hand where the colleges do not take vigorous action to prevent it is that being away from home and community encourages the fantasy that no one will ever know what is taking place. This creates in many girls the illusion that "it won't count." In other words, she tells herself that she will not be upset because she will pretend it didn't happen. Because no one in her home town will ever know, she can forget all about it—she thinks. The catch here is that a girl can never be sure in advance of how she is going to feel after she has become intimate with a boy. She is not familiar with her unconscious beliefs, for one thing. In addition, she has no way of knowing how the young man who has professed love and demanded intimacy is going to behave to her. The more sensitive, the more feminine, the more high-minded she is the greater will be her dependence upon the boy's devotion and consideration and affection for her and the greater will be her shock and despair if he lets her down. A boy who is far away from *his* parents and his girl back home can easily talk himself into believing that he "loves" a girl at college—not enough to ask her to marry him during the next vacation, but enough to use it as an excuse to himself and to her that it makes intimacy permissible.

Girls should be on guard against talking themselves into or allowing themselves to be talked into this snare and delusion. Sex with love means marriage. What kind of love is it that gives nothing but asks everything, and, moreover, carries the potential in many cases of destroying the girl's emotional stability and peace of mind, perhaps for the rest of her life? Many girls are completely shattered by a "first love" which later turns out to have been nothing more than the gratification of a boy's sexual drives and which may end in abortion. The disillusionment, the wounded self-esteem, the hurt pride, the heartache and the feeling of having been duped by a man can warp a girl's outlook on life. In many instances, it leads to a breakdown and the girl drops out of college.

A college boy who has in advance proclaimed manly responsibility for untoward complications may turn out to be a frightened little boy when put to the test. Sometimes what looks like heartless callousness is terror in disguise. But what difference does that make to the girl who finds that she is pregnant and is no longer "loved"?

In the same way that girls deceive themselves about their attitude towards sexual intimacy, boys can fool themselves about how mature and responsible and even noble they are going to be when faced with the responsibility for an abortion, or the necessity of a hasty marriage, or the responsibility for a girl's suicidal depression. Many boys find themselves involved in such affairs purely as a result of the pressure from their dorm-mates or fraternity brothers who have planted the seeds of doubt as to their masculinity and feel they must prove themselves. With no sensible adult to turn to for a discussion of his conflicts and uncertainties, a young man may feel that his reputation depends upon persuading a girl to have an affair.

A girl *has* to be more concerned about sexuality than a boy. She can never say that the baby inside her isn't hers, and she cannot escape the feelings of dependence upon her lover which arise in the normal female. Nor can she escape her longing for tenderness and love which are so completely fused with her sexuality.

Life is infinitely easier for the girl whose moral conviction or understanding of female psychology has given her an incorruptible self-control against "going all the way." She does not consider an affair as part of college life. Instead of being faced with one emotional crisis after another, her mind is free for learning, her world is predictable and safe. She can relax and have fun and enjoy all aspects of college life, including husband hunting, if that happens to be her primary goal. There will be no momentous decisions to make which may disturb her equilibrium, no desperate need to determine whether or not she is really in love and what to do about it if she is. She is at peace with herself because her actions are in harmony with her beliefs, and, therefore, her self-esteem is intact.

Fractured Freud

A smattering of knowledge of Freudian theories, misunderstanding of some of Freud's discoveries and mistaken application of others may be at least partially responsible for the current lack of restraint in sexual behavior. "Inhibitions are bad for your adjustment." "It's unhealthy to have ungratified sexual urges," college students often say, confident they are accurately quoting Freud. If we had no inhibitions, we would not be civilized. All of our instinctive, primitive impulses, the expression of which we have gradually learned to inhibit as we grew up, would characterize our actions. We would go around dirty and naked, hit each other when irritated, kill when enraged, steal from each other, and engage in unlimited sexual activity with family members. What did Freud actually say?

Freud Unfractured

When Freud discovered that his patients with anxiety neuroses always suffered some interference with the discharge of sexual tension, he concluded that the accumulated sexual excitation was being discharged in the form of anxiety. He apparently formulated this theory in 1894, and although he seemed to have some doubts about it, he adhered to it for many years. But by 1925—more than thirty years later—he had accumulated sufficient clinical evidence to prove to himself that he had been mistaken. In "Inhibitions, Symptoms and Anxiety," which was published in 1926, he rejected his original theory and stated his belief that neurotic anxiety was a reaction to a situation viewed as dangerous by the ego, as judged by childhood beliefs. He still felt, however, that perhaps the old theory held in certain cases, but *by 1933 he wrote that he no longer adhered to it at all.* (Lecture XXXII of the *New Introductory Lectures,* Standard Edition, Hogarth Press.)

Failure to distinguish between normal and neurotic inhibitions may be the cause of the confusion. Normal inhibitions are obviously the automatic control of primitive impulses and drives which our civilization requires. A neurotic inhibition refers to an unconscious restriction of the expression of an instinct needed by the individual to function at his full potential. He may be inhibited in intellectual functioning, such as in emotional blocks to learning. He may be inhibited in motor control, as in the case of people who are unusually clumsy (when there is no neurological basis for it). He may be inhibited in speech under certain circumstances as are those who are incapable of speaking to a group regardless of being expert in their subject. Normal aggression may be neurotically inhibited, as in the case of the person who trembles with fear at the thought of asking the boss for a much deserved raise or promotion. And, of course, people can be sexually inhibited in that they are unable to function adequately in the sexual sphere.

All neurotic inhibitions come about as a result of anxiety-arousing experience in childhood. Freud discovered that if little children were made to feel deeply ashamed and guilty about their childish sexual drives and curiosity, they grew to adulthood suffering from some degree of permanent inhibition of normal sexual functioning. This type of inhibition also produced many neurotic symptoms, because every time the individual became aware of the sex drive he immediately felt anxious and would feel the need to *avoid* becoming aware of the sex drive. The additional symptoms which he might exhibit could be a feeling of illness when it was time to go on a date. In this way he would avoid being in a situation with a girl which could cause him to have sexual thoughts and feelings. In fact, many psychosomatic illnesses are traceable to sexual inhibitions.

As to how the creation of the sexual inhibition takes place, the following illustrations may serve: A little boy is severely punished for masturbating. When he becomes an adolescent, and is out on a date, he may find that he ejaculates immediately upon feeling sexual sensations, an occurrence which is very much in opposition to his desires. This happens because the voice of his parents in childhood—*You are a bad boy for wanting sexual pleasure; it is wrong, bad, we won't love you if you don't stop that*—continues to be heard in the unconscious, making him feel anxious whenever sexual feelings arise. To be threatened with the loss of the parents' love is a terrible danger to the child. When a young man is overwhelmed by such childhood fears, his sexual functioning becomes inhibited as an unconscious means of avoiding the dangers attendant upon displeasing the parents of his childhood.

Similarly the little girl who was shamed and made to feel excessively guilty because of childhood expressions of sexuality, including Oedipal rivalry, may always react to the imminence of sexual feeling with anxiety. This can, for instance, create frigidity in a young wife who on a conscious level desperately wants to be able to respond to her husband's embraces. Her normal sexual response is thus inhibited because it unconsciously is equated with forbidden childhood wishes.

The kinds of inhibitions Freud showed to be harmful are those which produce an unconscious avoidance of sexual feeling, stemming from childhood fears and guilt. They impair normal functioning.

Freud discovered that sexuality was a normal part of life from birth. Some people have taken this to mean that the exercise of rigorous control over its gratification in adolescence or adulthood is harmful. Healthy adjustment of the young adult requires that he accept his feelings, but *become master of his actions*. Intelligent, conscious control is healthy. It has never been known to harm anyone.

Promiscuity

Some teenagers who regard themselves as free and emancipated, engage in one love affair after another. Actually they are enslaved by unconscious childhood needs. In a recent study of unwed teenage parents it was found that many of the boys expressed concern because there was so little pleasure for them in the sexual act. Similarly, it is well known that promiscuous girls usually experience very little sexual feelings, if any, but are looking for mother-love from men. In other words, all they enjoy of the relationship is the fondling and caressing which unconsciously represent maternal affection. Other girls express to the world their deep feelings of worthlessness by making themselves available to any man. Some promiscuous girls suffer from an unconscious wish to have a baby which will belong only to them. These girls often refuse to marry the father of their child.

Promiscuity may represent a frantic attempt to escape from too strong an attachment to a parent, or it can be caused by spite and rebellion against a parent. Sometimes it serves as a flight from an awareness of homosexual tendencies. The pop-

ular notion that promiscuity is caused by unusually stron
sexual desires couldn't be more mistaken. Sex for the promis
cuous becomes depersonalized and meaningless. Promiscuit
is always a sign of deep disturbance in personal relationships
an inability to trust, to form meaningful and lasting ties.

An Affair with Someone Who Is Married

Adolescents who fling themselves into love affairs wit'
married people often deceive themselves that it is a sign o
sophistication and maturity. The reverse is true. These teen
agers are usually very much tied to a parent and the love af
fair is an expression of it. To the unconscious, every marrie
person is a parent and so they leave one parent for another.

The most dangerous aspect of a love affair with someon
who is married is that the adolescent cuts himself off from th
normal social experiences of adolescence. He then fails t
learn to cope with the tensions and uncertainties of teenag
dates and courtship and fails to learn to know more abou
other people and about his own reactions to different types o
people. As a matter of fact, these affairs often serve the pur
pose of a retreat from the trials and tribulations of the ado
lescent growth period.

An even greater danger lies in the fact that the teenage
may remain involved for many years, feeling unable to breal
this childlike attachment to the parent substitute, even
though he (or she) realizes that precious years in which th
world is teeming with possible mates are slipping away. Th
lack of genuine interest in single young people communicate
itself to them, and, therefore, dates are few and far between

If you've had an affair, you need to understand what le
you into it, what you were unconsciously seeking. Under
standing the hidden forces which have driven you into a
unwise or uncontrolled action provides the first step in findin
out how to arm yourself against a repetition of it. You shoul
try to find an adult whom you trust and respect to talk it ove
with, preferably someone who understands psychologica
problems.

The sensible thing to do about all experiences which hav
left an aftermath of unhappiness is to learn as much as yo
can from them. In this way, they may in the long run be con
verted into assets, purchased, alas, by disillusionment, heart
ache, fear and misery, and, therefore, very dearly bought
But if they lead you on to greater understanding of yoursel

and others and greater self-discipline, you become a wiser and better person than you might otherwise have been. The important point is for growth to take place as a result of insight.

Should a Girl Confess?

There is no reason ever to discuss your sexual experiences with anyone other than the person to whom you go for help in avoiding a repetition of them. Confessing really means that you want reassurance or forgiveness, both of which are childlike attitudes and do not belong in an adult love relationship. A girl's worth is not in any way dependent upon whether or not she has had a sexual experience. Such an attitude is a throw-back to the days when women were the property of their fathers and then of their husbands, when men made the laws to suit themselves and women had no choice but to obey.

Excessive Guilt Feelings

Some adolescents, most often girls, have been subjected from earliest childhood to excessively severe moral teachings. They react with fear to the adolescent urges for freedom and the hunger for love and choke them off by means of excessively rigid moral principles and a total renunciation of the love-making and the social life typical of the teens. They suffer from neurotic inhibitions. They avoid real experiences and depend heavily on fantasy, which of course leads to neurotic symptoms and behavior, such as the continuous and exaggerated fear of being attacked by men, which one so often sees in unmarried women.

The standards of what is right and wrong are taken over from our parents in the course of early childhood upbringing. They form that part of our thinking which is popularly called a conscience, and which psychoanalysis refers to as a superego, because it tells the ego how to evaluate certain situations. Therefore, the superego influences the way in which the ego perceives a situation. If a girl has been taught that sexual feelings are wrong, when she experiences them in the normal course of development, she will regard them not as natural but as a sign of her own badness and will feel anxious and inferior. The girl who has been taught to regard them as normal and healthy desires, the expression of which needs to be brought under control, will experience a certain amount of

anxiety as to whether they are going to control her or sl
them, but armed with the knowledge that they are norm
she will be in a better position to come to terms with the
She will be able to make a sensible decision which conform
to the culture in which she lives.

With her self-esteem intact, she will find a solution to bo
expression and control. Her ego will not have been cripple
by a harsh and unrealistic superego. Therefore, she will pe
ceive reality accurately and be able to enlarge her unde
standing of her developing self and move toward adulthoo
with an expanding grasp of the reality of adulthood, of whi
sexuality is such an important part. In other words, she ha
developed a healthy ego, which is in harmony with her supe
ego, as contrasted with the first girl whose ego strivings a
at odds with what her superego considers to be proper; there
fore, her knowledge of reality is constricted as well as di
torted. She acquires false notions about herself, and, there
fore, is prevented from understanding the adult world.

The person who is always cringing before the disapprov
of a harsh superego remains in the position of a child continu
ally fearful of the parents. He is never able to think for hin
self, but always goes by what mother or father would co
sider proper. The strange thing about the superego is that
is usually much more severe than the actual parents of th
person would be under the circumstances. For instance,
parent may have viewed with alarm and strong disapprov
the sight of a four-year-old child handling its genitals. Fro
their attitude the child acquires the belief that anything whic
produces a sexual sensation is bad. These same parents wh
did not know that sexuality is a normal part of childhoo
might understand that sexual feelings are part of adolescenc
and not be nearly as disapproving of them as they were in th
four-year-old. But the superego attitude, formed when th
child was four or five and reinforced in its severity perhap
by guilt feelings connected with coming to terms with th
Oedipal problem, will respond to the new desire for sexu
experience with all the disapproval which the little child fe
from his parents, plus an extra dose.

Another superego attitude which creates difficulty for bot
adolescent boys and girls and can have far-reaching harmf
effects is the belief that sexual feelings and desires are no
part of the life of girls and women of refinement. Sometim
parents actively promote a split between love and sexualit
by urging a young man who is tied up in a long engagemen

have sex relations with someone who means nothing to him
order to be certain that he won't persuade his fiancée to
ave premarital relations.

An Individual Moral Code

It should be clear by now that some form of sexual activity
characteristic and normal for every period of development.
Nature seems to have taken great pains to guarantee that
the sexual instinct would not fail to be given expression, thus
ssuring the continuation of life. Civilization, in regulating
the expression of this powerful instinct has not only vastly en-
iched the earth by means of derivatives of the sexual drive,
ut in so doing has added emotional and spiritual dimen-
ions to sexuality which have made of it the deepest and
most powerful expression of love.

The problem is one of finding a balance between control
nd expression which conforms with other demands made
pon the individual at each stage of his life. In early child-
ood the control rests with the parents. From the ages of six
to ten or eleven, the youngster usually responds to his own
internalized controls taken over from the parents. During this
time, normally, sex drives are at a minimum and the child's
chief interests are in learning. In adolescence, for the first
time in the life of the individual, his sexual drives involve the
well-being of another person, the possibility of doing harm
to the other person as well as to himself. At the same time,
his sex urges become stronger and more insistent than they
ave ever been *and* the responsibility for achieving the balance becomes his own, very largely, although parents and
society try to help. Small wonder that adolescence is an age
f anxiety.

In finding an individual moral code for the expression of
ove and sexuality, if teenagers guide themselves by kindness
nd consideration for all aspects of the other person's well-
eing and happiness, combined with serious regard for their
bligations to themselves to make the most of all opportunities
or constructive self-development, they cannot, it seems to
me, do wrong or fail to become responsible, thinking members
f society.

SECTION III

14

FOR PARENTS

Nature is wise, but also cruel. All biological drives impel the individual to cast out the parents at adolescence. Animals shed all attachments to the mother at maturity. Human beings shed the childhood attachment and trade it in for a mature and friendly attachment. At times the trading-in period can be even more rough on the parents than on the adolescents. The happier and the healthier the relationship between parents and children has been up to this time, the greater generally will be the confidence on the part of the parents that things will eventually straighten themselves out and they will have their children back as young adult friends before long.

Nevertheless, even under ideal circumstances, parents usually experience a painful sense of loss when these delightful young companions suddenly become completely absorbed in others and in life outside the home. Only when they dash in to shower, dress and bolt a mouthful of food do the parents see them. The loss of their company can be a very great deprivation to the parents, but they must try to accept it for the healthy development it is and to avoid interfering in one guise or another, attempting to pull the youngsters back to the former relationship of closeness.

Teenagers are not really difficult to understand even though they are a mass of contradictions and lightning speed mood changes. Parents can get to know what the contradictions consist of and to understand why teenagers at times are so unpleasant, and thus become helpful and interested observers of the rapidly changing scene instead of helpless and harassed victims or anxious and restrictive joy killers. Instead of being irritated and alarmed, they can enjoy the zany antics of their offspring and take pleasure in their uneven but touching strides towards adulthood.

Hints for Getting Along with Teenagers

It has been noted that adolescents ask very few questions of their elders. The reluctance to question is typical and is caused not only by the fact that the adolescent, in striving for independence, is averse to showing dependent behavior by turning to his parents and other elders for advice, but also because some of his deepest concerns are related to sexual activity and functioning and it is embarrassing to approach an adult for such a discussion. Moreover, it also puts the youngster in the position of being preached at, something they all hate.

A fifteen-year-old girl from a happy family in which both parents were quite ready to discuss any problems with her made an overture to her mother by mentioning that a certain magazine had an article which was interesting. After initially brushing aside the comment, the mother later thought about her daughter's remark and secured the magazine. She found that the article dealt with premarital intercourse and realized that her daughter wanted to know what she thought of this practice. "I almost lost her," the mother reported, "by saying, 'I've read the article. What do you want to know?'" The daughter replied, "Oh, nothing," and was about to leave the room, pretending great indifference to the whole matter. She couldn't bear her mother's adopting the role of the authority. The mother fortunately understood the oversensitivity of her adolescent and quickly added, "I was very much interested in the article and I'm sure it must make you girls wonder whether it is the right thing for you to do. I guess it also makes you wonder what *I* think is the right thing to do." This brought her daughter right back to her side for a discussion.

The single most important thing for adults to learn in order to get along with teenagers is to remember that intellectually they are young adults, and, therefore, entitled to be treated as equals as far as discussions of ideas about life, love and everyday activities go. Because the adult may have a greater number of ideas or view the situation differently does not mean that he should thereby automatically consider himself vastly above the teenager. The situation is akin to a relationship between an old professor and a young teacher at a university. A wise head of a department will treat with respect and courtesy the ideas and suggestions of a young, inexperienced colleague, and if he is in disagreement with some of the plans will use the greatest tact in pointing out certain pitfalls which he feels may present themselves.

The second most important thing for adults to remember is that adolescents cannot help being overly sensitive to everything. This oversensitivity is produced in part by the rapid physiological changes taking place in the body. It has been proven that adolescents show an increased sensitivity to stimuli of all kinds, and it is well known that their reactions to stimuli are more rapid than at any other time of life. Anyone who has ever watched a teenage boy of the constitutionally active type take off in an automobile or change the recordings on a phonograph will realize that the dizzying speed with which the youngster performs is phenomenal, and it is indeed a phenomenon of adolescence.

Another cause of oversensitivity is that the teenager swings back and forth between feeling entirely able to be independent, and then becoming anxious and feeling that perhaps after all it would be safer to remain a child for just a little longer. The adult who approaches the teenager can never be sure in advance at just what point in the pendulum swing he is catching the youngster. Tact, kindness and respect for the youngster's ideas and feelings are important qualities a parent needs in order to get along with teenagers. He also needs a rhinoceros hide to be able to withstand his adolescent's periodic need to prove his parents' ideas and preferences are stupid.

The parent or educator who understands what to expect of the teenager does not become as easily offended nor feel as painfully rejected by the youngster and is therefore better able to maintain a friendly attitude. Those who feel threatened and hurt by the youngsters either fight back or withdraw in aggrieved silence; in either case adding to the guilt and confusion of the teenager.

Normal Adolescents

Dr. Anna Freud described, in 1958, adolescent behavior as follows:

Adolescence is by its nature an interruption of peaceful growth. . . . I take it that it is normal for an adolescent to behave for a considerable length of time in an inconsistent and unpredictable manner; to fight his impulses and to accept them; to love his parents and to hate them; to revolt against them and to be dependent on them; to be deeply ashamed to acknowledge his mother before others and, unexpectedly, to desire heart to heart talks with her; to thrive on imitation of and identification with others while searching unceasingly for his own identity; to be more idealistic, artistic, generous, and unselfish than he will ever be again, but also the opposite: self-centered, egoistic, calculating. Such fluctuations between extreme opposites would be deemed highly abnormal at any other time of life. At this time they may signify no more than that an adult structure of personality takes a long time to emerge, that the ego of the individual in question does not cease to experiment and is in no hurry to close down on possibilities.

If parents understand that these fluctuations are inevitable and healthy, and, therefore, desirable, they will not find them alarming nor nearly as irritating. Being prepared for unpredictable and inconsistent behavior puts parents in a frame of mind in which it will not be upsetting to them. What is unexpected or inexplicable creates anxiety. Parents have the feeling, "What is going on here? I don't know where I stand or what's what." But if you know that it is normal for your teenager to be gay one day, feeling that the world is his oyster, and depressed the next, sure that all is hopeless, the knowledge should fortify you against being infected by the black moods or being irritated by his overexuberance.

If you know that before a personality trait or character trait crystallizes, both sides of the quality will unconsciously be experimented with in perhaps an extreme form—such as being noble and perhaps even foolishly generous on one occasion and a veritable demon of selfishness and low cunning on the next—when you observe this behavior you can understand what is taking place.

Similarly, there are times when the teenager will be loving and dependent upon you, then suddenly behave as though nothing could be less important than your existence on this earth as long as a money tree is growing in the backyard. You shouldn't be offended although it is admittedly hard to take. It only means that the path towards maturity and independence which the youngster is treading has an uneven rhythm: two steps forward and one step back, and then perhaps three steps sideways and one step forward. And when life is cruel—a broken romance, a humiliation, a school failure— the youngster may take three steps or even four steps back towards childish dependence coupled with adolescent irascibility before sprinting ahead again in the direction of super-independent adulthood!

Your teenager is often just as baffled by his mood swings and inconsistent behavior as you are. He doesn't know "which is the real me" and is often quite worried about it. Being on a continual seesaw and merry-go-round sometimes makes him dizzy and queasy.

Attitudes Toward Sex

Naturally what worries teenagers the most is sexual behavior. What is right, wrong, dangerous, safe, normal, abnormal? Using the standards of the home as a starting point, they must evolve their own if they are to be truly mature individuals some day. Their behavior must be dictated not by blind fear, which is childlike, but by knowledge, logic, reason, and consideration for the well-being of others as well as of themselves. In many cases one finds overanxious parents very disturbed at the thought of even the smallest intimacies; one finds the other extreme too, where parents make the serious mistake of approaching their teenagers with the offer of contraceptive devices. The overanxious parents are beaming unspoken alarm messages to their children, "Sex is bad and dangerous, we don't want you to be involved." The ultramodern are in effect saying, "There's nothing specially important about it, c'mon along and be one of us." There is a large in-between group of parents who, feeling uncomfortable and uncertain as to what their attitude should be, ignore the entire matter, uneasily hoping for the best. Then there is a small group of lucky parents who, feeling comfortable and happy about their own sexuality and respecting the place of sexuality in the lives of their children, communicate to the child by their whole attitude and an occasional discreet twinkle in the eyes, that love, sex and romance are great and one of life's most wonderful and important experiences, deserving to be treated with due regard for all of its important aspects. These parents are able to allow their children a proper amount of freedom and privacy, trusting to their judgment and good sense, knowing that any kind of detailed discussion of date behavior and sex is an invasion of privacy and an embarrassment to the youngster.

The parents who always insist upon knowing what went on in the course of the evening are unconsciously trying to live through the romantic and sexual aspects of the date, as well as keeping control of the youngster's sex life. The attitude is unhealthy and no good will come of it. Parents who simply can not stop themselves from doing this (some actually feel a compulsion to do it and become terribly anxious if they try to stop) should seek professional help. Such behavior represents a sexual involvement with the teenager which can only be injurious to the teenager's adjustment. This is also true of the parents who offer their teenagers contraceptive devices (as distinguished from the normal situation of giving *information*, in response to the teenager's *request*). It is an inappropriate intimacy to share with one's teenagers. It means urging them to have intercourse, practically under the parents' noses, making it a shared sexual experience. Such behavior always makes the teenagers embarrassed and uncomfortable and adds to their problems, even though on the surface they may appear to take it all quite calmly and even brag about how modern their parents are. Moreover, such an attitude pretends that this most intimate and important relationship between a man and woman is a quite ordinary, unimportant and everyday affair. It's a great pity if parents actively prevent their children from acquiring a true appreciation of the meaning and significance of sexual intimacy in which love, tenderness, ardor and passion transport the individuals into an ecstatic other-world. In a happy marriage where the couple's sexual instincts have not been crippled, the memory as well as the anticipation of the joy and pleasure which they can give to each other filters through their daily life, binding them closely and making them tolerant of each other's faults and weaknesses and of the setbacks, disappointments and burdens of normal living.

The importance of helping teenagers achieve normal sexual attitudes cannot be overemphasized. Thousands of marriages which end in the divorce courts with complaints of incompatibility could have been entirely successful marriages if one or both partners were not suffering from sexual difficulties which caused feelings of frustration and anger, instead of joy and gratitude, to make them completely intolerant of each other, each convinced that he has fallen in love with the wrong person, and frequently moving on to another unsuccessful marriage.

Troubled Teenagers

Not all teenagers display the typical fluctuations between love and hate for the parents which is considered normal for adolescence. In some cases the adolescent is so overwhelmed by anxiety that he is unable to go through a process of gradual detachment marked by these fluctuations. He suddenly breaks with the family and transfers all of his affection outside to people who usually represent the opposite of the parents. There are new passionate ties formed to age-mates of either sex and to a group, and the parents then are continuously treated with callous indifference. Although at first glance this might look like normal adolescence, the suddenness of the change, the selection of direct opposites of the parents as idols, and the overemphasis on the new attachments reveal this form of development to be "a too hasty anticipation of normal growth rather than a normal developmental process." These youngsters are inconsiderate and indifferent to everyone in the home and are exasperating to the parents.

This behavior represents the teenager's response to anxiety and there is nothing that the parents can do to change it. The adolescent was not strong enough to cope with the anxiety and quickly closed down on other possible ways of dealing with it. If parents try to bring about better and more considerate behavior it only makes the situation worse. All that parents can do is to unobstrusively try to be aware of the caliber of the people to whom the adolescent has given his allegiance because the ideals of these new attachments will be taken over wholeheartedly and without criticism since these teenagers cast out the family standards with the family ties. Should the teenager attach himself to bad company, the parents will need to seek professional guidance in attempting to rescue the youngster and attempting to interest him in airing his views to a specialist.

Some teenagers deal with the anxiety aroused by the attachment to the parents by turning their childhood feelings towards them into their opposites. Anna Freud states, "This changes love into hate, dependence into revolt, respect and admiration into contempt and derision." As a result of this reversal of feeling, the adolescent imagines himself to be free, but actually he remains as securely tied to his parents as he was before, while reassuring himself through churlish behavior that he has broken the attachment and no longer has feelings of love for his parents. The youngster does not continue to develop but remains in a state of compulsive opposition to the parents.

This unhappy situation may take one of two turns. Unable to bear the hostility he continually feels and expresses to his parents, he may ascribe that hostility to his parents (project the feeling of hostility from himself onto them) and then regard them as his oppressors and persecutors.

Or, the extreme hostility and aggression may be turned inward against himself. He may become very depressed, seriously accident-prone and even become suicidal. This type of disturbed adolescent is very greatly in need of professional help, and is usually so unhappy that he welcomes it if the opportunity is tactfully presented to him. The best approach is for the parent, without rancour, to remark, "Something is the matter. We can't seem to get along and I know you aren't happy. I don't know how to improve the situation. There are people who know all about the things that make teenagers unhappy and can help them. It might be a good idea if you had a chance to talk confidentially to someone like that." If this is said with quiet dignity by the parent and without a trace of anger, it is highly unlikely that the offer will be refused.

Some teenagers although they are able to withdraw from the childhood attachment to the parents are nevertheless prevented by anxieties and inhibitions from finding anyone to love or become attached to in the outside world. The love feelings, called libido in psychoanalytic psychology, remain within the self and may give these persons very inflated notions about themselves, their abilities, accomplishments and achievements. In other words, they love and idolize themselves, sometimes even having the fantasy of being a second saviour of mankind.

When the dangers of adulthood appear overwhelmingly threatening, some adolescents retreat to very childlike behavior and dependence upon the parents, and still others, fearful of giving in to any of the normal adolescent impulses, fight against all impulses and against all needed satisfaction. All pleasures are forbidden, even sufficient food, sleep and body comfort. The teenager becomes an ascetic.

Parents will recognize that all teenagers occasionally exhibit behavior which fits into these disturbed categories. What distinguishes the troubled teenager from the normal teenager is the *fixed quality* of the troubled response. They are not experimenting with different kinds of responses and moods. They have hit upon a certain reaction which makes them feel relatively safe and they don't budge from this position. Therefore, growth and development towards adulthood are stopped. Sometimes the youngster will be able to abandon the rigid defense against anxiety after a while without help, but most often the situation warrants attention.

Causes of Friction

Those parents who feel certain that their adolescents fall within the normal range of behavior and yet find that there is a great deal of friction between them and their children about dating and general behavior need to ask themselves some questions.

Do you, for instance, understand that all parents need to brace themselves for removal from the pedestal on which their children's overestimation of them has placed them? To the degree that parents were overestimated, they will now be temporarily underestimated. (Mark Twain remarked that when he was a teenager he couldn't understand how his father could be so ignorant, and when he reached twenty he couldn't understand how his father had learned so much in such a short time.) In homes where parents are habitually courteous to each other and to their children, they will help their teenagers have some measure of stability during these turbulent years by courteously insisting upon courteous dislodgement from the pedestal. Not that the highly emotional teenager will always be able to live up to the standard but it should never be entirely lost sight of. If this is done consistently and kindly it can only be a help to the young person in learning to behave with at least a measure of dignity at other difficult times in his life.

But do you belong to the group of parents who politely nag their children to distraction? Is what is termed a demand for courtesy really a disguised demand for submission to the old parental authority? If you consider a refusal to obey you as lack of courtesy, then courtesy is being used as a demand for submission. Also, parents need to guard against using verbal politeness as a mask for needling and nagging. Sometimes adults use exquisitely polite phrases in tones of hardly veiled contempt and sarcasm. Such insincerity or sarcasm goads the teenager to a frenzy of helpless rage. If you make use of these techniques, don't be surprised at the result. And don't expect a polite response if a youngster comes home obviously deeply upset and you insist upon knowing what has gone wrong, or demand that some chore be attended to forthwith. Just quietly tell him that you're sorry he's feeling bad and then continue with your usual activities. If the youngster shuts himself up in his room, leave him undisturbed for an hour or so. You can then bring him a snack. His facial expression and attitude will let you know whether he wants to talk to you or be left alone. His wishes must be respected. If he feels able to, sooner or later he'll tell you what's bothering him. However, he may not, and you should not pry. Many youngsters prefer not to tell their families about humiliating experiences. Sometimes, a teenager will be in a terrible mood without having any idea of what has caused it. He just needs to be left alone to work out of it.

If you sense that something really disturbing has happened and that your youngster needs your help, then gently tell him that you are deeply worried about what could have happened to cause him such distress and that nothing can be worse for *you* than to be left to imagine disasters of various kinds. If it is a serious difficulty, he needs to know that you will stand by and help him do what is right and proper, and to make amends wherever possible.

Some parents fail to understand that teenagers need to remain aloof from them. "I can't reach her (or him)," a parent often laments. "Reaching" often means unconsciously trying to keep the youngsters in the old relationship of closeness. Attempts to "reach" the balky teenager who is obeying the unwritten laws of his own psychological development (it would be more correct to say psycho-biological) only intensify the youngster's anxiety and attempts to break away in order to retain his newly developing sense of independence. Under those circumstances, it may become absolutely impossible for adolescents to maintain even a semblance of courtesy towards their parents so frantic can they become at feeling the noose of parental involvement tighten around them.

An important source of antagonism is to be found in the unfortunate parental practice of listening in on telephone calls and reading the youngster's mail. This is an unpardonable invasion of privacy and guaranteed to keep teenagers in a fury of resentment. Another cause of friction is the tendency on the part of some parents (mothers in particular) to use their own adolescent experience as a blueprint of what is permissible for their teenagers. If mother didn't date until she was seventeen, there is no reason why daughter should. If mother felt anxious and insecure and nervous and unhappy through most of her teens, why shouldn't her daughter accept it as inevitable? Sometimes fathers adopt the same attitude towards their sons' social problems. Teenagers resent these attitudes and well they may, for there is nothing constructive in them. The knowledge that a parent went through the same misery is poor consolation to a dateless boy or girl.

A very common cause of friction between adolescents and their parents (again, mothers are the worst offenders) is a tendency on the part of the parent to continually offer suggestions and criticisms as to clothing, appearance and behavior. All are meant to help the teenager be successful but usually have exactly the opposite effect. Continual criticism of the youngster's efforts or ideas of what is good taste and what is attractive paralyzes the teenager and destroys any self-esteem or feeling of independence which may be budding. If Mother or Dad always knows best, that is another way of saying, "Your taste and judgment aren't good and we have no confidence that it will develop in the right direction, so just do as we say." This breeds great resentment which spills out in all contacts with the parents.

Parents who do this must make a great effort to be more detached and to allow the youngster to experiment. Nothing disastrous will happen if the outfit or the hairdo or the makeup isn't what you would like it to be. If you succeed in imposing your taste and your teenager leaves the house looking perfect on the outside and feeling resentful and inadequate on the inside, what have you accomplished? He (more usually she) is off to a bad start. Whereas, if an adolescent goes out to a party or to school feeling pleased with the way he looks according to his own standards, his confidence and self-esteem will be infinitely greater and his whole approach to people will be more cheerful and relaxed. Gradually, he will acquire a sureness of taste which, if circumstances do not keep him in a continuous state of rebellion against you, will closely resemble your own, or at least be strongly influenced by it. But this takes time, which means that you must be patient— and sensible. Some mothers carry on as though the family honor were at stake if any detail of daughter's appearance would fail to win the approval of a fashion or beauty editor. In so doing, they invariably are expressing some anxiety and insecurity of their own which makes them see their daughters only as an extension of themselves; hence, they treat the daughter's body and appearance as though it were their own. How can a girl's individuality, sense of identity, and self-esteem blossom under such adverse circumstances? Obviously they cannot. Irritation and friction inevitably follow.

In searching for possible sources of tension and antagonism between your teenagers and yourself, the areas to investigate are those in which typical adolescent development is taking place. Problems arising from a need for emotional and physical privacy and a need to be allowed to develop independent taste and judgment have been mentioned.

In view of the fact that sexual feelings and awareness are so strong at this time and that the need to renounce the early love ties with family members is a paramount task, we should not be surprised to find that very often difficulties can be traced to entanglements which are perpetuated by certain types of behavior on the part of all the family members.

Inappropriate intimacies of all kinds create problems of which people may not be consciously aware. Teenage boys are not indifferent to the sight of mother walking around in her underwear or nightgown. Fathers are not untouched by the sight of a teenage daughter in similar undress. And brothers and sisters are certainly aware of each other's developing bodies. To keep tensions at a minimum, no one should present himself to view without appropriate clothing. Little children may march around in their pajamas and undies, but parents and teenagers should not. That's what bathrobes and dressing gowns are for. Some parents find it almost impossible to believe that their children are in any way affected by seeing them in various states of undress or even in the nude. But in therapy one hears a great deal about just how disturbing such things are. Either the teenager has to pretend not to see anything or he has to cope with the uncomfortable feelings aroused in him. And parents (especially unhappily married parents) are bound to have a response to the beautiful young bodies being displayed to them. It can make them feel more attached and more possessive of their youngsters at a time when the teenagers want less and less of that feeling from the parents. Some kind of tension and irritation is bound to ensue.

A sixteen-year-old girl was beside herself with anxiety because she was expected to kiss her pajama-clad father good night every evening as he sat in his easy chair. She was painfully aware of the fact that his pajama pants were partially open and she could not resist looking. This in turn made her feel so ashamed and guilty that the good night kiss became a dreaded event. Needless to say the circumstances added greatly to her tension and self-consciousness with boys, and made her irritable and jumpy with her father who would have been most surprised to know what was causing it.

Sometimes, as a result of unresolved childhood attachments, a teenage boy or girl will insist upon walking around in seductive stages of undress. In a very kindly but firm way, this should be forbidden. Sometimes, under these circumstances, the parent unconsciously tries to ward off a feeling of attraction by becoming overly severe and critical of the youngster.

Sharing bathroom intimacies and sexy and off-color stories between parents and teenagers are other forms of seduction and should be avoided. Privacy about every single aspect of living which is in any way connected with sexuality should be thoroughly respected, if tensions and conflicts are to be kept at a minimum, and if the youngsters are to be unhampered in carrying their sexual interests outside the home for fulfillment.

Two men were waiting for a college train to pull in at the station at Christmas. One was waiting for his daughter and he began to describe her to his friend. "Boy, is she stacked," he exclaimed. "Wait till you see her figure. She really is beautifully built. I can't understand why she doesn't think much of herself." Eventually his daughter arrived. She probably did have a beautiful figure, which she did her best to hide in shapeless rather masculine clothing and her face was a mixture of sullen irritation and shyness. One couldn't resist conjecturing that her father's too great awareness of her as a sexually attractive female created so much anxiety that she defended herself against being attractive to anyone of the male sex and was very unhappy as a result.

In one home where the father frequently walks around his room in the nude, but with the door open, his teenage daughter never goes to sleep without first putting on a pair of tight panties under her pajamas. The nature of the fear aroused in this girl is obvious. It also should not be unexpected that she is extremely shy and withdrawn and has great difficulty in relating to boys despite the fact that she is very pretty. With her parents she is irritable and withdrawn.

A teenage boy is in a continual state of anger with his mother for her habit of barging into his room scantily clad and not troubling to find out whether he is dressed either.

A teenage girl is almost distraught because her very neurotic father refuses to knock before coming into her room and has often caught her undressing. She is in a continual state of tension and irritation and her parents find her impossible to get along with.

It is to be hoped that no teenager would dream of entering his parents' bedroom at any hour of the day or night without first knocking and waiting to be asked to enter. And it is just as fervently to be hoped that no parent would even for a moment consider entering a teenager's room without first knocking and asking permission to enter.

If the teenager's need for privacy, for independence, for reassurance that intimacies won't be forced upon him is clearly understood and respected by his parents, such understanding should automatically bring about changes in parent attitudes and behavior towards the adolescent which will go a long way toward reducing tensions at home, and enable the youngster to be more at ease outside the home.

How Parents' Problems Affect the Approach to the Teenager

There are many ways in which parents unwittingly create some of the difficulties of which they complain.

If parents are in the habit of being untruthful with their children, of pretending to believe something they don't believe in order to influence the youngster's actions, they are bound to either have a great many difficulties with their teenagers, or be the recipients of the same kind of insincerity and double-talk. One often sees a mother saying something to a young teenager (or younger child), punctuating her remarks with winks and grimaces, intended to convey to the adults in the room that she doesn't mean a word she says. Children are never fooled by this kind of behavior and with great justification they feel distrustful and antagonistic towards the parent who behaves in this way.

Nothing but sincerity and honesty can bring about a good relationship between you and your children, no matter what their ages. A mother of a seventeen-year-old girl was finding it extremely difficult to get along with her daughter, as was the father. They found that she was lying to them and seeing a neighborhood boy whom they did not want her to see as often as she desired. The mother, as the result of a sense of guilt lingering from her own adolescent romantic activities, had said when this baby girl was born "If she tries to do what I did, I'll break her neck." She kept an abnormally close watch over her daughter and pretended to have a very puritanical attitude toward adolescent romance. Her deceit bred deceitful behavior in her daughter. And it was all based on a misconception of what was right or wrong for the mother to have done as a dating teenager. She actually hadn't done anything unusual, but her very puritanical parents would have considered it wrong and she never was able to feel comfortable about having failed to live up to their standards. As a result, she determined to make of her daughter a better daughter than she felt she had been. In other words, her daughter's purity was to make amends for what she considered to be her own impurity. Therefore, a spontaneous, open, sincere and natural relationship with due regard for her daughter's need for freedom, privacy and growing independence was ruled out from the very beginning because of the mother's unresolved problems about herself.

Unbeknown to themselves, many parents develop a great sense of rivalry with their teenagers. The father who belittles his son's achievements with the claim that he doesn't want him to get a swelled head may be struggling with strong feelings of jealousy if he himself is lacking in true self-esteem. Some fathers express the feeling of rivalry through giving their sons less-than-average allowances even though the father has a higher-than-average income, the rationalization being that they want the youngsters to know the value of money. By this maneuver they can seriously curtail the young man's activities. These attitudes breed nothing but resentment in the teenagers who usually sense the underlying attitude.

A father's jealousy of his daughter's suitors may unconsciously take the form of belittling them to spoil his daughter's pleasure in their attentions or setting such unreasonably early curfews as to discourage them from wanting to take his daughter out.

Sometimes without being at all aware of the cause, a mother can be continually at odds with her daughter because of the mother's unconscious envy. It is not easy for many mothers, especially those who have set great store by their beauty, to see their daughter's radiant blooming beauty at a time when they themselves are beginning to fade. One of the first things a mother needs to search for within herself if she is getting angry criticism and complaints from her daughter is the possibility of an underlying envy impelling her to do things which spoil her daughter's pleasures. The mother who can detect pangs of envy along with the pride in her daughter's appearance and accept the combination of feelings without guilt is able to exercise conscious control over the expression of it. Difficulties arise when the envy is strong and the mother, unable to bear facing this emotion in herself, must for her own peace of mind deny to herself that it exists. Then the expression of it crops up in various disguises: it's too exhausting to go shopping for beautiful clothes with her daughter; everything is too expensive or unnecessary. Mother may object to sessions at the beauty parlor, to the use of make-up, to the wearing of high heels, etc. When birthdays and Christmas roll around, somehow all the gifts may turn out to be dull, utilitarian items like flannel pajamas, bluejeans, sensible black umbrella, etc., instead of any number of inexpensive yet glamorous items such as gaily colored little half-slips, pretty compacts, eau de cologne in glamorous bottles, chi-chi little dressing-table items, filmy scarves, and all the other frivolities so dear to the feminine heart.

Being given attractive clothing and little glamorous gifts makes a girl feel that her mother wants her to be successful as a woman. Moreover, good looking clothing is of vital importance to teenagers for other psychological reasons as well. Feeling insecure about their changing bodies they take especially great comfort and confidence from good looking and becoming clothes. Some people, as we all know, never outgrow this insecurity and rely all their lives upon a never-ending succession of glamorous new outfits to make them feel attractive. In the teens the feeling of insecurity is natural. Parents should do whatever they can to help the youngsters have an attractive wardrobe.

In some mothers the sense of rivalry takes the form of making statements which tell her daughter that everything bought for her means the mother is deprived of something. Of course this makes the daughter feel guilty, resentful and unhappy about everything she manages to get. Being thus thrown into a competitive situation with her mother hampers her pleasure in social life. Dimly, she feels forbidden to grow up, to equal or surpass her mother, to be attractive to young men; in short, she feels restrictions against taking her rightful place in the world, because it is unconsciously connected in her mind with taking it away from her mother. Under such circumstances, there is a great deal of unpleasantness between mother and daughter, usually taking the form of friction over unimportant matters because neither one feels able to speak about the real cause of the dissension between them. Often it is because they aren't clearly aware of what the trouble is. The daughter frequently ends up continually carping at her mother, the expression of her anger and disappointment at major frustrations being displaced onto minor or even nonexistent frustrations. Of course, the mother can not understand what makes her daughter so unreasonable.

Very difficult relationships between mothers and sons are sometimes brought about by the mother's resentment that her sons do not take her out. This may happen where a marriage has been unhappy and the mother has indulged in fantasies of having her sons make up to her for the attentions and social pleasures which her husband has failed to give her. In extreme cases, the mother is so successful that her son remains a bachelor until she dies, feeling unable to leave her for another woman. The mother's possessiveness and her displeasure at her son's budding social life quickly communicate themselves to him, however subtly, and, if he does not run away in complete rebellion, he is likely to remain tied to her. Here again the frustration of his normal desires to find his place outside the home can result in explosive, friction-filled behavior at home. This will most likely be apparent from adolescence, with the mother usually unable to understand why her son is often so disagreeable and difficult since she is so utterly devoted to him. One such mother when told that her twenty-seven-year-old son should be taking girls out instead of squiring her around, replied, "His life is much too interesting for him to be bothered taking out young girls They don't know anything, how could they interest him?" An extreme case, to be sure, but proof of the kind of life situations which can be created when drives on the part of a parent, which usually remain unconscious, become a reality.

Disciplining the Adolescent

I often wonder whether the parents who fly at their teenagers in a rage when the youngsters come home later than they are supposed to really believe it when they say that the only reason they behave this way is because they *care* about their children. Of course they care about their children, but do they realize they are implying that other parents love their children less because they don't work themselves up into a lather when their adolescents have exceeded a curfew, who are easygoing and friendly, who assume that if a youngster is late he probably has a good reason for it?

Parents who sit up and wait for their teenagers with an ever-increasing conviction that the youngster is lying dead in a ditch are naturally going to get into a wild state of agitation if the youngster is late. The problem is for the parent to find out why such morbid thoughts keep coming to mind when their teenagers are somewhat delayed in arriving home. Are the teenagers reckless and irresponsible or is it a problem of exaggerated parental anxiety?

If you cannot trust your teenage boys to be sensible and careful when driving, or your teenage girls to insist that a boy drive carefully, and to trust both to keep away from questionable places and dangerous areas, the difficulty may lie in the type of discipline you have used in training them to be prudent, responsible, reliable and considerate of others.

If you have relied upon whipping, coercion and harsh punishments in the past, then you may expect difficulty. Unless the youngsters have become completely intimidated, they will most likely have stronger than average feelings of rebellion as well as less self-control because whipping and harsh punishments usually prevent the development of a strong conscience. If you have played the part of a harsh policeman, with club always in motion, unless you change your method of dealing with them, your youngsters are likely to kick up their heels somewhat recklessly and try to get away with whatever they can when the policeman isn't present.

A most important reason why harsh punishments work

against conscience formation is that they take away the guilt feelings which arise when a child does something of which the parents disapprove. Because a child loves his parents and is completely dependent upon their continuing love for him, he feels anxious when his actions bring disfavor in their eyes. The only way to build a conscience, which is nothing more than an inner policeman, is for the child to feel guilty about bad behavior and to have retained a strong desire to please his parents. If he sees that his actions make them feel disapproving and disappointed in him, he will feel that way about himself. He will feel unhappy, ashamed, remorseful and anxious about retaining their love and approval. These twinges of guilt, remorse and lowered self-esteem are extremely painful to the child. His only relief from them is to give up the naughty behavior. Severe punishment from the outside immediately sweeps away the guilt feelings and the child comes to rely upon this type of relief and control. Some children actually keep provoking a parent into spanking them when they are aware of some wrongdoing which has escaped the parent's notice. Parents judge the situation accurately when they say, "Why, he practically asks for it, and it clears the air." Surely, he asks for it, but who taught him that that was the way to get relief from guilt feelings? The air is cleared because the parent has vented his aggression and anger and the child has been cleared of guilt. But the child has learned nothing of value and his development of self-control has remained at a standstill.

Constructive expressions of disapproval mean that the parent retains control of himself. He does not hide his displeasure, but neither does he overwhelm the child with it, predicting dire consequences and a black future. It is enough for the child to know that his parents are greatly annoyed and ashamed of the way he has behaved, that they expect better of him and that they are disappointed by his failure to live up to their standards. Firmly maintaining a sober demeanor, or being stern as distinguished from having a chip on the shoulder, for a length of time commensurate with the "crime" and the age of the child, and then quietly and wholeheartedly forgiving the child with a serious but fundamentally friendly reminder that better behavior is expected of him, can not fail to gradually bring about the desired results, provided the parents are completely sincere and are not trying to veil bitter anger with polite words.

It is best for parents who are quickly aroused to great anger to keep away from the child until they have gotten themselves under control. A parent who has lost control of himself cannot teach a child anything. The parent who in a rage sets out to "teach the child a lesson" usually ends up teaching him how spiteful, childish and full of vengeance it is possible for an adult to be. Parental example is the most potent factor in developing inner controls. Through love, guilt for backsliding, effort, and absorbing the example of the parents, the child gradually learns to take his parents' standards into himself and be his own policeman. Then he can love himself, know that he is good, and bask in the knowledge that his parents are happy and gratified by his behavior. The happy child who reaches adolescence with a strong and reliable conscience can be relied upon to behave sensibly. He knows that his parents trust him and have confidence in him and he is not likely to betray their trust.

Expressions of Parental Anger

An important distinction in the ways of expressing anger needs to be made for many parents. There is nothing wrong with allowing a child to see how angry his behavior has made you, provided your reaction is appropriate to the misbehavior, and the child's age. If you roar mightily and furiously at something a four-year-old has done, no matter what, it can only be out of a lack of understanding of the extent of self-control possible for four-year-olds, and you will surely terrify the child because you will appear at that moment to be transformed into a raging monster. In that case, your reaction would be inappropriate and the child too young to remain undamaged by the fear aroused in him.

But, even if you tend to blow your top too often, or get nervous and irritable too easily, older children from the age of nine or ten can learn to accept your peculiarities and eccentricities without damage to them. However, you must fully understand the enormous difference between angrily describing what you don't like, a method which is educational because it gives the child a clear picture of what you disapprove of and what upsets you, and name-calling, sarcasm, nastiness and cutting remarks, all of which humiliate and hurt the child, and tell him mainly how hostile you feel toward him.

When parents make a practice of hurting and humiliating their children, they do permanent damage. Going to the other extreme and trying to undo the damage by exaggerated praise when in a good mood, becoming momentarily over-indulgent or buying a gift for the child does not undo the damage. One sees this over and over again in therapy. The hurt child simply does not believe the parent when it swings over into praise, and the consolation prize does very little consoling. A mother told her ten-year-old son she wished she had died before giving birth to him, and then in remorse treated him to an ice cream soda, which ordinarily her children were not permitted to have, since sweets were considered dangerously unhealthy.

A father kicked his seventeen-year-old daughter down a flight of stairs and called her a tramp for coming home later from a dance than she was supposed to. The next evening he brought her a dress as a gift when he returned from work. Another father furiously called his nine-year-old son an animal for accidentally breaking a vase and later presented him with a baseball.

What's wrong with the consolation prize? Isn't it better than if the parent did nothing at all to show he was sorry? No, it is not. The consolation prize is to salve the parent's guilt feeling. It does nothing for the child, except to confuse him if the consolation prize is something usually forbidden. The parents' guilt feelings should not be reduced by this means, anymore than a child's guilt feelings should be reduced by spanking. The parent *should* feel guilty but he should let the guilt and remorse force him to try to exert better control over his temper the next time a provoking episode occurs, or to seek professional help if he finds that despite his heartfelt intentions, he cannot acquire self-control through his own efforts.

When parents try to square themselves by becoming temporarily indulgent about things which are usually forbidden, nothing can be more confusing to the child. Wavering standards of what is good or bad for him leave him with no standards at all.

Parents who have fallen into the deplorable habit of calling their children insulting names or of sneering and jeering at them, or making scathing denunciations, have, without knowing it, abandoned all meaningful educational procedures. Nothing constructive, nothing worthwhile is ever accomplished through humiliating, hurting, or frightening youngsters (or adults either, for that matter). They lose respect for parents who behave this way and they distrust the parents' love and good intentions on more favorable occasions.

Worst of all, they believe the insults down deep in their hearts.

A father who had always irritably and unrestrainedly expressed his dissatisfaction and displeasure with his son's personality, behavior and achievements was baffled by the fact that when it came time for the young man to go off to college no amount of praise and reassurance on the father's part could pull the boy out of an acute anxiety state, the result of fear that he would be a complete failure at college, socially as well as academically. The boy simply could not bring himself to believe one reassuring word his father uttered. In therapy it became clear that what he did believe, and believed firmly, were the cutting and humiliating estimates of him which it had been the custom of both parents to voice to him as a means of spurring him on to greater achievements as he grew up.

Effects of Corporal Punishment

It is difficult to think of anything more humiliating and degrading to an adolescent than to be struck by the parents, but, unfortunately, it happens in many homes. Many people firmly believe in spanking. They claim that their childhood spankings and whippings did them a great deal of good. If they give enough information about their upbringing, it soon becomes apparent that their good qualities developed *despite* the spankings, because of other strongly positive elements in their home and in their relationship with their parents. If they continue to reveal facts about their behavior, quirks and difficulties, it becomes evident that they have been reacting negatively to the whippings all through their lives without being at all aware of it.

A young man may reveal that he deeply regrets having wounded his parents by eloping because he lacked the courage to tell them of his decision to marry, knowing they would have disapproved. In other words, he was frightened of his parents at an age when he considered himself old enough and mature enough to establish a home of his own and become a parent. Can this be unrelated to the fact that he was always whipped for misbehavior by parents who loved him very dearly? An elopement implies fear, rebellion and defiance, three states of mind which whipping produces.

A young woman who has left her parents' home in the west and lives and works in New York reveals a peculiar quirk which she cannot understand: she always starts her meals with a dessert whenever circumstances permit. When we learn that she was always spanked for behavior displeasing to her mother, including refusal to eat disliked foods, it seems reasonable to assume that in breaking away from her parents' home and going to live in another part of the country she was motivated perhaps primarily by the desire to be free of her mother's control. The urge she felt to always eat dessert first was an expression of a continual declaration of independence from her strap-wielding mother, who never would have tolerated such a practice. If this girl were truly emancipated from her mother, however, she would not feel the need to behave in this eccentric fashion, not that dessert-eating is a matter of grave importance, but it may safely be assumed that the need to do the opposite of what is usual and what her mother would have tolerated permeates other areas of her life as well. In fact, there is ample evidence of it. Therefore, she is not free to allow her own unique personality to unfold, but is a slave to a negative pattern based upon rebellion. Although she has removed herself from her mother geographically, emotionally she is still back home with mother.

If a gentle and kindly young man sternly announces to his bride that he is to be the final and undisputed authority in their home in all important matters from this moment forth, it may seem completely out of keeping with his character unless we know that his upbringing included frequent whippings administered by his well-intentioned but extremely aggressive mother. Because his childhood had been spent with a woman whom he loved and who loved him, but who had bossed and beaten him he was taking no chances that the next woman in his life was going to dominate and intimidate him. Since his fear was so strong, he felt compelled to adopt an autocratic attitude in order to be certain of maintaining his cherished freedom. In temperament and personality, he was very much like his calm and kindly father, who had permitted the mother to be the boss and disciplinarian, having little taste for those roles himself. But, as a result of his childhood experiences, this young man will probably always have an exaggerated sensitivity to any attempt on the part of his wife to assert herself. It is not difficult to foresee how much his behavior with his wife will be influenced by his fear and resentment of his mother, both emotions having been intensified by her frequent whippings. He, too, is still involved in the struggle with his mother which will be fought out with his wife all their lives.

Whipping and harsh punishments do not create responsible, relaxed, considerate, mature adolescents. If they did, our delinquents and criminals would be our most responsible citizens. Although there are notable exceptions, as a group, one finds these harsh methods to have been the ones most favored by the adults in their environment throughout childhood and adolescence.

Overly Strict Parents

The counterpart of the parents who say "we're strict, angry and worried only because we love you" are the teenagers who say "if you really loved me you wouldn't be so strict and spoil all my fun."

Parents who are overly strict are usually that way because they are overly anxious. A variety of unconscious factors are to be found under the strictness to explain why these parents seem to have so little concern about how unhappy their strictness makes their teenagers. It *is* hard for teenagers to believe their parents love them when the parents regularly spoil their fun.

Setting curfews which are earlier than those of the rest of the group, arbitrarily deciding that the teenager may accept only one invitation per weekend no matter what happens to be going on, refusing to allow a teenager to date a certain youngster because the parent disapproves of the current custom of "going steady" and demands that the youngster make dates with others as well, when none are available, refusal to allow a girl to date any boy who drives a car, rage at tardiness in arriving home are some of the things overly strict parents do which make their children very unhappy.

Setting an absolute curfew with older teenagers is just looking for trouble. Such an attitude only inflames the normal tendency of the adolescent to rebel. Asking teenagers what they think would be a reasonable time to expect them, and making some adjustment from that, is likely to bring much more favorable results. It is most distressing to be forced to leave a party when it is going full blast instead of being allowed to go home with the others when it breaks up. The entire evening can be ruined for a teenager who comes to a party dreading the fact that when the clock strikes a certain hour, he alone must leave all the fun or else be turned into a criminal in his parents' eyes.

This is not a bid for anarchy. A good home cannot be a democracy as some people mistakenly think, with children having equal voting power with the parents. A good home is a *benevolent* dictatorship, gradually moving towards democracy as the children approach adulthood. Some adolescents are so responsible and mature by seventeen that they really can be left very much on their own, but others need the protection of a measure of parental authority for a longer time. As children move into the teens, their growing needs for independence must be taken fully into account or the dictatorship is no longer benevolent. It no longer serves the needs of the people but the needs of the dictator.

"You'll do it because I said so." This is a perfectly reasonable statement for a parent to make to a small child who is trying to see how big an argument he can provoke, or how many times he can get the parent to explain reasons of which he is perfectly aware all the time. It reassures the child that the parent is strong and in control, especially if he has said it with firmness which contained no hostility.

But if a parent issues an order to an adolescent which will cut him off from a group activity, because it doesn't entirely measure up to what the parent thinks is ideal, it is bound to create subversion of some sort. The adolescent has ideas of his own of what is right and wrong and they merit consideration.

Overly strict parents are prone to say, "I don't care what other parents permit their children to do. You'll do what we think is right, period." If you are living in a community of responsible people, why shouldn't you be interested in what they permit their children to do? On the other hand, if you live among people who dismiss drunkenness and vandalism with "Oh, boys will be boys" then you really should consider moving to a neighborhood where your standards will be shared.

There are scores of sensible, devoted and loving parents who disapprove of some of the customs prevalent among young people today, but who say, "I can't bear to put my children in the position of being the only ones in the group who are not permitted to do a particular thing, as long as it is not really harmful." Before forbidding your youngsters to engage in an activity, ask yourself if it is truly dangerous and harmful.

Some things are unwise, to be sure, and should definitely be changed, such as going steady in the early teens, but they will have to be changed by group action on the part of parents in a community, or at a particular school, not by an individual parent or child. It is foolish for twelve and thirteen-year-olds to be dancing in the dark and otherwise aping adult behavior. It does not help their development at all. In fact it creates anxiety in many youngsters. But if that's the kind of party everyone in your child's class gives, the PTA or the principal's office is the place to start a reform movement, not in your living room on the night your child is entertaining his classmates. And it isn't helpful to telephone another mother and berate her for allowing her child to give that kind of party. Such action will only get your child into the school's dog house, if the other mother, as usually happens, tells her child about your call.

Some parents are confused. They think these customs are cute. They must be educated to the fact that they are unwise. These parents need to be worked on with tact, patience and determination. If you are unwilling to become involved in the effort, then it might be best to consider the possibility that another school would be a better choice for your youngster.

But none of the things that the average older teenager desperately wants to be allowed to do and which enable them to feel part of the group are truly dangerous. Extreme behavior is the province of the seriously disturbed.

If you observe that your youngster admires the irresponsible and the delinquency-prone outer fringe of adolescent society and makes even tentative overtures towards being accepted by them, you do have something to worry about. Clamping down is not the way to handle it, although that surely is a perfectly natural reaction for a parent to have. If circumstances in your youngster's life have made him feel drawn towards bad company, the only sensible thing to do is to seek guidance of a professional person, so that your approach to the youngster will not be frantic and uncontrolled, thereby making the situation worse. Desperate pressure brought to bear on rebellious teenagers usually drives them further into the very behavior the parent is trying to eradicate. Many an unfortunate marriage, an elopment or allegiance to bad company has been precipitated by the uncontrolled approach of desperate parents, frantically trying to break up the ill-advised relationship. Without the restraining influence of sustained professional guidance, it is almost impossible for parents to control themselves and do the opposite of what they instinctively feel a great need to do; namely, to attack the problem head on.

For the most part, the average teenager simply wants to be trusted by his parents to behave sensibly. He craves freedom at the same time that he feels the need of some protection, and he needs privacy as well as some leeway with regard to curfews. In short, he wants to be treated like the young adult he is, or is becoming. These are reasonable demands. If a youngster gets a little, or a lot out of hand from time to time, a firm expression of disappointment and disapproval on the part of the parents and a reminder that better behavior is expected are usually all that are required to bring him reasonably back into line, if the relationship has been one of friendliness, love and mutual respect. And if it has not been, now is the time for the parent to try to bring some of those qualities into his approach to the teenager.

Panicky Parents

How is it that some parents are always in a state of anxiety when their teenagers are out and find it impossible to remain calm if the youngster is at all delayed in arriving home? They die a thousand deaths before the youngster appears. A variety of unconscious factors can usually be discovered under all the anxiety and anger.

The parent who is always sure that the tardy youngster is at least half-dead from some form of violence generates these ideas from his own thoughts and feelings, which then are used to torture himself. There is nothing more painful for a parent than to lose a child in death, yet that is all some parents can think of when their children are late. Some mothers go into this state if their children are a bit late in coming home from school through having stopped to chat with a friend for ten or fifteen minutes. Other parents have this type of reaction only when their children are out on dates with members of the opposite sex, and in the evening.

Along with the love these parents unquestionably feel for their children, there is also unconscious hostility. As was mentioned earlier, sometimes a child unconsciously represents to a parent a brother or sister from their own childhood, and feelings of antagonism may be transferred from brother to son, or sister to daughter. This often accounts for unusual anxiety about a child's safety from the moment it is born. The parent then is a helpless victim of these fears. The feeling of hostility arises spontaneously. Because the parent loves the child, it automatically and also unconsciously tries to neutralize or compensate for the hostility by overprotective attitudes.

If exaggerated anxiety about a youngster's safety first arises when the child becomes an adolescent, it sometimes is caused by one or a combination of the following: anxiety and reluctance to face the fact that the teenager is becoming an independent young adult; fears and anxieties about the possible sexual activities in which the young people may be engaging; unconscious jealousy that the youngster is beginning to give his strongest feelings of affection to people other than the parents; and, sometimes, unconscious envy of the teenager who may be very much happier and more successful than the parent was at that age or is at the moment. This last is really a carry-over of childhood rivalry.

Feeling guilty about their hostile feelings, these parents punish themselves with the fantasy of the most terrible thing that could actually happen to them. Then, reassured by the sight of the returning child, the cycle starts all over again, with the original anger turned once more against the teenager who again becomes the villain who *caused* all that upset to the parent.

One mother, who had a great many problems which caused her to be overprotective and overanxious about her seventeen-year-old daughter, asked her daughter to bring her dates home after a party or theatre date, rather than stay out late since the mother became so apprehensive about the girl's safety. The girl obliged, and would ring the door bell lightly to let her mother know she had arrived. To the mother's surprise she found herself becoming extremely anxious about the young couple being in the living room alone. When silence had reigned for about half an hour, she became convinced that her daughter was being sexually assaulted. Unable to restrain herself, she finally threw on a robe and burst into the living room to find them seated about four feet apart conversing in low tones in order not to disturb her parents. Did this experience prevent the mother from becoming anxious on the next occasion? No. Each time she was convinced that *this* time it was really happening.

Quite obviously, the mother's own fantasies of rape and her over-identification with her teenage daughter were creating the difficulty. Dissatisfied with the restrictions of marriage, she would have much preferred to be the one who was dating and engaging in romantic encounters. In an extreme case such as this, it is plain that the mother is seriously in need of help.

It is not nearly as obvious, but nevertheless just as true in less severe cases where the parents pace up and down in ever-increasing agitation waiting for their teenagers to return.

The father who kicked his daughter down the stairs for exceeding her curfew was in a panic as well as a rage. He was positive that the lateness signified immoral behavior. He had been a gay blade before marriage, spending a great deal of time in the company of women whose favors he enjoyed but whose morals he frowned upon. If his daughter was not a model of submissive obedience, then he could think only of one other alternative—she was a tramp. Clearly this was his opinion of the women with whom he had consorted in his youth. His problems were making it impossible for him to be a kindly and understanding father. And his daughter's attitude towards men and sexuality as well as towards her own femininity were being warped by his angry suspicions and harsh and uncontrolled behavior towards her.

Adolescence is a test of parents' endurance, understanding, humor and emotional stability. Difficult situations call for flexibility and kindly understanding. If your teenagers are bitter and unhappy about your attitude towards them and their activities, there may be something mistaken in your approach. A better solution can perhaps be found by calmly trying to examine the reasons for your demands and restrictions and trying honestly to see how many of them stem from your own problems. Don't think that because you've taken a stand on something, you have to stick to it. It takes a secure and big person to say to a youngster with whom he has been at war, "I've thought about it and I see it differently now." Learn to close your eyes to the many little unimportant and irritating things they do, gross exaggerations of other youngsters' privileges and similar underestimation of their own being chief among them. They're not lying. One might say that adolescence is the time when the world is viewed alternately through one or the other end of an opera-glass. Exaggerations and distortions are typical. In evaluating a communication, you simply correct for the opera-glass effect. Alter the statistics by about forty per cent and you'll have a pretty clear idea of what's going on. Don't fuss, fret and fume. Relax!

With the average teenager, if your daily attitude shows that you have confidence in his good sense, it will do more than a thousand lectures to encourage him to behave sensibly.

Unquestionably, the most difficult group for parents to live with are those teenagers who have turned love into hate, admiration into contempt and obedience into rebellion as a means of emancipating themselves from childhood ties. All that parents can do in these extremely painful and trying circumstances is to give the adolescents a wide berth. By remaining dignified and somewhat aloof from the irascible teenager, they reassure him that they are not going to prevent him from becoming independent. In this way, they refrain from increasing flare-ups of hostility and rebellion. It may then be only a matter of time before the troubled teenager realizes he needs help. With no provocations on the part of his parents to point to as the cause of his hostile feelings, he is much more likely to realize that something is wrong with his feelings and behavior.

In the case of teenagers whose struggle for emancipation takes the form of being away from home most of the time, it is best to allow them to do so without criticism. If occasionally they have dinner with the family, teasing is not in order. Questions such as "What have we done to deserve the honor of your company?" may make them feel foolish, resentful and determined never to expose themselves to ridicule again.

As difficult as some teenagers unquestionably are, they almost always show some response to self-control, kindness and sincerity on the part of their parents. These qualities have a leavening influence on the instability so characteristic of adolescence. And what better qualities are there with which to identify and to carry over to the handling of their own children in the not so distant future?

Ultramodern Parents

Some parents have become so confused by the many different theories with which they have been bombarded that they have lost confidence in their own intuitive understanding of what is appropriate behavior for youngsters in the pre-teens and teens and they go to the other extreme of the overly strict parent.

They will, for instance, leave teenage boys and girls alone in the home for hours on end. This is an unwritten invitation to sexual activity. It is neither proper nor fair to expose adolescents to such temptation. Under these conditions even young teenagers of thirteen (with neurotic problems) have been known to try everything. Two sets of highly educated parents were astounded to find that the fifteen-year-old son of one pair and the same-aged daughter of the other pair had become involved in a complete sexual relationship in the course of a winter during which they were left alone at the boy's home evening after evening when the two sets of parents went out to theatres, concerts and openings of art exhibits. Both youngsters loved classical music. The boy had a fine record collection. And the parents were content for them to spend the evening at home "listening to music" while they went out. It was, needless to say, a highly unrealistic approach to teenage sexual drives.

Some parents, fearful of being old-fashioned, permit their teenagers to entertain a member of the opposite sex in the teenager's bedroom at any hour of the day or evening. Just because a teenager has his own TV set or record player in his bedroom is no reason the two young people should be allowed to use that room as a parlor. Some parents become so confused as to what is "modern" that they permit the young couple to lie on the bed together and watch TV and even to fall asleep together.

In permitting this, the parents are sending an unspoken message to the teenagers. They are saying, "You are just babies. Your bodies cannot mean anything to each other because they are not yet sexually attractive bodies so we need not be at all concerned." Or it may appear that the message is, "Do whatever you wish, the responsibility is all yours."

Parents can guide themselves by whatever would be appropriate if the parent were entertaining a friend of the opposite sex in the home. One doesn't take him into the bedroom and lie on the bed with him, either to watch TV or to rest up after an exhausting outing, unless one intends to arouse expectations of less innocent behavior.

The living room should be made cheerfully available to the teenagers and record players can be moved in temporarily. Books, comics, photographs or anything else the adolescents want to look at together can be brought in from the bedroom.

The same applies to parties. A responsible adult, not an indifferent houseworker, should always be somewhere in the house. That doesn't mean that the adult has to continually buzz in and out like a distracted detective in search of a misplaced magnifying glass. But he is there, and wide awake and fully clothed, ready to make a friendly appearance if it sounds as though a rumpus is starting. All the youngsters have the reassurance of knowing that while no one is going to sit and stare at them or eavesdrop and they can have all the fun they want no one can get into trouble of any kind.

It remains for some future sociologist to reveal all the forces which have led us into the situation we now face, in which eleven-year-olds are allowed to go steady, go to co-ed parties where lights are turned out and they dance in the dark.

Some observers see it as a frantic American desire to make children grow up fast and force them to mature socially before their time, hence eleven and twelve-year-olds are treated as teenagers. They see adult pushing as being responsible for the pairing off of grade school children, with junior high school romances turned into junior betrothals.

Very likely, an important element in this unhealthy change in the social customs of the very young is traceable to a misapplication of psychoanalytic knowledge and the confusion arising from a failure to distinguish between methods which are appropriate to conducting psychoanalytic treatment and methods which best serve to educate a child and help him to learn to tolerate frustration, handle anxiety and learn to sublimate his primitive instinctual drives. When news got around that psychoanalysis revealed the damage resulting from a repressive upbringing, many well-intentioned parents and educators took this to mean that the key to mental health had at last been found in the complete permissiveness which characterizes the therapeutic procedure. When the children thus raised and educated were later analyzed, it was found that lack of boundaries and parental authority created anxiety in the children, that they were overstimulated and unable to achieve proper mastery over their primitive infantile impulses, and they had no clearly established standards of what was right and wrong.

The Need for Reform

To bring up children with a healthy acceptance of sexuality does not mean that the child should not learn as it moves through early childhood to sublimate sexual drives into other activities. In the chapter, "First Lessons in Love," the importance of being aware of childhood sexual games so that they can be healthily limited is discussed. The same principle applies to all other forms of childish behavior. On a level appropriate to his age, the child needs to be allowed expression of his drives and feelings: greediness, messiness, destructiveness, clinging and dependence, jealousy and hostility. But little by little, as he becomes capable of internal controls, he must be helped to develop and use those controls so that his behavior becomes acceptable in polite society.

Bringing up children with a healthy acceptance of sexual feelings does not mean that the preteens should be a preparatory period for sexual freedom in the teens. The fact that many eleven and twelve-year-olds are eager to act as though they are full-blown adolescents is no reason to encourage them to, or to allow them to, except in limited ways. Here again group action is required because it is too painful for an individual child to have to be a martyr for his parents' ideals. If your child is the only one who is not permitted to go to teen-type parties or have a boy friend or girl friend, it may place the child in an agonizing position and make him lose confidence in your understanding and affection and good-will. But if even a small group of parents get together and agree on certain restrictions such as no going steady, no "formals," no dancing in the dark, and no parties where "couples" dance only with each other all evening, the little group of preteen pioneers, while they will at first have a tough time as pioneers always do, won't be exposed to isolated martyrdom. Meanwhile, their parents can be pressuring civic and religious leaders and PTA members to continually enlarge the group. Parents should explain their point of view and their program to their children. If they remain friendly and kind, while sticking to their guns, the youngsters will not lose confidence in their good-will. A high and mighty and indignant you'll-do-no-such-thing-while-I-have-anything-to-say-about-it attitude will only arouse anger and resentment. The child's gripes should be listened to (but not incessantly) and discussed.

It is important to remember that the preteens have real desires to be and act grownup. At the same time they have fears of being expected to be grownup. The parent can respond to the desire for adulthood by reassuring the child that it isn't too far off and by giving increased responsibilities wherever possible. Under no circumstances should a parent use ridicule and sarcasm. "Who do you pups think you are?", "Getting married tomorrow?", "Is your sweetheart faithful to you?" and similar remarks are humiliating and strengthen the desire to rebel. When properly handled most children, however secretly, will welcome this parental control.

Premature dating and the aping of adult behavior at parties create anxiety and tension as well as feelings of inadequacy and inferiority in most children. Often, in an attempt to still these feelings, the youngster will throw himself into amorous activities, trying to live up to teenagers and the vicious circle has started. If he does respond with sexual excitement, the preteen feels quite unable to cope with the feelings. If he fails to respond, he begins to believe that something is wrong with him. In either case, anxiety is aroused which disturbs the youngster's peace of mind, usually interferes with his ability to study and also interferes with his normal development and personality growth. Whenever we jump the gun on a developmental stage, something is lost which is needed to stabilize and enrich the character and personality of the youngster. The same applies to the custom of going steady in the early teens.

Perhaps one of the reasons these practices have developed is that so many parents, feeling insecure themselves, cannot bear to see the agony their young teenagers often go through, particularly the girls, over whether they will be asked to some party or for a date and by whom. Life seems to be much less hectic for everyone when these diminutive debutantes have their steady beaux. Bearing with the acute agony of the break-up, when it inevitably comes, isn't quite as wearing on everyone as coping with a continuous succession of major-minor crises day by day, week by week, and month by month.

But it is a dearly bought peace, purchased by the sacrifice of precious experience in getting to know others, in learning to live through frustrations of an intensely personal nature which should enable the young person who is moving through his teens to know his own strength and make him a wiser and more mature person. The price also includes the unwelcome effects of premature sexual arousal. Going steady tends to gradually break down the normal inhibitions and restraints. This is fine as a prelude to marriage but it is entirely inappropriate for youngsters who have at least eight to twelve years of study and work ahead of them before they will be ready to settle down. Moreover, it surely must destroy some of the pleasure and excitement of real courtship when the time comes. In short, encouraging behavior which is pseudo-adult and pseudo-mature not only puts today's youngsters under a great strain but also tends to impoverish personality and prevent the fullest measure of normal development from taking place. Being deprived of the opportunity to gradually unfold, enrich and expand his personality through relationships with many different people is bound to result in a less adequate adult.

If premature "steady" dating and premature sexual experience and marriage are to be avoided, parents must be aware of what their teenagers are doing and maintain an active, friendly interest in them and in the dating customs of the community. Permitting busy and successful teenagers to make all their own plans does not mean that the parents pay no attention to their youngsters. There is no substitute for a parent's feeling of affectionate pride and interest in his budding young adults. No matter how indifferent to it the teenager may appear to be, it gives him a warm sense of security and protects him from loneliness and despair at difficult times.

A study of high school students who were about to marry revealed that many felt their parents were not interested in them at all. A good number had started to date early and seriously with no restriction whatsoever placed upon their social behavior and obviously soon felt that they were ready for a complete sex relationship. Many were marrying because of loneliness and unhappiness. (Welton)

In suburbs and small towns, adolescents not only need the feeling of parental interest, but the parents' full cooperation and help in establishing recreational centers and activities of various kinds. In one town in the east, as a result of unfavorable publicity about their teenagers, the parents snapped to attention and showed what could be done to help their adolescents have fun and keep out of trouble. They helped establish theatre groups, run block parties and expand Y activities, especially dances and athletics, all with the happy participation of the teenagers.

Sensible codes of behavior acceptable to both teenagers and parents have been arrived at by committees of parents and adolescents, who worked out agreements on such vexing questions as going steady, curfews, the use of the car, drinking, behavior at parties and in public places, manner of dressing, party crashing, etc. Thus, parents and teenagers have a meeting of minds in a neutral setting, after which both groups are fully aware of what their community expects of them. With clearly established standards, both can feel more confident.

Alert, friendly, community-minded parents seldom have

serious behavior difficulties to cope with in their children. Their teenagers usually follow in their footsteps. Accounts of adolescent drinking, vandalism and sexual misbehavior in privileged neighborhoods usually leave out the rest of the story: parental indifference, neglect, and, often, the parental example of heavy drinking and lax moral standards.

All adolescents need to feel that their parents are available for a discussion when serious problems arise. (A common complaint of delinquents is that there is no adult in the environment whom they can trust and with whom they can have a serious talk.) The teenager who is confident that his parents would never make light of his problems but will treat them with the dignity and seriousness they deserve feels he can approach his parents when in distress. The adolescent who has learned to expect indifference, ridicule, criticism or authoritarianism isn't likely to say a word. At the other extreme are the parents who cannot resist becoming so involved emotionally that the teenager who has come for a discussion feels as though the problem has been taken entirely out of his hands and is now the parents' problem. His natural struggle for independence may make him very reluctant to risk being engulfed by his parents' emotionalism and over-identification with him.

The adolescent needs to feel that his parents are his discreetly affectionate, interested friends who have confidence in him. Where such relationships exist there is very little likelihood of irresponsible sexual behavior, unless it is promoted by the parents' mistaken attitudes towards sexuality. The father with doubts about his own potency is not helping his college-bound son's sexual and moral development by urging him to have affairs while he is away at school. Nor is the mother, whose horrified recollection of her naïveté as a co-ed who failed to recognize that she was the target of lesbian passes, furthering her daughter's development by suggesting that she have a "couple of heterosexual affairs" while she is at college. Such advice can make teenagers extremely anxious. They may feel that they are obliged to carry it through as an assignment from the parents. Pressures of this kind constitute a serious and disconcerting interference with the adolescent's academic education, with his emotional development and with his establishing of a satisfactory personal moral code, one which will be in harmony with the highest purposes of our society.

BIBLIOGRAPHY

Barron, Jennie Loitman:
 "Too Much Sex on Campus," *Reader's Digest,* May, 1964.
Bealer, Robert C., Fern K. Willits and Peter R. Maida:
 "The Rebellious Youth Subculture—A Myth," *Children,* volume II, No. 2, U. S. Dept. of Health, Ed. & Welfare, March-April, 1964.
Bell, Anita I.:
 "The Role of Parents," *Adolescents: Psychoanalytic Approach to Problems and Therapy,* Eds. Lorand, S. and H. Schneer, Paul B. Hoeber, Inc., Division of Harper & Brothers, New York, 1961.
Blos, Peter:
 On Adolescence, Free Press of Glencoe, Division of Crowell-Collier, New York, 1962.
Bornstein, B.:
 "Masturbation in the Latency Period," *The Psychoanalytic Study of the Child,* vol. VIII, International Universities Press, Inc., New York, 1953.
Brazelton, T. Berry:
 "Why Some Babies Cry So Much," *Parents Magazine,* April, 1964.
Carson, Ruth:
 "How to Keep Teens out of Trouble," *Parents Magazine,* June, 1964.
Christoffel, Hans:
 "Male Genital Exhibitionism," *Perversions: Psychodynamics and Therapy,* Eds. Lorand, S. and M. Balint, Random House, Inc., New York, 1956.
————:

"Creativity," Carnegie Corporation of New York *Quarterly*, July, 1961, vol. IX, No. 3.

Day, Donald:
The Evolution of Love, The Dial Press, New York, 1954.

Deutsch, Helena:
The Psychology of Women, Grune and Stratton, New York, 1944.

Eidelberg, Ludwig:
A Comparative Pathology of the Neuroses, International Universities Press, New York, 1954.

————:
"Analysis of a Case of a Male Homosexual," *Perversions: Psychodynamics and Therapy*, Eds. Lorand, S. and M. Balint, Random House, Inc., New York, 1956.

Escalona, S.:
"Feeding Disturbances in Very Young Children," *American Journal of Orthopsychiatry*, vol. XV, no. 1, Jan., 1945.

Feldman, Sandor:
"On Homosexuality," *Perversions: Psychodynamics and Therapy*, Eds. Lorand, S. and M. Balint, Random House, Inc., New York, 1956.

Fenichel, Otto:
The Psychoanalytic Theory of Neurosis, W. W. Norton & Co., Inc., New York, 1945.

Fraiberg, Selma:
"Homosexual Conflicts," *Adolescents: Psychoanalytic Approach to Problems and Therapy*, Eds. Lorand, S. and H. Schneer, Paul B. Hoeber, Inc., Division of Harper & Brothers, New York, 1961.

Freud, Anna:
"Adolescence," *The Psychoanalytic Study of the Child*, vol. XIII, International Universities Press, Inc., New York, 1958.

————:
"Observations on Child Development," *The Psychoanalytic Study of the Child*, vol. VI, International Universities Press, Inc., New York, 1951.

Freud, Sigmund:
"Inhibition, Symptom and Anxiety," *The Standard Edition of the Complete Psychological Works*, vol. XX, The Hogarth Press, London, 1959.

————:
"Neurotic Mechanism in Jealousy, Paranoia and Homosexuality," *Collected Papers*, vol. I, The Hogarth Press, London, 1924.

————:
"Psychogenesis of a Case of Female Homosexuality," *Collected Papers*, vol. II, The Hogarth Press, London, 1924.

————:
"Three Essays on the Theory of Sexuality," *The Standard Edition of the Complete Psychological Works*, vol. VII, The Hogarth Press, London, 1953.

Friedan, Betty:
   The Feminine Mystique, W. W. Norton & Company, Inc., New
   York, 1963.
Fries, Margaret and Paul J. Woolf:
   "Some Hypotheses on the Role of the Congenital Activity Type
   in Personality Development," *The Psychoanalytic Study of the
   Child*, vol. VIII, International Universities Press, Inc., New
   York, 1953.
Geleerd, Elizabeth R.:
   "Some Aspects of Ego Vicissitudes in Adolescence," *Journal of
   the American Psychoanalytic Association*, vol. IX, No. 3, July,
   1961.
Greenacre, Phyllis:
   "Problems of Infantile Neurosis," *The Psychoanalytic Study of
   the Child*, vol. IX, International Universities Press, Inc., New
   York, 1954.
———:
   "Special Problems of Early Female Sexual Development," *The
   Psychoanalytic Study of the Child*, vol. V, International Univer-
   sities Press, Inc., New York, 1950.
Greene, Gael:
   Sex and the College Girl, Dial Press, New York, 1964.
Harley, Marjorie:
   "Masturbation Conflicts," *Adolescents: Psychoanalytic Approach
   to Problems and Therapy*, Eds. Lorand, S. and H. Schneer,
   Paul B. Hoeber, Inc., Division of Harper & Brothers, New York,
   1961.
Harlow, Harry F.:
   "The Heterosexual Affectional System in Monkeys," *American
   Psychologist*, vol. XVII, no. 1, Jan., 1962.
Kagan, J. and H. A. Moss:
   Birth to Maturity, John Wiley & Sons, Inc., New York, 1962.
Keiser, Sylvan:
   "The Adolescent Exhibitionist," *Adolescents: Psychoanalytic Ap-
   proach to Problems and Therapy*, Eds. Lorand, S. and H.
   Schneer, Paul B. Hoeber, Inc., Division of Harper & Brothers,
   New York, 1961.
Kestenberg, Judith:
   "Menarche," *Adolescents: Psychoanalytic Approach to Problems
   and Therapy*, Eds. Lorand, S. and H. Schneer, Paul B. Hoeber,
   Inc., Division of Harper & Brothers, New York, 1961.
Kinsey, A. C., W. B. Pomeroy, C. E. Martin and Gebhard:
   Sexual Behavior in the Human Female, W. B. Saunders Co.,
   Philadelphia and London, 1953.
Konopka, Gisela:
   "Adolescent Delinquent Girls," *Children*, vol. II, no. 1, U. S.
   Dept. of Health, Ed. & Welfare, Jan.-Feb., 1964.
Lampl-DeGroot, Jeanne:
   "On Masturbation and Its Influence on General Development,"

The Psychoanalytic Study of the Child, vol. V, International Universities Press, Inc., New York, 1950.

Miller, Milton:
"The Relation Between Submission and Aggression in Male Homosexuality," *Perversions: Psychodynamics and Therapy,* Eds. Lorand, S. and M. Balint, Random House, Inc., New York, 1956.

Muensterberger, W.:
"The Adolescent in Society," *Adolescents: Psychoanalytic Approach to Problems and Therapy,* Eds. Lorand, S. and H. Schneer, Paul B. Hoeber, Inc., Division of Harper & Brothers, New York, 1961.

Nunberg, H.:
"Homosexuality, Magic and Aggression," *Practice and Theory of Psychoanalysis,* Nervous and Mental Disease Monographs, International Universities Press, New York, 1948.

Pannor, Reuben:
"Casework Service for Unmarried Father," *Children,* vol. X, no. 2, U. S. Dept. of Health, Ed. & Welfare, March-April, 1963.

Reich, Annie:
"The Discussion of 1912 on Masturbation and Our Present-Day Views," *The Psychoanalytic Study of the Child,* vol. VI, International Universities Press, Inc., New York, 1951.

Salisbury, Harrison E.:
"Lost Generation Baffles Soviet: Nihilistic Youth Shun Ideology," *The New York Times,* Feb. 9, 1962.

Savitt, Robert A.:
"Psychoanalytic Studies on Addiction: Ego Structure in Narcotic Addiction," *Psychoanalytic Quarterly,* vol. XXXII, no. 1, 1963.

Schwartz, Eugene J.:
"Why Babies Cry," *Today's Health,* American Medical Association, Sept., 1963.

Spiegel, Leo A.:
"Identity and Adolescence," *Adolescents: Psychoanalytic Approach to Problems and Therapy,* Eds. Lorand, S. and H. Schneer, Paul B. Hoeber, Inc., Division of Harper & Brothers, New York, 1961.

Spitz, Rene A.:
"Authority and Masturbation," *Psychoanalytic Quarterly,* vol. XXI, no. 4, 1952, pp. 490-527.

————:
"The Truth About Teenage Divorce," *Ingenue Magazine,* June, 1964.

Welton, Shirley:
"Heading off those Risky Teenage Marriages," *Parents Magazine,* March, 1964.